The Educational Leader's Guide to Improvement Science

The Educational Leader's Guide to Improvement Science

Data, Design and Cases for Reflection

EDITED BY Robert Crow,
Brandi Nicole Hinnant-Crawford,
Dean T. Spaulding

Myers Education Press

Myers Education Press is an academic publisher specializing in books, e-books, and digital content in the field of education. All of our books are subjected to a rigorous peer review process and produced in compliance with the standards of the Council on Library and Information Resources.

Library of Congress Cataloging-in-Publication Data available from Library of Congress.

13-digit ISBN 978-1-9755-0095-5 (paperback)
13-digit ISBN 978-1-9755-0094-8 (hard cover)
13-digit ISBN 978-1-9755-0096-2 (library networkable e-edition)
13-digit ISBN 978-1-9755-0097-9 (consumer e-edition)

Printed in the United States of America.

All first editions printed on acid-free paper that meets the American National Standards Institute Z39-48 standard.

Books published by Myers Education Press may be purchased at special quantity discount rates for groups, workshops, training organizations, and classroom usage. Please call our customer service department at 1-800-232-0223 for details.

Cover and text design by Sophie Appel

Visit us on the web at **www.myersedpress.com** to browse our complete list of titles.

CONTENTS

SECTION THREE
Contextualizing Improvement Science in K–12 Education

FOREWORD

A movement. That is how Robert Crow, who edited this volume with Brandi Hinnant-Crawford and Dean Spaulding, refers to the growing interest and activity that improvement science has garnered among those concerned with educational leadership. One way to describe a movement is as a noteworthy change in the way people from a broad swath of a field go about their work. Crow, Hinnant-Crawford and Spaulding, have assembled an impressive collection of papers, from thoughtful authors, that suggest that such a transformation, in how the work of leadership is conceived, is now underway among practitioners, scholars and practitioner-scholars across the landscape of educational leadership.

No doubt you happened upon this volume because you are concerned with leadership and education. Perhaps you happened to open this book because you heard that something called *improvement science* is making its way into leadership discussions. Maybe you are here because this text has been assigned as a part of a course. Or you may be considering assigning this book for a course that you are about to lead. However you arrived at this volume, you will, almost certainly, come to see that this book will make an important sense-making contribution to charting the landscape at the nexus of educational leadership and improvement science.

The editors of this book represent a wonderful group of intellectual guides who will help you chart your journey through the nexus of these domains of knowledge. Each editor has been taught educational leadership. And born of practical experience in attempting to help school leaders build higher performing organizations, each has come to see how the practice of education leaders can be enhanced by the ideas of improvement science. Improvement science, from an organizational perspective, is a discipline that aims to support organizations in deepening their capacity to learn. These editors have a deep and abiding interest in helping schools build equitable learning environments. They, and the authors they have assembled for this volume, will guide you on a most interesting exploration, at the end of which I suspect you will also see how ideas from improvement science can help school leaders help their organizations to improve.

Movements create a new narrative. Improvement science's marriage to educational leadership is no different. It is forging new ways to think about problems and how to go about addressing them. In this volume you can expect to see how the improvement science narrative is carving a new niche in the educational leadership discourse. Improvement science offers leaders a new palette of tools with which to do their work. In reading this volume, you will see how the tools are being used in diverse teaching and learning contexts. The volume is chock-full of good examples of how improvement science is offering educational leadership an enhanced core of analytic practices that are capable of offering new insights into problems that have vexed the field for a long time. These tools form the basis of what is so often essential to make progress, a common, analytic discourse that helps leaders see and address problems differently. A reader of the volume will see, for example, how organizations can dig deep into problems and make steady progress toward durable solutions. Rather than being stuck, as we often are today, with data regarding average differences between schools, classrooms, or groups of students, that offer few, if any, insights about how to make things better, in the volume readers can see that more can be learned about long-standing teaching and learning problems by exploring the micro-details of variation. In essence, IS scholars and practitioners argue that much that is important to organizational improvement is obscured by attending only to average differences. In the volume, you will encounter several sample of *use cases* where practitioners effectively explore problems by studying variation.

I think that, in this volume, the editors and the authors are leading us down a reasoning trail that ends with the case being made for improvement science as a consequential coupling to educational leadership studies. Specifically, the chapters in this volume point to a general consensus that improvement science is a worthy candidate to become, what Lee Shulman coined a "signature pedagogy" for the study and practice of educational leadership. Signature pedagogies, according to Shulman, provide the guideposts that enculturate people "to think, to perform and to act with integrity" [Shulman, 2005, p. 52] in a profession. Heretofore, educational leadership practice has never had a signature pedagogy or method. The editors, and authors, give us good examples about how to integrate improvement science in courses and capstone projects so that the next generation of leaders who aspire to a range of credentials, including the EdD and the master's degree, have in their toolkits a coherent form of disciplined inquiry that is particularly well suited to the problems they will encounter in practice.

Crow, Hinnant-Crawford and Spaulding have assembled a book that is approachable by both practitioners and scholars, who have experience at the intersection of educational leadership and improvement science, as well as for those who have little experience with these ideas. The book is well suited to serve as a tool, to be used in the practice of education leadership, as well as a course text. I congratulate the editors and their team of authors on the production of a very useful volume.

Louis Gomez,
UCLA & The Carnegie Foundation for
the Advancement of Teaching

Reference

Shulman, L. S. (2005). Signature pedagogies in the professions. *Daedalus*, *134*(3), 52–59.

The Science of Improvement Science

CHAPTER ONE

Considering Improvement Science in Educational Leadership

Western Carolina University

W e see every now and then where instances of revolutionary thinking lead to dramatic changes in education. At the turn of the century, we witnessed the promise of technology to revolutionize gains in learning, particularly as the Internet began its now ubiquitous presence in classrooms. A second wave of revolutionary thinking led to articulating what are now known as metacognitive strategies, such as mnemonics and self-regulation—real skills learners could learn to apply to enhance their own learning, leading to leaps in educational attainment outcomes. As encouraged as school and college leaders must have been by what in hindsight should be considered paradigm-shifting moments for enhancing the capacity to affect student learning, it is now that we see another promising revolution in thinking. Borrowing from our colleagues in the business and healthcare industries, educators are field-building around the science of improvement. Distinctive and systematic procedures for describing and applying improvement frameworks to educational contexts allow for the development of the science to serve as a philosophy and a methodology for enhancing school leaders' capacity for institutional and organizational improvement.

Educational leaders who are current in their practice are amassing a knowledge base comprising the *whys* and *hows* of integrating improvement science into leadership programs as well as into the districts and schools where they practice. As we build a collective understanding for the role that improvement science plays in institutional process and system improvement, it becomes imperative that the practitioner develop an understanding of this systematic approach to problem-finding and subsequent problem-solving. *The Educational Leader's Guide to Improvement Science* presents a collection of chapters designed to describe and illustrate applied organizational improvements using various methods of improvement science (IS) in educational leadership scenarios. Early chapters provide the reader with an introduction to improvement science, along with an overview, rationale and challenges for exploring this emerging paradigm. Following this, the reader is led through a logical sequence as cases of various educational dilemmas are presented and matched with principles of IS. Most important, examples of research methodologies are applied in context. Consider the following:

- How does an organization such as a school or district determine or measure whether its initiatives are "successful" when they are unable to use "traditional" research designs such as a control or comparison group?
- How does an organization working to improve a program in the school conduct rigorous data analysis when working within the realistic framework of small sample sets that do not meet the traditional assumptions of parametric analysis?

These and other questions will be explored in the text. Generalities can be transferred to individuals' settings, particularly as related cases are presented and discussed.

An Emerging Field in Graduate Development

Improvement science is an emerging field that has found its way into graduate education. Under the larger umbrella of improvement research, the science of improvement is gaining popularity as efforts continue to redefine the purpose and characterization of doctoral-level degrees of practice. Like other practice-oriented degrees, such as the JD or MD, the role of the doctor of education (EdD) degree has historically suffered obscurity compared to her sister degree, the PhD. Historically perceived as PhD-lite, the doctor of education degree has had a similar trajectory; the typical coursework and subsequent dissertation products involved have relatively mirrored the same requirements of candidates seeking the research-based PhD degree.

Improvement science is gaining recognition as a signature methodology and core subject area of inquiry in the field of educational leadership. Currently, faculty and administrators in the area of educational leadership are witnessing a paradigm shift, where improvement science is becoming a preferred methodology for developing doctoral candidates' skills in organizational improvement. One movement spurred by this reform is in establishing methods of organizational improvement as a core component of the curriculum in practice-based doctoral degrees.

Work done by the Carnegie Foundation for the Advancement of Teaching's Improvement Science Fellows, as well as efforts by the Carnegie Project on the Education Doctorate, have reinforced the idea that a structural renovation would be necessary in order to establish the unique nature of the degree as a practice-based designation. Requiring a near-complete overhaul of a curriculum that has historically mirrored the course sequence of PhD coursework and, in particular, the inquiry line of courses (i.e., the research methods courses) would be a major focus in this restructuring. Originally, during this overhauling of programs in early form days (the mid-2000s), faculty and administration were led by a scant but emerging literature, largely borrowed from the fields of healthcare and business, to provide basic foundational knowledge about improvement science. As a unique science, characteristic features include the generation of practical learning that is applied in real-life situations (Marshall & Dixon-Woods, 2013). Moreover, accumulation of new knowledge for practice, in turn, enables practitioners to generate theories for positive change. Therefore, a main goal of this text is to contribute to the knowledge base by providing concrete examples through illustrative cases designed to strengthen our understanding of IS principles and applied frameworks.

It is only currently that those who are in the throes of graduate education reform see an apparent migration of principles and process of improvement science from the healthcare and manufacturing industries to the field of education. Focused on organizational improvement, graduate schools, particularly those that grant practitioner-oriented terminal degrees, are recognizing that the tools and methods of improvement science are necessary components of practical and evidence-based leadership skills development.

Improvement initiatives, and the subsequent research written about them, that use the science of improvement for a guiding set of conceptual and applied tools appear different compared to traditional action or experimental research designs. Tightly controlled randomized trials are the gold standard for determining causation in linear relationships, yet social change research demands rethinking our methodological approach based upon the charge to generate rich, yet disciplined, ways to learn (Berwick, 2008). The model of improvement presents four fundamental questions:

1) What is hoped to be accomplished?
2) What changes made would result in improvement?
3) Why are these changes thought to lead to improvement?
4) How might one recognize that a change made led to an improvement? (Bryk, Gomez, Grunow, & LeMahieu, 2015, p. 9)

Defining features characterizing the science of improvement include cyclical rather than linear approaches, emphasize collaborative over administrative research designs and focus on formative data to guide improvement projects and initiatives. Considered the starting point for eliciting systematic measures in areas in need, improvement science focuses on process variance. Typical improvement work requires a shift in research considerations; where a traditional hypothesis translates into a practical prediction, a random sample becomes a purposive stakeholder group, and a *p*-value parallels the human side of value. Faculty are recognizing the experience practitioners bring to the classroom as student candidates in leadership programs in higher education. Learning to integrate improvement science into the milieu of existing institutional problems of practice that these very students bring to programs provides a trajectory for great promise, as we aim for expert insight to drive the development of testable strategies to overcome once seemingly insurmountable barriers.

As more published research becomes available on the topic of integrating improvement science into the field of educational leadership, there appears to be three general types of description that are currently most prolific. The first genre consists of conceptual writing that describes the emerging field of improvement science and its role and relationship with programs in educational leadership. As a methodology, the problem-focused, user-centered approach that characterizes the science of improvement naturally lends itself to the daily problems faced *in situ* by educators. Practical measures, focused on processes and systems, yield just-in-time data that directly impact the strategies and tactics used, as well as the next steps employed in the lines of attack on problems of practice. And yet, despite this great progress in foundational knowledge-building, the current state reflects a lack of wholesale integration into academic programs in educational leadership. Among myriad avenues of exploration, faculty are interested in producing a graduate with a scholar-practitioner toolkit while researchers in this area are currently exploring institutional preparedness of academic programs to develop in their graduates a skillset that includes the knowledge, skills and dispositions comprising the field of improvement science.

Research and dissemination on best practices for the teaching and learning of improvement science in graduate leadership programs are related topics currently appearing in the literature. Formal and informal groups investigating the subject of IS integration into graduate programs have considered making content relatable using personal improvement projects, whereas others have considered creating and using educational games as an instructional method. What is known, however, is that it is only now that there appears to be a critical mass in higher education heeding the call to incorporate improvement science into the inquiry strand in leadership program curricula.

What is helpful, and is now the most widely disseminated form of illustration, is the bevy of case studies whose features and frameworks of improvement science are highlighted in a variety of settings and exemplify a range of problem-focused scenarios. As illustrative models, description and assessment of these works, highlighted through narrative and graphics, allow the reader to draw from the cases pertinent bits of information found relative and personally attributable to one's own professional practice. The amalgamation of information on developing, testing and modifying interventions is then reinterpreted by the reader. Applied at a later time is a unique configuration that, while keeping the distinctive features of IS intact, is reconstituted in consideration of the particular circumstances at hand. Illustrative cases will typically provide the reader with a structure where a problem of practice, existing within the educational organization, is well described and to which one or more of the ubiquitous structures or frameworks of improvement science, such as a process or system map, causal systems or fishbone analysis, a driver diagram, or an iterative Plan, Do, Study, Act (PDSA) cycle, is applied and followed subsequently by an analysis of the data generated during the inquiry cycle regarding new learning. Consider the following example:

> The change in student body, compiled with the current curriculum and instruction practices, resulted in the building now being placed in receivership by the state department of education. This designation requires the building to develop a plan and as part of that plan show adequate yearly progress toward improvement. One area noted during the state's review is the need for improvement in student performance on the annual state's ELA assessment, especially Grade 4. The belief among many in the school is that along with redistricting, the recent decline in student scores is due to an influx of new teachers joining the faculty and an exit of experienced teachers retiring. Many believe that much of the knowledge and effective instruction walked out the door when these experienced teachers left. They also believe that in order to solve the problem the district needs to move more experienced teachers from other buildings to the Jackson Spring building or hire more

experienced teachers from the outside to assist new teachers in delivering better reading instruction. However, the recent placement of the building in receivership has made teachers weary of relocating or applying for a position at the school altogether.

Today, many school leaders face the same improvement dilemma as Jackson Spring but, instead of conducting careful investigation, simply select another curriculum or program "off the shelf" in hopes that it will solve the problem. In the example above, the school leadership team is careful to avoid being solutionists (Bryk et al., 2015) who believe they know the fix before fully understanding the system that is producing the problem. Using an improvement lens, the leadership team will typically employ a series of improvement frameworks, including the PDSA model, a cornerstone of the methodology used by IS practitioners and supported by experts in the field (Langley et al., 2009). During the initial Plan stage, the team will work to gather a wide variety of stakeholder perceptions about the reading and literacy curriculum currently being used, documenting the challenges as well as the benefits. Next, during the Do stage, the team will conduct observations of instruction in the classroom. And finally, the team will examine student scores on the state's ELA assessment for the past few years, along with the formative data they collected during the Study phase. Recognizing the need to conduct a small pilot study, the team chooses one fourth grade teacher and implements a six-week reading intervention. The group will then examine the outcomes of their pilot study to determine the results and to learn from the process overall. Based on these results and the team's new learning, they will move to scale the intervention to other teachers in the building and conduct additional series of PDSA improvement cycles in the Act phase of the improvement cycle.

The Improvement Science Movement and Its Historic Roots

The emergent field of improvement science grew from two major areas outside of education: business and healthcare. The world of business brought to bear organizational improvement processes based on automation. Systems were the major foci, and ensuring quality was the major driver. Total quality management and other such philosophies led to creating many of the frameworks that are now ubiquitous in IS, such as process and system mapping.

The healthcare industry is another field that has had an impact on the migration of improvement science philosophy and frameworks into education. As in business, healthcare professionals focus on process and system efficacy. Improvement science includes the philosophy of utilizing well-defined measures to evaluate efficacy in improvement initiatives in the educational realm rather than in the clinical context. It is a goal of this book to expand coverage of improvement science from the worlds of healthcare and business to education by incorporating the models and structures that are presently used in improvement work.

The Need for Improvement Science in Education

Graduates from educational leadership programs emerge with a disciplinary way of thinking that is distinct for the profession. Although programs have historically produced graduates who can apply leadership and other theoretical perspectives to institutional problems, often these same graduates are prepared by coursework in traditional research methods, usually developing their skills at analyzing the research published in academic journals or drafting research proposals on a topic. However, this lineup of traditional inquiry coursework (i.e., research classes) did not include improvement science research as a core course. Today, institutions are responding to this omission by heeding the call for including improvement and other design-based research courses as part, if not a core, of the required inquiry coursework. Due to this reform, graduates are becoming increasingly more prepared to use their foundational knowledge of improvement science research garnered while in their educational leadership programs. Furthermore, these graduates are prepared to utilize and apply improvement science principles and frameworks in order to evaluate changes implemented to obtain improvements.

Prior to this inclusion, there was a void of practical tool use in the skillset of yesterday's graduates. This is not the case today.

Those who are graduating with a terminal degree in educational leadership should be the cadre the academy is sending out into the professions, prepared to use improvement science as a signature methodology in improvement-oriented work. Because of the nature of the practice-based degree, the doctor of education (EdD) coursework and its associated culminating project should reinforce the acquisition and development of improvement research methods.

Considering the Tenets of Improvement Science

Currently, there are varying philosophies about what constitutes and defines the field of improvement science research. Consider two sets of philosophies in the defining parameters (Table 1.1).

Table 1.1. Comparison of Essential Tenets of Improvement Science

Philosophy Based on Model of Improvement	Carnegie's Principles of Improvement
• Knowing why you need to improve	• Make the work problem-specific and user-focused
• Having a way to get feedback to know if improvement is happening	• Focus on variation in performance
	• See the system that produces the current outcomes
• Developing a change you think will result in an improvement	• We cannot improve at scale what we cannot measure
• Testing the change in pilot	• Use disciplined inquiry to drive improvement
• Implementing change to larger system	• Accelerate learning through networked communities

Source: Langley et al., 2009, 6–8 (Col. 1); Bryk et al., 2015, 172–173 (Col. 2)

Either implicitly or explicitly stated, these essential tenets relate to the four components described in the early work by Deming (1994) who, among others, describes the concept of profound knowledge as comprising the (a) development of an appreciation for a system, (b) gaining an understanding of the variation the system yields, (c) building practical and foundational knowledge for improving the system and (d) developing an understanding of the role the human side of change plays in organizational improvement initiatives. It is, as some research suggests, that the foundational underpinnings of improvement science builds on and adapts the benefits profound knowledge affords practitioners.

References

Berwick, D. (2008). The science of improvement. *Journal of the American Medical Association, 299*(10), 1182–1184.

Bryk, A., Gomez, L., Grunow, A., & LeMahieu, P. (2015). *Learning to improve: How America's schools can get better at getting better.* Cambridge, MA: Harvard Education Press.

Deming, W. E. (1994). *The new economics for industry, government, education* (2nd ed.). Cambridge, MA: MIT Press.

Langley, G. J., Moen, R. D., Nolan, K. M., Nolan, T. W., Norman, C. L., & Provost, L. P. (2009). *The improvement guide: A practical approach to enhancing organizational performance.* San Francisco, CA: Jossey-Bass.

Marshall, M., & Dixon-Woods, M. (2013). Promotion of improvement as a science. *Lancet, 381*(9864), 419–421.

CHAPTER TWO

Tools for Today's Educational Leaders

The Basic Tool Box

DEAN T. SPAULDING
Z Score Inc.

BRANDI NICOLE HINNANT-CRAWFORD
Western Carolina University

Improvement science is a member of a family of improvement methodologies that have been used across many disciplines to drive continuous improvement. In many ways, improvement science is a methodological framework that helps guide scholar-practitioners as they define problems, implement changes and determine whether or not those changes are actually improving outcomes and practice. As such, it is not as didactic as traditional research designs, nor does it have prescribed criteria that must be applied in every situation. However, improvement science does offer tools for practitioners to use at every step of the improvement process, from problem definition to scaling up improvements. This chapter will introduce you to tools to help you answer two of the fundamental improvement science questions:

1. What is the exact problem I am trying to solve?
2. What change might I introduce and why?

The other fundamental question (How will I know a change is an improvement?) is answered in greater detail in the following chapter.

Problem Definition:
What Is the Exact Problem I Am Trying to Solve?

When problems arise in an organization, it is common for individuals within that organization to blame others (Doggett, 2005). Root cause analysis (RCA) is a tool or process that organizes and categorizes potential causes of a particular problem or issue (Rooney & Vanden Heuvel, 2004). In addition, RCA reminds us that in these situations it is not only important to know *what* occurred and *how* it occurred, but it is also critical to know *why* it occurred in the first place. This is especially important if the organization is interested in preventing these events from happening again in the near future (Cohen-Vogel et al., 2014). The following examples demonstrate issues that might occur within an educational organization that members of that organization believe would need to be addressed:

1. A middle school's percentage of students scoring at the proficiency level on the state's annual state ELA assessment suddenly drops by 23%.
2. A college's percentage of first-year students persisting to their sophomore year drops by 15%.

Faced with these issues one might ask the following questions: What was the cause for the changes? Who or what do we blame? With the middle school example, it is easy for members of that organization to blame the assessment itself:

1. The assessment was too difficult.
2. Students weren't taught the correct content.
3. The test was poorly written.
4. The test came at a bad time of year.

But what about the higher education example? What might be the cause of the decline in student persistence?

1. Money—college is too expensive for a lot of students.
2. High schools are not preparing students for college.

3. Introductory classes are too large.
4. Gateway courses are poorly taught.

The list for both of these issues could go on and on. But if you take a moment to examine them, you may see a pattern emerging: all of these beliefs pertaining to low scores or low enrollment are hypotheses. At this point they are just the beliefs or intuitions of members from the organization. Members do not know for sure the *true* root cause for these problems.

Basic Components of an RCA

Root cause analysis (RCA) is a systematic and logical exploration of causes that underpin a current problem. Although there are many different approaches or models to conducting an RCA, all of these models have some overlapping characteristics. Presented below are some basic characteristics that you can find when you begin to dissect any RCA model:

1. *Problem must be identifiable.* First, the issue or problem has to be something that can be identified. Experts in RCA note that there is generally more than one single cause of a current problem. RCA allows for multiple causes to be identified and for these multiple causes to be sorted during the process. You will see that this is a unique feature to the tools presented in this chapter.
2. *Something that can be fixed.* In addition to being able to identify a cause (or multiple causes), RCA can only be used for identifying problems that can be fixed or addressed by management. For example, the state education department increasing the difficulty of its assessment in ELA is not something that the RCA could affect or change because a school district has little authority in the state's test development; however, a school leadership team would have the ability to increase professional development training for its teachers in literacy to "match" classroom instruction with the rigor of this new assessment.

3. *Members must be on board.* The RCA has to be conducted by members of the organization who have honest intentions and want what is good for the overall outcome of the organization.

Four Different RCA Approaches

If you review the literature on RCA you will quickly discover that there are many different models or approaches an organization can use to conduct an RCA. The RCA process typically occurs at the beginning of the improvement process; however, it should be noted that although this is customary, RCA could take place at any point in time, with practitioners reexamining the data to confirm their ideas and hypotheses or exploring new ones (Creswell, 2014). Although there are many approaches to RCA, there are four approaches that are widely cited in the literature: cause-and-effect diagrams (CED), interrelationship diagrams (ID), current reality trees (CRT) and the five whys method.

According to Doggett (2005), although these approaches have been validated and confirmed in the literature, there has been little written about what criteria one should use in selecting a particular RCA for a certain task. Doggett also notes that although these approaches certainly have their benefits, they also have limitations. Practitioners using or contemplating using these root cause approaches should be aware of their limitations to make the best selection for their particular situation. Practitioners should also be aware of the propensity for some stakeholders to view root causes through a deficit lens.

In addition to identifying root causes experts in RCA also note that these approaches should provide a forum that fosters discussion among key stakeholders, as well as helping to develop a sense of community and a capacity among stakeholders that did not exist prior to engaging in root cause practices. This creation of knowledge at a community level is beneficial because an organization that does not properly identify the core problem or issue is one that is merely treating the symptoms and not the actual cause (Anderson & Fagerhaug, 2000; Dew, 1991; Sproull, 2001).

The Cause and Effect Diagram (a.k.a. Fishbone Diagram)

Originally developed by Kaoru Ishikawa in 1943 to address quality control issues in steel manufacturing plants, this model became widely used throughout Japanese industry and eventually recognized around the world. Although it was originally known as the Ishikawa diagram, it became better known as the fishbone diagram because of the image a successfully completed model portrayed (Doggett, 2005).

The creation of a fishbone diagram is meant to identify causal factors for a problem, but it is also designed to foster a conversation about the issues surrounding those factors and, in turn, increase knowledge and awareness within the organization itself. There are four steps to developing a fishbone diagram:

Step 1: Identify the Problem

In this first step, a problem or event has to be identified. This problem should be written on the right-hand side of a piece of paper. Next, draw a line from the left side of the page to the right, connecting to the problem (see Figure 2.1).

Figure 2.1. Step 1 in developing a basic fishbone diagram.

Step 2: Identify Major Causes

Next, draw smaller lines off of the main line as shown in Figure 2.2. On each of the smaller lines list separately a major cause that is contributing to the problem. Although many times we like to think that a problem or event is caused by only one factor, in reality there are usually multiple factors at work. It is important at this part of developing your fishbone diagram to be sure to provide as much breadth as possible when it comes to generating all the possible causes that contribute to the problem. A discussion among team members or vested stakeholders is an effective way to generate these ideas; however, members have to come to consensus for the diagram to be successfully developed.

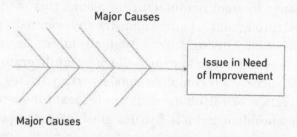

Figure 2.2. Step 2: Major causes for fishbone.

Step 3: Identify Minor Causes

Now draw a line off of each major cause you have listed and identify any minor causes. These minor causes form the small lines or branches, as they are sometimes referred to (see Figure 2.3).

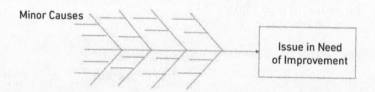

Figure 2.3. Step 3: Minor causes for fishbone.

Step 4: Confirm Breadth of Categories

The last step is to refer to the major and minor categories that you or your team have proposed in order to determine if there are any remaining categories. Experts in the field recommend having no fewer than three and no more than eight categories listed on a single fishbone diagram. Less than three categories creates a fishbone that is so vague that no meaningful work can come from it; however, more than eight creates an environment that is not focused enough.

In addition, it may be useful to have sections of the fishbone with particular themes. As you can see in Figure 2.4, one section could pertain to people, another to process, another to equipment and so on (Hristokski, Kostoska, Kotevski, & Dimovski, 2017).

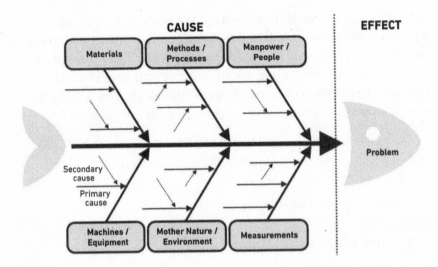

Figure 2.4. Step 4 in developing a fishbone.

Proponents of the fishbone diagram method note that this RCA model is easy to develop and creates meaningful thought-provoking dialogue among participants. This model can help in developing new knowledge and new perspectives for the program at hand by those involved in its development. Critics of this model point to the fact that there is no final analysis or method for determining what the real root cause of a problem is and leaves this up to team members to decide, usually through a shared consensus about what members believe is the root cause.

Interrelationship Diagram (ID)

Many believe the problems or issues that are identified within an organization are not linear in nature (as shown by the fishbone diagram) but have dense intertwined relationships. Based on this idea, the interrelationship diagram (ID) was developed. It works by visually displaying all the relationships and interrelated factors (Doggett, 2005).

Step 1: Identify a Problem or Issue

Members of an organization are asked to come together and identify a problem or issue. It is advised to do this activity using a whiteboard or newsprint. It should be noted that there are different types of ID approaches and, depending on which type you use, you may place the issue or problem differently in the model. For this approach, we are placing the problem at the top of the page (see Figure 2.5).

Low parent
involvement

Figure 2.5. Step 1 in developing an ID.

Step 2: Identify Possible Causes

Once this has been done, members should brainstorm about possible causes. These causes should then be placed in a circle around the page, as shown in Figure 2.6.

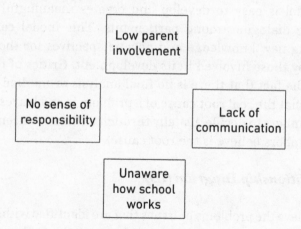

Figure 2.6. Step 2 in developing an ID.

Step 3: Connect Causes and Outcomes

Next, use arrows to connect the boxes. Arrows that point away from
a box are causing it to happen, whereas those that point into the box
comprise the outcome. Again, a group discussion should be used in
order to come to a consensus as to the direction of each arrow (see
Figure 2.7).

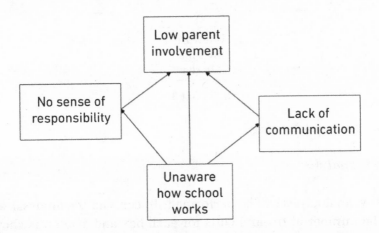

Figure 2.7. Step 3: Connect causes and outcomes.

Step 4: Determine Intensity

Now it is time to determine the intensity of the arrows. Darken
arrows where the members feel that there is a more intense cause
or outcome associated with it (see Figure 2.8).

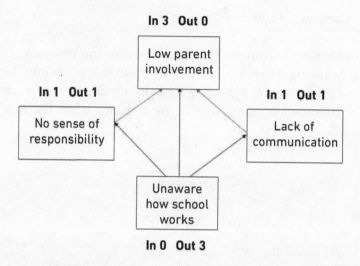

Figure 2.8. Step 4: Intensity.

Step 5: Analysis

Finally, an analysis can be performed. To conduct the analysis, add up the number of Ins and Outs for each box and display as shown in Figure 2.9. Which cause has the most number of each? The team should focus on the causes that have the greatest number of Ins and Outs. In this example about parent involvement, members of the data team quickly realized that parents' lack of awareness about how school "works" was an underlying or root cause of many of the other causes and a main contributor to low parent involvement. Interestingly, parents' lack of responsibility (which many members of the team thought was a central issue due to their deficit understanding and talked about a great deal at school meetings) played very little into the equation when mapped out using the ID method.

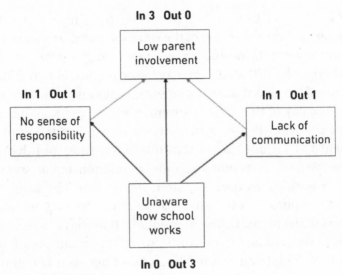

Figure 2.9. Step 5: Analysis.

Benefits of ID are that it is relatively easy for members to create, and, like the fishbone diagram, it increases an organization's knowledge and capacity. Unlike the fishbone, the ID approach also allows an organization to not only analyze the relationship between causes but to establish quantitative findings to confirm those relationships; however, a main barrier to this approach is that it still requires members of the organization to reach a consensus, whereby the majority perception prevails.

Current Reality Tree (CRT)

The third RCA tool is what is called the current reality tree (CRT). Developed by Goldratt (1994), the CRT is based on the notion that people know how to solve problems but lack the methodology to focus their intuition. In fact, Goldratt notes that without such methods people do the exact opposite, compounding the crisis within their organization (Doggett, 2005; Spaulding & Falco, 2013). Rather than isolate causes as individual components, the CRT recognizes the interrelationship of causes and guides practitioners into understanding the links between these causing factors and the core issue at hand. These factors are referred to as undesired effects (UDE). In doing so, the CRT is designed to show the reality of the situation and the collective causes that contribute to the problem from various angles (Doggett, 2005).

Although the CRT diagram may look complex, in reality it is similar to the ID in that it uses statements, boxes and arrows to present a visual display of the current situation within the organization. As you can see from Figure 2.10, statements are inside of boxes and represent the various causes that ultimately underpin the current problem. Arrows represent a significant relationship between those causes or entities, as they are often referred to. The word *significant* here implies that in some instances causes may be listed but members of the organization may not feel that they are contributing enough to warrant an arrow. An "If, then" statement should be used in order to validate an arrow being placed between two entities. If you look at the example in Figure 2.10, members from the organization would validate the linking of the arrows by discussing if the following statement rings true: "If . . . then . . ." CRTs are typically designed from the top down, but read from the bottom up.

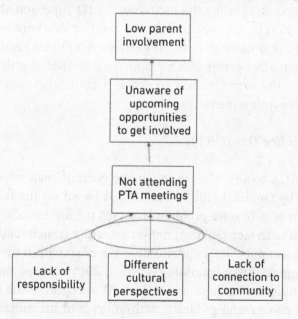

Figure 2.10. Overview of completed CRT.

In addition to arrows, the CRT also uses ellipses. Ellipses in this diagram represent interdependent causes (Doggett, 2005). Where causes in the CRT are considered interrelational, interdependent causes are those that cannot exist without the assistance of another cause or several causes. As you see in Figure 2.10, lack of responsibility, different cultural perspectives (when it comes to the purpose of education), and lack of community connection are interdependent, in that all three must be present in order to impact not attending PTA meetings. Through discussion members of an organization would determine which causes are interrelational and which are interdependent.

Benefits of the CRT approach are that once again it provides a clear visual as to the relationships between causes and the problem. Another benefit of the CRT is that it allows for various "strengths" of relationships to exist where there isn't enough significance between causes to support the use of an arrow. The CRT also shows where two or more causes are interdependent on one another. The two previous approaches do not entertain this idea; however, a key barrier to using the CRT is that it is more time and labor intensive than the fishbone or the ID approach.

Five Whys Questioning Technique

Not all RCA models require a visual framework using arrows, boxes or ellipses. Developed by Shakichi Toyoda for the Toyota Industries Corporation, the methodology for the five whys approach follows its own name (Serrat, 2017). In order to accomplish this approach, one would pose a problem statement and then ask *why* this is the case and continue to "drill down" asking why to the responses team members generate.

The first step in this method is to establish a team. Once this has been accomplished the team should put forth a problem or issue. Ideally flipchart paper, a whiteboard or even Post-it Notes stuck to a wall should be used so everyone can see the process and respond accordingly. The problem or issue should be clearly stated on the flipchart paper. A consensus should be established among team members that this is indeed a worthwhile problem or issue that needs to be addressed.

Next, pose the question *Why?* to the problem and have team members generate ideas in response. Approximately, four to five ideas work best. From each of the proposed ideas generated from the first why, ask why to each of these. Continue this process until you have asked five times why. If executed correctly, there should be a gradual narrowing of the cause for the problem (see Figure 2.11).

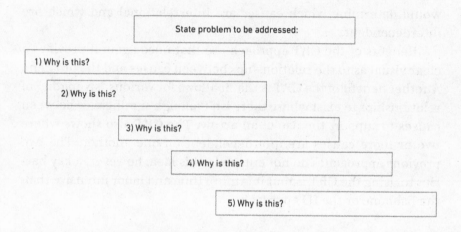

Figure 2.11. The five whys technique.

In Figure 2.12 you can see how we have taken the same theme of low parent involvement and from a discussion among team members have "drilled down" using the five whys technique. Notice how the result or root cause is somewhat different from the previous models. It is clear here that lack of parent involvement isn't so much that they don't care but that they have to work multiple jobs due to the lack of opportunities. How might this new understanding affect how you and your team members go about addressing the issue. Holding more PTA meetings, increasing communication so parents know when PTA meetings will be held and disseminating information about school-related issues at PTA meetings now appear to be ineffective strategies for increasing parent involvement.

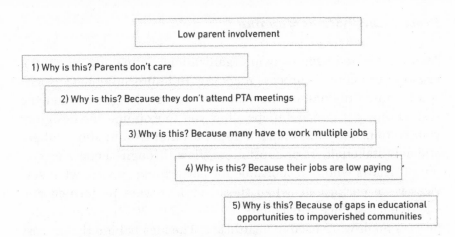

Figure 2.12. Applying the five whys technique.

After the five whys have been completed, the team should examine all the original reasons for the problem (as well as their supporting reasons) and decide which cause is the most valid for the problem. It is also important for validity purposes that there is a consensus among team members in selecting the cause that makes the most sense. Once this has been achieved the team should work to develop an action plan to address the problem.

The five whys method has been criticized for being superficial in nature and not getting to the "authentic" root cause of the problem, because stakeholders often don't know what they don't know and may give responses that are self-serving in nature or politically correct. As stated earlier, it is important that stakeholders are both accurate and honest in their responses; however, it should be recognized that the makeup of the team can play a role in that level of honesty. If the team is made up of an administrator and workers, workers may be apprehensive about expressing their true feelings during the five whys method and may in fact adhere to the administrator's agenda (Spaulding & Falco, 2013; Spaulding & Smith, 2018). If this is the case, it may be beneficial to the validity of the five whys method to form a team that is made up of all employees or in the case of parental involvement, go through the process with a group of parents.

Process and Systems Mapping

Another method used to help organizations define and locate the origin of problems is process mapping. In improvement science, it is a common understanding that systems are designed to get the results they get; process maps allow you to examine the design of your system. A process map is a flowchart that visually shows where and how stakeholders or consumers "flow through" a complex system. It shows who is responsible for performing service, what services were performed, when these services were performed and where each service was conducted (Marriott, 2018). Traditionally, process maps were used in healthcare. The idea behind the process map is once the process map is created and shows all possibilities of how people flow through the various aspects, then matrices or measures can be added to the maps. For example, how long does it take for an individual to be served at the clinic? In this situation, a process map would be created of all the possible treatments available at the clinic, including signing in, paperwork, insurance forms, sitting in the waiting room and so on. Then members from the organization would select individuals who are at the clinic and follow them through the process, timing them to see how long it takes to be served. As part of this process a clinic could conduct this investigation and determine an average time for treatment in the clinic. In addition, surveys could be administered to gather data about how satisfied patients were with the services they received. In the end new goals could be set to decrease the time it takes to serve patients and increase patient level of satisfaction.

In education, we have similar processes in that we serve students; however, instead of providing healthcare services we provide curriculum, coursework and sequencing of coursework for majors, to name a few. Using a process map a school district could document how parents are informed about student registration, what forms have to be filled out, where these certain forms have to go within the district, how parents are notified about which school building their child will attend or how parents are notified of any changes. You may have some experience with mapping already and not realize it. Curriculum maps are not dissimilar from process maps; you identify objectives and where they are covered in the coursework throughout the sequence of a program or school year and what course/teacher is responsible for ensuring that standard/objective has been covered. You can see the possibilities with process maps in educational settings.

Process mapping can also be used in higher education settings. An organization could construct a process map about how students register for classes, how they find out about their advisors, how they find out about information about financial aid and the forms students need to fill out. The steps in the process are virtually endless. Once this process map is delineated and in place, then the institution could examine students as they move through this process and gather data at critical moments in time. Perhaps through process mapping the institution is able to see the specific point in the system that is contributing to the lack of persistence of first-year students. Presented in Figure 2.13 is an example of a basic process map regarding first-year student registration. The University Innovation Alliance has described process mapping as a "critical strategy linked to our success" that is also "low-cost, low-tech, and high interaction" (Burns & Aljets, 2018, para. 2).

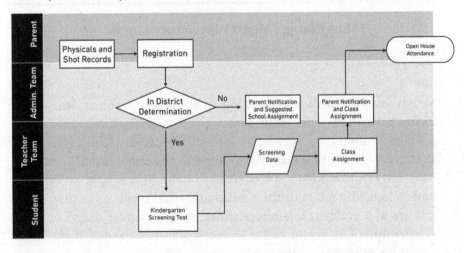

Figure 2.13. Basic process map: Fictional kindergarten registration.

Tools for Creating Process Maps

The tools used for creating process maps are the same tools that are traditionally used in creating basic flowcharts. Presented below are the basic tools (shapes) that are used. Process maps can be easily created using Microsoft and Word software. The shapes presented below can be created using this software; however, there is specific software for flowcharts that make this easier.

An Oval. An oval is used to signal the beginning and end of the process.

Box. A box is used to show activity of a process.

Arrow. The arrow is used to link between process steps.

Diamond. A diamond indicates that a decision is being made in the process. This usually creates two pathways: a "Yes" or a "No," based on how this decision is made.

What Change Might I Introduce and Why?

The Driver Diagram

When an organization is working to address a problem, it is often difficult to know what steps or actions to take first. It is also challenging to know if a certain action will eventually lead to the goal that the organization wants to achieve in the first place. The driver diagram (Figure 2.14) is a tool used to help members of an organization logically map out their goals and what needs to be done (i.e., drivers and actions) to achieve those goals. A driver diagram is an illustration of an organization's theory of improvement. If you have taken program evaluation or worked in education for a while, you may be wondering how a theory of improvement is different from a *theory of change or a theory of action,* both common terms used in the educational lexicon. A theory of change explains the rationale behind a change in a particular context, and a theory of action is the operationalization of the theory of change. Although not dramatically different, a theory of improvement recognizes that all change does not lead to improvement, and it identifies both changes that should lead to improvement and the actions that must accompany those changes.

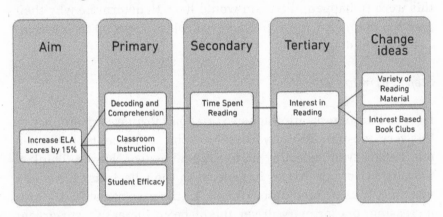

Figure 2.14. An example of a simple driver diagram.

Steps in Designing a Driver Diagram

A driver diagram, as with many of these other tools, should be developed collectively, because together a team knows more than any single individual. Prior to completing the driver diagram, the problem and the goal should be identified. Although steps in developing a driver diagram may vary from project to project, presented below are five core components that every team should include as they work through the driver diagram process.

Step 1. The Goal or Aim

As with the other improvement tools, a team within the organization needs to be formed to determine the overall goal for the driver diagram. In identifying the goal, team members may need to examine data or records to support their claims. A goal may be a written statement but may also have a quantitative aspect to it. For example, in Figure 2.12 the goal is to increase sixth-grader ELA scores in the school building by 15% annually. This type of goal provides a clear target in order to determine if the goal has been met. If for example the student ELA scores were to increase only by 10%, this would be nice but not achieving the organization's original goal. If this were to happen, the team would have to determine why their goal was not met. They would have to decide to revamp their actions in the driver diagram.

Step 2. Primary Driver

How will the organization achieve this goal? Primary drivers answer this very question. Primary drivers are the components that, when put in place, will logically lead to the goal being achieved. Think of primary drivers or drivers in general as the wheel that turns in a machine, thus turning other wheels. In the case of the ELA scores increasing, one primary driver might be to increase sixth-grader decoding and comprehension skills, as evidenced on the district's benchmark ELA assessment. This ELA exam is created by the district and given to students three times throughout the school year for progress-monitoring purposes (which would serve as a driver measure—see more in chapter 3). The belief may be that if students improve decoding and comprehension skills as evidenced on the district-level ELA assessment, they will improve on the state's assessment and reach proficiency. Other primary drivers for this goal might be improved ELA classroom instruction, alignment of classroom instruction with assessment and increased student efficacy as learners. In general, a team should look to generate three to four primary drivers, because more than that amount makes the diagram becomes too cluttered, losing its original purpose and focus. Too few primary drivers and the exercise does not have the breadth to make it meaningful or illustrate the complexity of the problem.

Step 3. Secondary Drivers

Once the primary drivers have been established, it is time for the management team to develop secondary drivers. Secondary drivers are those initiatives that cause the primary drivers to occur. For example, student improvement throughout the year on the district assessment was noted as a primary driver. What secondary driver would contribute to this? Perhaps an increase in time spent reading. Students have to read to increase literacy skills. Student scores on the district-level ELA assessment will never improve if students do not practice reading.

Step 4. Tertiary Drivers

Tertiary drivers are those components that play a role in secondary drivers occurring. Student interest may play a role in their willingness to read beyond class-assigned reading tasks. This tertiary driver, interest in reading, would play a role in increasing student time spent reading (a secondary driver).

Step 5. Actions/Interventions

Last but not least are the actions or changes that need to take place. An action could be an intervention, an activity or a program. A program is a temporary set of activities or services that come together to address a particular problem within an organization (Mathison, 2005; Spaulding, 2014). Developing change ideas should be a group activity and nothing should be eliminated while ideas are being developed. When selecting a particular action or intervention, it may be useful to use a difficulty/impact matrix to quickly determine what gives you the most bang for your buck. Design thinking activities are quite useful when developing change ideas. *Innovating for People: Handbook of Human-Centered Design Methods* by the LUMA Institute and *Design-Based School Improvement* by Rick Mintrop have examples of activities you could use during the development of change ideas. For this particular example, the change might be increasing the variety of reading material within sixth grade classes. Another possible action that may occur along with the increased variety in material is the creation of book clubs around student interest—for example, a Marvel versus DC Book Club, where you read comics, graphic novels and books about the history and development of the characters. You may even watch movies related to what they are reading. This action would certainly increase student attendance!

Your driver diagram illustrates the logic from your change idea back to your aim. If the problem is unfamiliar or it is the first time you have encountered it, you may want to read a bit about it before developing your theory of improvement. Walter A. Shewhart developed a concept entitled "degree of belief" (Langley et al., 2009). In essence, it questions to what degree you trust your theory of improvement. You cannot develop a strong theory with little background information. There are two things that determine the degree of belief—the first is whether or not there is evidence that the change idea has had an impact elsewhere. Second is how similar the current context is to the context where the change worked. This is critical for doctoral- and master's-level scholar-practitioners. Unlike research for discovery, where the goal is to see if some new thing works, improvement research is sometimes research of application—finding something that has already worked and determining how to make it work in a new context. Literature and/or evidence from similar organizations should justify support for particular change ideas (especially if being used for a thesis or dissertation in practice).

In addition to implementing an action, it is important that team members keep in mind that the driver diagram is an ongoing, ever-evolving document. One should not create a driver diagram and then store it away in a desk drawer. A successful driver diagram is a "living document" in that it is made to be revisited and revised over and over as new knowledge comes to light. Many experts who use driver diagrams want team members to know that the interconnectedness between drivers, actions and goals will vary from setting to setting. What one organization finds may not necessary be what another one with similar demographics and characteristics determines to be true. An action that has "worked" in one setting will not necessarily transfer to another setting with the same results.

The Plan, Do, Study, Act (PDSA) Framework

Having not been best served by traditional research methods, many administrators these days unfortunately default to a type of "knee-jerk" reaction when addressing problems or issues. They identify the issue while simultaneously identifying its cause (or what they believe to be the cause) and select the intervention to fix it. In addition, after they have implemented their new approach, they provide little to no real monitoring or studying to discover whether they were right in their hypothesis. The following year the problem is still there and it has grown.

Also referred to as the Deming cycle, the Plan, Do, Study, Act (PDSA) framework (Figure 2.15) is a method used by those wishing to make ongoing programmatic decisions at their institutions or educational settings. The PDSA framework is a unique improvement tool that requires the organization as a whole to learn and build knowledge, both about the problem or problems that need to be addressed, as well as their causes. In addition, the PDSA approach requires organizational members to study the problem through collecting data and using the data to make informed decisions and programmatic refinements as they work.

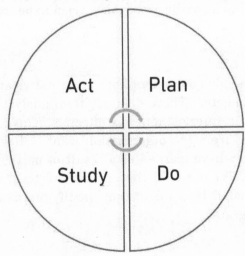

Figure 2.15. PDSA framework.

Overview of Basic PDSA Framework

Plan

When making changes to an organization we often don't take the time to plan. In this first step, stakeholders come together to discuss the issue that has been identified and to brainstorm its causes and possible interventions. Typically, organizations participate in this planning stage by holding meetings where members who have direct in-depth knowledge of the settings and the overall situation would come together and discuss the problem.

Do

In this step, the organization implements the intervention. The intervention can be many different things. It can be a new program or a modification of a current program or practice. It can also be a change in a policy; however, a change in policy typically results in some type of change in practice. In any event, it is important for this step that members clearly articulate and operationally define this new program or intervention. A clearly defined intervention will later transfer into an easily replicable project to be scaled up.

Study

As part of the study component both quantitative and qualitative data can be collected. These data are then analyzed in order to determine if the intervention was effective. This is also a time when members from the organization want to have discussions about what they have learned as a result of participating in the PDSA process. What would they do differently if they were to repeat the process? How might they modify or change the intervention or program?

Act

In most cases the responsibility for this last step falls to the original group of stakeholders who came together in the planning stage; however, as noted by (Spaulding & Falco, 2013), the implementation or change in policies and or practices within an organization may require the approval or assistance of members of the organization who outrank those members serving on the planning committee.

Regardless of who will implement this new plan, the important thing is that some action has to be taken. Working through the PDSA process without taking some action is a waste of the members' time and resources that could be redirected to another part of the organization. In the Act stage, members must reflect on what was learned in the Study stage and from that new knowledge change practices or policies altogether or modify them. All of these changes are based on evidence from this original PDSA cycle. If, for example, the intervention that was put into place during this first cycle was deemed successful and evidence from it promising, then it warrants being expanded within the organization to more sites.

PDSA Cycles

The PDSA framework was not meant to be a one-shot attempt to implement an intervention to see if it works. The PDSA framework was meant to have multiple cycles (Langley et al., 2009). As shown in Figure 2.16, the first cycle is built around the premise that it is a pilot study. In the pilot study the organization wants to "test" some aspect of the bigger intervention. As part of this process, the organization wants to have the first round of PDSA to take place in a short period of time—a week, month or a couple months at the most. One does not want the first cycle to continue for too long of a period (e.g., an entire year) because you want to "test" the intervention in a small setting for a short period of time. This allows one to study it first to see its effect before introducing it to the entire organization.

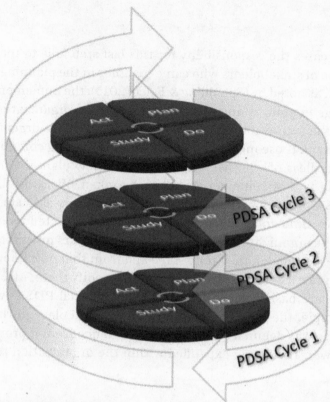

Figure 2.16. PDSA Cycles.

The most important aspect of the Do step is that the intervention be first studied in a small setting. Although a pilot study will vary from project to project, there are some key characteristics that need to be in place in order for the pilot to be successful and provide members with the information they need to optimize the PDSA approach:

1. Making sure that the time period for the pilot is short in duration. A couple of days, a week or maybe a month is ideal. What is not ideal is if you treat the pilot as a full-fledged study and allow it to take place over an entire year. It is important in an organization to quickly identify and fix issues as they arise. A pilot study over too long a time period is counterproductive in nature to the PDSA approach.

2. Also make sure that your pilot study will provide you with some quick data for members to make a decision. Keep in mind the data that are collected during this quick data feedback loop may not be the ultimate outcome data members of the organization may want to see improve. In the earlier example, the district had identified that there was a notable percentage of students who had "slipped" out of proficiency on the state's annual ELA assessment. Implementing an intervention to correct this and waiting to see if the following year's state assessment shows improvement is too long a time period for a pilot. In cases such as this, one would want to select another outcome variable to use as a measure in order to judge whether the intervention was successful or not. Some other marker for improved literacy scores would need to be identified and agreed upon by the members of the organization. One possibility in situations like these is to select what is referred to as an intermediate outcome. An intermediate outcome is a "smaller" outcomes that in a logical framework would need to occur in order for the large end outcomes (e.g., test scores) to improve. In the example with student ELA scores the district may choose to select interim data collected four times a year by the district. This interim data could be used for the pilot study to provide the necessary information to determine whether there is evidence of the new intervention working.

Next, the organization would conduct a second PDSA cycle. During this second PDSA the above steps would remain the same; however, if the data from the pilot study was shown to be promising, then a larger, expanded study would be warranted. This second PDSA round might include expanding both the timeline as well as the number of sites or sample size. If the data from the pilot did not support the expansion of the program, then another pilot using a different intervention or modified intervention would need to take place before scaling up the study to include a larger portion of the organization. *The PDSA addresses this problem by creating cycles.* Cycles are studies that take place in a short amount of time.

Once an organization has scaled up the intervention to include the entire organization, it is important to continue monitoring to ensure the intervention is being implemented across the site with fidelity and that no new issues arise over time (Cohen-Vogel et al., 2014).

There is no one way to do improvement science; its adaptability is what makes it applicable to so many diverse problems of practice. Its tools can be used in a variety of settings. As you tackle complex problems of practice within your organization, remember to use root cause analysis and process maps to help you answer the question regarding what is the exact problem you are trying to solve. Develop and refine your driver diagram as you answer the question as to what change might you introduce and why. Employ the PDSA cycle as you collect practical measures to determine if your change is indeed an improvement.

References

Andersen, B., & Fagerhaug, T. (2000). *Root cause analysis: Simplified tools and techniques.* Milwaukee, WI: ASA Quality Press.

Burns, B., & Aljets, A. (2018). *Using process mapping to redesign the student experience.* Available from https://er.educause.edu/articles/2018/3/using-process-mapping-to-redesign-the-student-experience

Cohen-Vogel, L., Tichnor-Wagner, D. A., Harrison, C., Kainz, K., Socol, A. R., & Wang, Q. (2014). Implementing educational innovations at scale: Transforming researchers into continuous improvement scientists. *Educational Policy, 1*(21). doi: 10.1177/0896904814560886

Creswell, J. W. (2014). *Research design: Qualitative, quantitative and mixed methods approaches* (4th ed.). Thousand Oaks, CA: Sage.

Dew, J. R. (1991). In search of the root cause. *Quality Progress, 24*(3), 97–107.

Doggett, M. A. (2005). Root cause analysis: A framework for tool selection. *The Quality Management Journal, 12*(4), 45.

Goldratt, E. M. (1994). *It's not luck.* Great Barrington, MA: North River Press.

Hristokski, I., Kostoska, O., Kotevski, Z., & Simovski, T. (2017). Causality of factors reducing competitiveness of e-commerce firms, 3 (02), 109–130.

Langley, G. J., Moen, R. D., Nolan, K. M., Nolan, T. W., Norman, C. L., & Provost, L. P. (2009). *The improvement guide: A practical approach to enhancing organizational performance.* Charlottesville, VA: Wiley.

Marriott, R. D. (2018). Process mapping: The foundation for effective quality improvement. *Current Problems in Pediatric and Adolescent Health Care,* 1–5.

Mathison, S. (Ed.) (2005). *Encyclopedia of evaluation.* Thousand Oaks, CA: Sage.

Rooney, J. J., & Vanden Heuvel, L. N. (2004, July). Root cause analysis for beginners. *Quality Program.* Available from www.asq.org

Serrat, O. (2017). *Knowledge solutions.* Asian Development Bank. doi:10.1007/978-981-10-0982-9-32

Spaulding, D. T. (2014). *Program evaluation in practice: A core concept and examples for discussion and analysis.* San Francisco, CA: Jossey-Bass Wiley.

Spaulding, D. T., & Falco, J. (2013). *Action research for school leaders.* Boston, MA: Pearson.

Spaulding, D. T., & Smith, G. (2018). *What does your school data team sound like?* Thousand Oaks, CA: Sage.

Sproull, B. (2001). *Process problem solving: A guide for maintenance and operations teams.* Portland, OR: Productivity Press.

CHAPTER THREE

Practical Measurement in Improvement Science

BRANDI NICOLE HINNANT-CRAWFORD

Western Carolina University

Rooted in pragmatism, practical measurement helps scholar-practitioners address a series of questions related to a primary pragmatist question: "What works?" For years, educational leaders have been inundated with many types of data and an onslaught of research about what types of data we should use to drive our decision-making. This chapter will define practical measurement, or data collected specifically to inform improvement efforts, and provide guidance on how to develop, collect and analyze practical measures and practical measurement data. It will also describe other types of measurement commonly encountered by educational leaders—namely, measurement for research and measurement for accountability. To ground this chapter, we will examine practical measurement in the context of the problems of practice of three scholar-practitioners: Sharice, an assistant principal of an elementary school; Hector, the director of financial aid at a community college; and Jennifer, a dean at a research-intensive university.

Educational Leaders with Complex Problems and Opportunities for Improvement

Discipline at Urban Stars Elementary School

Sharice is an assistant principal at Urban Stars Elementary School in a metropolitan city. Her administrative duties are many; like many assistant principals, she is in charge of buses and behavior. Forty-eight percent of Urban Stars students are African American and 26% are Latinx, whereas the faculty and staff are 94% White. When reviewing the descriptive statistics of disciplinary referrals, she uncovered a pattern among the students sent to her: Black boys are referred more than any other group (consisting of 80% of all referrals). When she dug even deeper, she discovered most of their referrals were for more subjective offenses such as disrespect, insubordination and being disruptive, consistent with literature on disproportionality in discipline (Skiba, et al., 2014). Sharice believes the disproportionality in discipline may actually be a symptom of cultural mismatch between her teachers and students. After convening a team of stakeholders, including the school social worker, veteran and novice teachers, parents and a behavioral specialist, and completing a root cause analysis, she and her team created the driver diagram in Figure 3.1 to illustrate their theory of improvement.

After careful consideration of the group's change ideas, Sharice identifies cultural responsiveness training as a change concept and decides to use communities of practice to educate her teachers on cultural responsiveness. But how will she know if the change leads to an improvement?

Financial Aid at Bright Future Ahead Community College

Hector is the director of financial aid at Bright Future Ahead Community College (BFACC). In the last five years, he has noticed an increase of people registering who do not qualify for financial aid because they have defaulted on student loans. Although using federal loans is usually discouraged by financial aid counselors at community

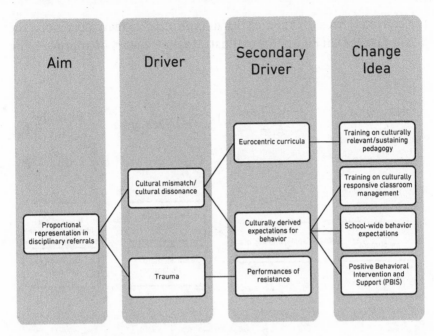

Figure 3.1. Sharice's driver diagram.

colleges (McKinney, Roberts, & Shefman, 2013), the extreme poverty facing the community he serves makes finding several hundred dollars for tuition and books out of reach for most of their population. Last fall semester, BFACC had to turn away 7% of its first-time students. Because BFACC is funded based on full-time equivalency (FTE), the president has asked Hector to figure out why so many students are ineligible for aid and what the college can do about it. After closely examining their records, Hector finds most of the students started but failed to finish at the local for-profit college—Get Your Degree Today University (GYDTU)—and had defaulted on their student loans. Hector, along with the director of admissions, academic advisors, a high school counselor and two students denied financial aid, sat down to examine the root cause of the problem. They found two issues needing to be addressed: (a) students attend GYDTU because they believe a bachelor's degree from a four-year institution is better than transferring from a two-year and getting a bachelor's, and (b) students do not understand the workings of financial aid and the consequences that come with defaulting. His team developed the driver diagram in Figure 3.2 to illustrate their theory of improvement.

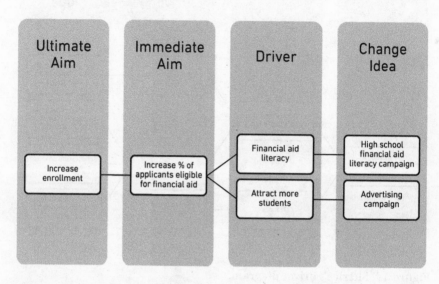

Figure 3.2. Hector's driver diagram.

Hector decides that recruiting students is not his area of expertise (he will leave that change idea for admissions), so he will launch a financial aid literacy campaign in the local high schools. But how will he know if the campaign is contributing to an increase in financial aid eligibility?

Promotion and Tenure at Intellectual Elite University

Jennifer is the dean of the College of Arts and Sciences at Intellectual Elite University. She has been recognized several times by the institution for the role her college has played in diversifying the faculty on campus. It is clear; her college hires the most faculty from underrepresented backgrounds. However, she is finding that the outstanding faculty members that she proudly hires are struggling with tenure and promotion. Three (of the eight underrepresented faculty she hired) were denied tenure this past year. Jennifer, who is a part of a national organization of female deans, reached out to some of her colleagues to get insights on how they support underrepresented faculty. She also met individually with the faculty denied tenure and asked what they felt they needed to be more successful. Last, she met with the tenure and promotion committee members (individually) to understand what they felt these tenure-track professors were missing in their dossiers. She found, as is well documented, underrepresented faculty

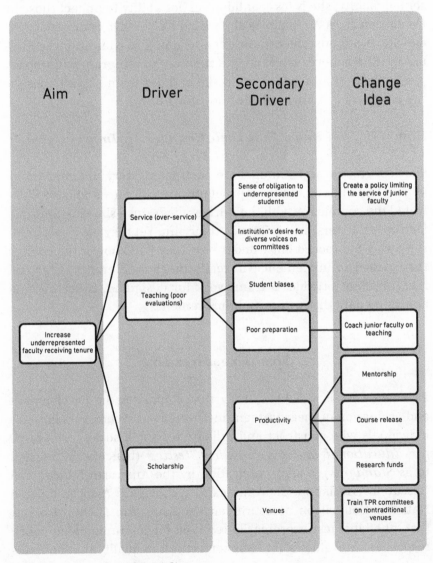

Figure 3.3. Jennifer's driver diagram.

have more service and less favorable student evaluations (Lilienfeld, 2016). She gathered her program directors and created the diagram in Figure 3.3 to illustrate her theory of improvement.

Whereas Jennifer (and her team) believe that student bias and institutional desire for diverse voices overburden her underrepresented faculty, she is less confident in her ability to impact those in the near future. As much as she would like to give course releases and startup funds, she cannot imagine doing so without it seeming unfair. She believes developing a mentorship program will impact productivity of junior faculty, so she and her team begin to design the program. But how will she know for sure?

How Will They Know That Their Changes Are Improvements?

Sharice, Hector and Jennifer are each facing very different problems. They understand their problems are complex and have illustrated the complexity with their driver diagrams—showing multiple factors (or drivers) will influence their aim. Yet they have each chosen a way to proceed but wonder how they will know if the change they picked to implement will really make a difference. Practical measurement provides a framework for designing, collecting and analyzing data that will drive improvement.

What Is Measurement?

Psychometrics is a field of study that comprises the development and evaluation of measurement instruments. Psychometricians are individuals who construct and validate tests and scales. *Standards for Educational and Psychological Testing* (henceforth referred to as *Standards*), a joint publication by the American Educational Research Association, the American Psychological Association, and National Council on Measurement in Education (1999), explains that "the label test is ordinarily reserved for instruments on which responses are evaluated for their correctness or quality and the terms *scale* or *inventory* are used for measures of attitudes, interests, and dispositions" (p. 3). Educators (and scientists of all kinds) develop instruments to measure constructs (i.e., characteristics, knowledge of a particular domain, etc.), either latent or observable. Early psychometricians used classical test theory (CTT) to evaluate instruments; CTT posits each score yielded from an instrument consists of the true score and some degree of measurement error. Classical test theorists were also concerned with the reliability and validity of an instrument. Reliability refers to the consistency of an instrument, when it is administered repeatedly, and validity is the degree to which the instrument accurately captures the construct it is designed to capture. Some psychometricians push back on the idea that an instrument is valid but argue validity lies more in if the instrument is used in ways it was intended. Psychometricians also use item response theory (IRT) to evaluate instruments; in contrast to CTT, IRT "models the relationship between latent traits and the responses to test [scale] items" (Rudy, 2007, p. 797).

In education, measurement is used for three purposes: research, accountability and improvement. Measurement in each case has a different function. Measurement for research attempts to quantify latent constructs (dependent or independent variables). Measurement for accountability serves as summative assessment and is used to identify outliers, be they exemplars or failures. Measurement for improvement is formative; it tells whether or not a change is working.

Measurement for Research

Psychometrics informs measurement in each of these fields, but more heavily in research and accountability. Yeager, Bryk, Muhich, Hausman and Morales (2013) explain that

> measures for theory development [research] often involve administering long, somewhat redundant question batteries assessing multiple small variations on the same concept. . . . By asking a long list of questions, researchers can presumably reduce measurement error due to unreliability and thereby maximize power for testing key relationships of interest among latent variables. (p. 10)

By designing instruments with many items, psychometricians can refine the instrument after piloting it and using factor analytic (CTT) or differential item functioning (IRT) procedures. The refinement process is to increase reliability and validity. Also, in the course of a research study, an instrument is administered a few times at most, not repeatedly and frequently. Therefore, longer instruments can be used, because the time burden to complete the instrument is not recurrent. As researchers, particularly those in the postpositivist tradition, attempt to make causal claims and predictions, as well as to model theories statistically, they need to ensure the instruments they are using to model phenomena capture the constructs of interest.

Measurement for Accountability

Similar to research, measurement for accountability is high stakes, when consequences, be they rewards or sanctions, are tied to scores. Measurement for accountability is characterized by data being "collected after the end of some cycle (such as the end of the school year), meaning that the people affected by a problematic set of procedures have already been harmed; [and] the causes that generated these results are often opaque and not tied to specific practices delivered at a specific time" (Yeager et al., 2013, p. 9). Individuals in all sectors of education, after the publication of *A Nation at Risk: The Imperative for Education Reform* (National Commission on Excellence in Education, 1983) and *Involvement in Learning: Realizing the Potential of American Higher Education* (National Institute of Education, 1984) are familiar with measurement for accountability. Standardized tests and the development of signals such as adequate yearly progress and college/career readiness indices, cohort graduation rates and college entrance exams are all functions of measurement for accountability. Measurement for accountability assesses outcomes—when it is too late to do anything to change the outcome.

Measurement for Improvement

Measurement for improvement or practical measurement addresses the questions posed by Sharice, Hector and Jennifer—"How do I know my change is an improvement?" Unlike researchers who attempt to develop long batteries of items to assess one construct that can be used in a variety of circumstances, practical measures are context specific and embeddable into daily work routines. The items are worded using diction unique to the context. Practical measurement data are collected frequently, analyzed frequently and acted upon quickly to expedite learning about "what works." Unlike measurement for accountability, which focuses narrowly on outcomes, measurement for improvement "require[s] direct measurement of intermediary targets (i.e., 'mediators') in order to evaluate ideas for improvement and inform their continued refinement" (Yeager et al., 2013, p. 12). Practical measures are tied to a theory of improvement, often depicted in a driver diagram (see chapter 2 for a greater description of a driver diagram). Without a working theory of how the change may impact the outcome, it is impossible to develop intermediary measures. Whereas the construction and evaluation of practical measures may not mirror that of measures for research and accountability, scholar practitioners engaged in improvement research also need measures that are valid and reliable. In fact, this is why, when possible, scholar practitioners will borrow and adapt previously established measures.

Understanding Practical Measurement

Practical measurement is pragmatic, yet it takes the question "What works?" and breaks it down into four more specific questions:

- Did it work?
- Is it working?
- How is it working?
- Is it working as intended?

Outcome Measures—Did It Work?

Practical measures are mapped onto the theory of improvement. The first practical measure is the outcome measure. Outcome measures address the question, "Did it work?" The outcome measure assesses the aim of an improvement initiative. It is also used as baseline data that illustrates the problem. The outcome measure will often feel like the easiest to assess. An outcome measure is what economists and businesspersons would call a "lagging" measure. Once the outcome is assessed, there is nothing that can be done to change it. In general, education tends to rely heavily on outcomes measures, in part because of its focus on accountability. When examining the aims of the three educational leaders, the outcome practically jumps out (see Table 3.1). The outcomes are obvious and once the outcome is assessed, there is clear evidence of whether or not improvement has taken place. Unfortunately, outcomes are not assessed that often and outcomes do not provide information on how to improve.

Table 3.1. Aims and Outcome Measures

	Aim	Outcome
Sharice	Proportional representation	Examination of referral records: • What percentage of referrals are Black boys? • What percentage of the school population are Black boys? • Are those percentages the same?
Hector	Increase the percent of students (in need) eligible for financial aid	Examination of financial aid eligibility in the incoming class: • What percent of last year's applicants were eligible for financial aid? • What percent are eligible this year? • Has the percentage increased?
Jennifer	Increase the number of underrepresented faculty receiving tenure	Number of faculty receiving tenure: • What percent of underrepresented faculty members have been awarded tenure?

Driver Measures—Is It Working?

Driver measures address the question "Is it working?" Changes in the primary and secondary drivers should eventually result in changes to the aim. Driver measures assess changes; they serve as intermediaries between the change and the outcome. The driver measure should have predictive validity for the outcome measure. Most improvement initiatives should establish a baseline for the driver measure as well as the outcome measure. A leader, in developing a theory of improvement, should be informed by empirical and theoretical scholarly knowledge about factors that may influence the outcome. Scholars have developed countless measures for a variety of latent concepts related to the outcome; preestablished measures may be useful to measure primary and secondary drivers. A search in a database such as PsychTESTS or disciplinary specific databases (ERIC) using the driver as the keyword along with *instrument/ questionnaire/scale/test/survey/measure* in a separate search field term may yield a preestablished measure for the driver.

Sharice Adopts Previously Established Measures

In the case of Sharice, she identifies *cultural mismatch* as a primary driver in the overrepresentation of Black boys in disciplinary problems. If she looks in the literature related to cultural mismatch theory and assets-based pedagogies, eventually she will come across the work of Siwatu (2007), whose Culturally Responsive Teaching Self-Efficacy and Culturally Responsive Teaching Outcome Expectancy instruments may be useful in gauging changes in her teachers' cultural orientations before, during and after the training.

Although Sharice may think she has hit the jackpot, she has to realize that these instruments were designed for measuring latent constructs for research. As such, the CRTSE scale has 40 questions and the CRTOE scale has 26. Although both have undergone rigorous psychometric evaluation, they are too long for her to administer monthly to her faculty. As she reads the literature about culturally responsive classroom management, she may want to home in on Siwatu's items that relate closely to Weinstein, Curran and Tomlinson-Clarke's (2003) five components of culturally responsive classroom management. If one of the components is not represented, Sharice may have to craft an item to add to the instrument. In Sharice's case, as she develops a driver measure, she does not have to start from scratch. However, she cannot simply use what is there without modification. She has to be selective in choosing her items.

Hector Designs a Test

Hector will measure change in his driver *financial aid literacy* using a test that he and several stakeholders created, borrowing items from established instruments and creating new items specific to the Bright Futures Ahead community. The assessment will cover two domains: financial aid literacy and financial literacy more broadly. Hector already had access to the federal student aid exit counseling survey items. From it, he borrowed multiple-choice questions about deferment, grace periods and ways to repay. However, because of the unique circumstances in his community, he added items about the consequences of defaulting on student loans and how defaulting impacts future aid eligibility. He also spoke to faculty in the business department about measures for financial literacy. He added several items about credit, what credit impacts and appropriate behaviors for maintaining good credit. Although he was pleased with what he could borrow from other instruments, Hector wanted to add a few items about postsecondary affordability that were unique to his state. Keeping with the multiple-choice format, he added the following questions:

- What is the average price difference, in terms of tuition and fees, between a four-year public and a four-year not-for-profit private school in our state?
    - a. $10,000
    - b. $15,00
    - c. $20,000
    - d. $25,000

- What is the average price difference between a for-profit and a
  four-year public school in our state?
  - a. $3,000
  - b. $5,000
  - c. $8,000
  - d. $10,000

His assessment could be completed in five minutes or less and consisted of 12 items: 5 on financial aid literacy, 4 on financial literacy, and 3 about postsecondary plans. One of his postsecondary plan items, which he planned to monitor closely, asked, "Would you consider transferring from a community college to a four-year college?"

To determine what students had learned from the workshop and if the workshop had any impact on his primary driver, Hector decided to have the homeroom teacher administer a preassessment a week before the workshop. This pretest would allow them to establish a baseline of financial and financial aid literacy prior to the workshop. At the culmination of the workshop, his team would pass out a postassessment, which contained similar items. Because this was low-stakes information, he had students put their names on the sheet, and he compared individual raw scores on the items related to financial literacy and the raw scores related to financial aid literacy.

Jennifer Creates a Mechanism for Data Collection

In some cases, the measures a leader will use as driver measures are already available; they just have to be collected in a uniform manner. In the case of Jennifer's scholarship driver, she could have faculty report their number of publications, the acceptance rate of each journal and the impact factor rating of each journal. These are all traditional metrics for scholarship. However, because publishing is an outcome measure of scholarship, she may want to add Likert-type items where faculty self-assess changes in the productivity around data collection, data analysis, grant proposal writing and number of manuscripts in various phases.

Compared to last quarter, how is your scholarship productivity in the following areas?

	Much Worse	Worse	About the Same	Better	Much Better
Research Idea Generation (planning, IRB)	❑	❑	❑	❑	❑
Data Collection	❑	❑	❑	❑	❑
Data Analysis	❑	❑	❑	❑	❑
Grant Proposals	❑	❑	❑	❑	❑
Manuscript Writing	❑	❑	❑	❑	❑
Manuscript Submissions	❑	❑	❑	❑	❑

These items will give a more holistic view of the scholarship productivity of her junior faculty. After creating a questionnaire, she could send it out quarterly. In addition to helping her stay informed about faculty productivity, she could use the data to highlight what's going on in the college in their newsletter.

As she designs her collection mechanism, she must ensure the design allows for quick completion as well as easy analysis. For impact factor she may use a textbox entry that has validation rules where respondents have to enter numeric values only. She could also use closed-ended items such as a scale for acceptance rate. Although she will administer the instrument to all faculty, she needs an item to disaggregate the data by career phase—clinical faculty, adjunct faculty, tenure-track junior faculty—so she can narrow in on the productivity of junior faculty.

Process Measures—How Is It Working?

Process measures are measures of fidelity that address the question "How is it working?" As a leader identifies a change that he or she believes will lead to improvement, the process measure(s) helps determine if the change is actually being implemented as intended. In chapter 2, Spaulding and Hinnant-Crawford discussed the development of process maps to aid in a leader's ability to see the system that produces the result. As a leader develops new processes, he or she must develop measures to make sure the process is being adhered to. The process measure should have predictive validity for the driver measure and subsequently the outcome measure. As implementation scientists Carroll and colleagues (2007) explain:

> If an implemented intervention adheres completely to the content, frequency, duration, and coverage prescribed by its designers, then fidelity can be said to be high. Measuring implementation fidelity means evaluating whether the result of the implementation process is an effective realization of the intervention as planned by its designers. (p. 3)

If a leader fails to get the desired results but the change was not carried out as designed, the failure could be in implementation and not the change idea. In subsequent iterations, he or she may need to focus on supporting the team during implementation. Implementation scientists have given leaders a framework to think about developing process measures. Examining components of the change idea in terms of content, frequency, duration and coverage helps guide our design of process measures.

Measuring Processes in a Community of Practice

Sharice has determined a sit-and-get training is not going to make a significant impact on the cultural mismatches taking place within her school. So she decides she will implement communities of practice within her school, focused on cultural competence, cultural responsiveness and classroom management. Using Wegner's model of communities of practice, she will adopt several texts for teachers to go through together and come to some shared understandings of what it means to be culturally responsive. They will also examine academic and disciplinary data to elucidate where they may be underserving some students. The communities of practice will take place as a part of the common planning and faculty meeting time. Grade-level chairmen may delegate someone to take notes, but Sharice has created a minutes template that uncovers the content and coverage of her

Community of Practice Minutes

UrbanStars

Attendees
_____
_____
_____
_____
_____
_____
_____

ate:_____

rade Level: _____

icilitator:_____

ipic: _____

Total in Attendance ____

xt : _____

y Questions:
_____
_____

Did you connect the material to any of the following?

❑ Academic Achievement at USE
❑ Discipline at USE
❑ Relating to USE Parents
❑ Teaching approaches
❑ Classroom Management Approaches
❑ Deficit Ideologies
❑ Personal Identity Work
❑ Other resources
❑ USE data

ractices To Implement or Things to Think About:
_____
_____
_____
_____

Figure 3.4. Sharice's process measure.

intervention (Figure 3.4). Her template asks for a roster of those in attendance and a total number, so she will be aware of how many people were exposed to the content. It also asks specific content questions such as what text was being explored and what key areas the text was connected to. The format of a checklist makes it easy to complete—while helping Sharice be able to see if they are making a connection to discipline and classroom management strategies.

Hector—Having Facilitators Self-Assess Workshops

Hector has designed an engaging workshop on financial literacy and financial aid literacy to conduct with students in his service area high schools. He has worked with guidance counselors and they have mapped out a plan where he or a member of his team will hit every senior homeroom/advisory class during the fall semester, when people apply to college. They will also complete reminders in the spring semester when students make their decisions. The content of the designed workshop will cover financial literacy, college affordability, financial aid options and consequences of different types of aid. Hector is not the only one teaching the workshop, so he created a rubric to have his staff self-assess each workshop.

Table 3.2. Hector's Process Measure

		Completed	Partially	Did Not Cover
Financial Literacy	Establishing Credit	□	□	□
	Credit Impacts	□	□	□
	Maintain Good Credit	□	□	□
Affordability	Community Colleges	□	□	□
	Public 4 Years	□	□	□
	Private 4 Years	□	□	□
	For-Profit Privates	□	□	□
Aid Options	Scholarships	□	□	□
	Fellowships	□	□	□
	Grants	□	□	□
	Student Loans	□	□	□
	Personal Loans	□	□	□
Consequences	Grace Periods	□	□	□
	Deferment	□	□	□
	Forbearance	□	□	□
	Default	□	□	□
	Eligibility	□	□	□

His rubric focuses on the content covered and will enable him to determine whether the workshops are covering all he intends. He tells his facilitators to complete this form while students are completing the postassessment; in doing so, he embeds data collection into the workshop process, so it is not something facilitators have to do once they return to the office. Hector will use these data to see if facilitators are focusing too much on one area to the detriment of another; he may retrain his workshop facilitators on how to get the most out of the time they have with the students so all of the content can be covered.

Jennifer Tracks the Hiccups

Jennifer has provided incentives for her senior faculty to serve as mentors. If they choose to mentor, they have no additional service requirements besides university and college committees. However, she has explained she wants her mentors to meet with junior faculty at least biweekly and collaborate on a project that will lead to publication (if possible). Her process measure determines the degree to which the mentoring is happening as intended. She has a simple questionnaire for her mentors that is automatically emailed to them every other Friday and can be completed on their phones (Figure 3.5a).

Her process survey is incredibly short and makes use of display logic, so there is a different set of questions for mentors who met with their mentees and mentors who did not meet with their mentees. The survey engine Jennifer used, Qualtrics, estimates it can be completed in one minute (see figure 3.5b), yet it gives her information on whether or not the change idea of the mentorship program is being implemented as intended.

After six weeks (three administrations of the survey), if there is no mention of collaboration, she may reach out to the mentors and remind them that collaboration is a component of being a mentor. Or if she notices mentors and mentees are discussing teaching every week, she may need to give mentors resources on teaching strategies to make them better equipped to handle the questions from their mentees.

Figure 3.5a. Jennifer's mobile friendly process measure.

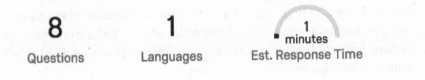

Figure 3.5b. Estimated time to complete Jennifer's process measure.

Balancing Measures—Is It Working as Intended?

The balancing measure answers the question "Is it working as intended?" The balancing measure measures other parts of the system, and may appear to be completely unrelated to the outcome in question. It attempts to capture the unintended consequences of a change. In complex organizations, it is critical to ensure that the intervention or change introduced has not upset another part of the organization. Senge and Sterman (1990) explain that "dynamic decision making is particularly difficult, especially when decisions have indirect, delayed, nonlinear, and multiple effects" (p. 1008).

For example, a leader who introduces a new reading curriculum wants to make sure it does not have unintended consequences on math achievement. Often in education, a balancing measure can be overall student achievement. An initiative may focus on motivation or attendance, but educators always want to make sure the introduction of some change to improve one area does not have a negative impact on achievement.

Balancing measures could be likened to vital signs: temperature, blood pressure, oxygen levels and pulse. They indicate the overall health of the system after the introduction of a change. Like driver measures and outcome measures, it is best to establish a baseline of the balancing measures prior to introducing a change. In Sharice's case, a balancing measure could be student achievement. As she focuses on alleviating disproportionality in disciplinary referrals, she wants to make sure the students at Urban Stars continue to achieve on the benchmark assessments. Hector may examine the amount of money students borrow while he is trying to increase the number of students eligible; he does not want students to begin borrowing excessively or more than is needed. Jennifer plans to make the mentoring available to all junior faculty, but she may watch the tenure and promotion rates of nonunderrepresented faculty as a balancing measure.

A Quick Word on Analyzing and Visualizing Practical Measurement Data

Data yielded from practical measures are no different from data yielded from measures for research or measures for accountability. If data are qualitative in nature, approach them with inductive coding techniques just like interview data. Multiple rounds of coding, an up-to-date code book, audit trail, interrater reliability and member checks are still necessary to ensure high-quality analysis of qualitative data yielded from practical measures.

If data are quantitative, the level of measurement, the design, and the number of groups determine what type of analysis to use.

Sharice and Hector's driver measures will yield a numeric (ordinal/ interval/ratio) score. Descriptive statistics are appropriate in both cases and should not be abandoned due to lust for more sophisticated techniques. Descriptive statistics are quite useful when communicating about the impact to lay audiences without a strong statistical background. Sharice and Hector can also use paired samples (dependent samples) *t*-tests to see if their scores postintervention differ significantly from those preintervention, if they do not deviate from assumptions. The fairly robust nature of *t*-tests makes them user friendly in improvement science, even when educational leaders do not have very large samples. For interventions with multiple groups, repeated measures ANOVA may also be used. Remember, the researcher sets the alpha level. The .05 cutoff for significance was one that was chosen arbitrarily. If a community college dean implemented an intervention in one academic program and did a *t*-test to determine the impact it had on student attendance before and after, and it yielded a *p*-value of .12, improvement scientists may not want to render that as ineffective. If 88 times out of 100, such a finding is not due to chance or sampling error, that may be all the evidence the dean needs to justify expanding the initiative to another academic program. Beyond statistical significance, as in traditional research, it is also essential to report practical significance. Effect sizes (Cohen's *d*, Eta squared, etc.) are critically important when determining whether an intervention should be adopted, altered or abandoned.

Practical measures will often use nominal or ordinal data, and they may not confirm to the assumptions necessary for parametric statistics. Although nonparametric statistics are often not a focus of inferential statistics courses, they may be quite useful in the analysis of practical measures. Permutation tests, for instance, can be useful for analyzing repeated measures that do not conform to assumptions of normality. When dealing with larger samples (N>12), a Wilcoxon signed rank test can be used in lieu of a permutation test (Siegel & Castellan, 1988). So even if it isn't covered in detail by your stats professor, do not disregard the chapters on nonparametric statistics.

Practical measures can often be depictured using a number of common graphing techniques. Some practical measures, like process measures and driver measures, are collected frequently and over time. If Sharice administers her driver measure monthly and wants to visualize the change over time, she may opt to display the data in a run chart (see Figure 3.6).

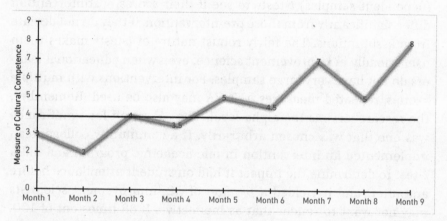

Figure 3.6. Chart 1: Sharice's run chart.

A run chart is a line chart that illustrates the fluctuation of a numerical measure over time. The mean of the occurrences appears as a straight line, as a reference. Run charts are also frequently used to display process measures that are collected daily.

If Sharice's instrument broke down into multiple domains, she could also examine the domains over time using a radial chart (see Figure 3.7). Imagine, in addition to self-report measures, that Sharice created an observation rubric to measure incidences of culturally responsive practices in the classroom. She and teacher leaders throughout the school observed classrooms over time for evidence of caring and supportive environments, scaffolding, real-world and authentic assignments, collaboration, high expectations and connections to previous knowledge throughout her intervention, establishing a baseline at the beginning of the year and once each quarter. This could be displayed with a radial chart, showing change by domain.

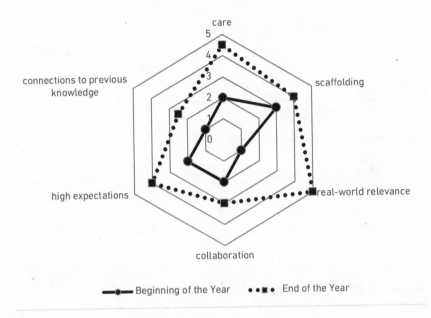

Figure 3.7. Chart 2: Sharice's radial chart.

Sharice and her colleagues could observe a great deal of change in the inclusion of real-world relevant and authentic assignments, but less change in scaffolding and collaboration. This type of data informs how she may want to tweak the intervention to encourage her staff to consider additional opportunities for collaboration. A radial chart would also nicely display perceptions of productivity captured each quarter by Jennifer's driver measure.

For her process measure, Jennifer tracked the reasons that mentoring meetings were not happening. Data on errors is often depicted in a Pareto chart. The Pareto principle suggests that 80% of the errors are due to 20% of the causes; therefore, improvement scientists can prioritize solutions to those 20% of causes, reducing 80% of the errors. Jennifer's Pareto chart may appear as shown in Figure 3.8. After viewing her Pareto chart, Jennifer will realize that hectic faculty schedules have the most significant impact on the failure of mentors and mentees to meet. And that is where she may need to focus her attention if she wants the intervention to work.

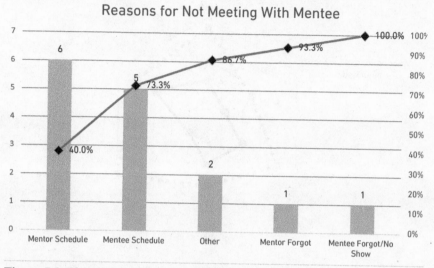

Figure 3.8. Chart 3: Jennifer's Pareto chart.

Summary

Improvement science is still science. Educational leaders do not abandon what they know about psychometrics and research design when developing practical measures and analyzing the data they yield. The goal remains to collect valid and reliable data, and validity is determined by how the data are used (in this case to drive improvement). Practical measures assess changes, provide predictive analytics and help leaders set priorities (Yeager et al., 2013). In *Learning to Improve*, Bryk, Gomez, Grunow, and LeMahieu (2015, p. 101) outline six requirements for practical measures. Practical measures must (a) operationalize a theory of improvement, (b) be specific to processes involved with the change, (c) inform next steps, (d) use language that is meaningful to those implementing the change, (e) yield data in a timely manner so it can be acted upon and (f) ensure that data collection is embedded in daily routines and does not feel like an additional task that busy professionals have to take on.

What methods courses teach about the design of surveys and interview protocols still rings true in the development of practical measures. The science is still there, but instead of generating new knowledge, the science is being used to improve our practice and to improve our implementation of what we already know to be good.

Septima Clark (1898–1987), educator and activist, said, "We must be action-research minded. We have to take a look at where we are and where we want to be." (Clark, 1964, p. 122) Although the method evolves, the premise is the same—use informed inquiry to make improvements. To paraphrase Bryk (2011), improvement science combines the context-rich inquiry of action research and the rigor of scientific investigation to create a methodological synergy that accelerates the improvement efforts of educational leaders. The psychometrics of improvement science is practical measures. Practical measurement takes "What works?" a step further by asking "Is it working?" (driver measures); "How is it working?" (process measures); "Is it working as intended?" (balancing measures); and after it is all said and done, the reflective "Did it work?" (outcome measure). These are the measures that will accelerate the efforts of educational leaders to transform education.

Readings About Sharice's Problem of Practice

Siwatu, K. O. (2007). Preservice teachers' culturally responsive teaching self-efficacy and outcome expectancy beliefs. *Teaching and Teacher Education, 23*(7), 1086–1101.

Skiba, R. J., Arredondo, M. I., & Williams, N. T. (2014). More than a metaphor: The contribution of exclusionary discipline to a school-to-prison pipeline. *Equity & Excellence in Education, 47*(4), 546–564. doi:10.108 0/10665684.2014.958965

Skiba, R. J., Chung, C., Trachok, M., Baker, T. L., Sheya, A., & Hughes, R. L. (2014). Parsing disciplinary disproportionality: Contributions of infraction, student, and school characteristics to out-of-school suspension and expulsion. *American Educational Research Journal, 51*(4), 640–670.

Skiba, R. J., Homer, R. H., Chung, C., Rausch, M. K., May, S. L., & Tobin, T. (2011). Race is not neutral: A national investigation of African American and Latino disproportionality in school discipline. *School Psychology Review, 40*(1), 85–107.

Weinstein, C., Curran, M., & Tomlinson-Clarke, S. (2003). Culturally responsive classroom management: Awareness into action. *Theory Into Practice, 42*(4), 269–276.

Readings About Hector's Problem of Practice

Deming, D. J., Goldin, C., & Katz, L. F. (2012). The for-profit postsecondary school sector: Nimble critters or agile predators? *Journal of Economic Perspectives, 26*(1), 139–164.

Luna-Torres, M., McKinney, L., Horn, C., & Jones, S. (2018). Understanding loan use and debt burden among low-income and minority students at a large urban community college. *Journal of Student Financial Aid, 48*(1), article 2.

McKinney, L., Roberts, T., & Shefman, P. (2013). Perspectives and experiences of financial aid counselors on community college students who borrow. *Journal of Student Financial Aid, 43*(1), article 2.

Mettler, S. (2014). *Degrees of inequality: How the politics of higher education sabotaged the American dream.* New York, NY: Basic Books.

Readings About Jennifer's Problem of Practice

Baez, B. (2000). Race-related service and faculty of color: Conceptualizing critical agency in academe. *Higher Education, 39*(3), 363–391.

Diggs, G. A., Garrison-Wade, D. F., Estrada, D., & Galindo, R. (2009). Smiling faces and colored spaces: The experiences of faculty of color pursuing tenure in the academy. *The Urban Review, 41*(4), 312–333.

Lilienfeld, E. (2016, June 10). *How student evaluations are skewed against women and minority professors.* Retrieved from https://tcf.org/content/commentary/student-evaluations-skewed-women-minority-professors/?agreed=1

Turner, C. S. V., González, J. C., & Wood, J. L. (2008). Faculty of color in academe: What 20 years of literature tells us. *Journal of Diversity in Higher Education, 1*(3), 139–168.

For Further Reading on Practical Measurement

American Educational Research Association, American Psychological Association, & National Council on Measurement in Education. (1999). *Standards for educational and psychological testing.* Washington, DC: American Educational Research Association.

Bryk, A. (2011, March 31) It is a science of improvement [Web log comment]. Retrieved from http://blogs.edweek.org/edweek/futures_of_reform/2011/03/it_is_a_science_of_improvement.html

Bryk, A. S., Gomez, L. M., Grunow, A., & LeMahieu, P. G. (2015). *Learning to improve: How America's schools can get better at getting better.* Cambridge, MA: Harvard Education Press.

Carroll, C., Patterson, M., Wood, S., Booth, A., Rick, J., & Balain, S. (2007). A conceptual framework for implementation fidelity. *Implementation Science, 2*(1), 40–49.

Clark, S. (1964). Literacy and liberation. *Freedomways, 4*(1), 113–124.

Ginty, A.T. (2013) Psychometric properties. In M. D. Gellman & J. R. Turner (Eds.), *Encyclopedia of behavioral medicine* (pp. 1563–1564). New York, NY: Springer.

Langley, G. J., Moen, R. D., Nolan, K. M., Nolan, T. W., Norman, C. L., & Provost, L. P. (2009). *The improvement guide: A practical approach to enhancing organizational performance.* Charlottesville, VA: Wiley.

Rudy, T. E. (2007). Psychometrics. In N. J. Salkind (Ed.), *Encyclopedia of measurement and statistics* (pp. 797–798). Thousand Oaks, CA: Sage.

Senge, P. M., & Sterman, J. D. (1990). Systems thinking and organizational learning: Acting locally and thinking globally in the organization of the future. International Conference of the System Dynamics Society, Chestnut Hill, Massachusetts, 1990. Albany, NY: System Dynamics Society.

Siegel, S., & Castellan, N. J. (1988). *Nonparametric statistics for the behavioral sciences.* New York: NY: McGraw Hill.

Turner, J. R. (2013) Psychometrics. In M. D. Gellman & J. R. Turner (Eds.), *Encyclopedia of behavioral medicine* (pp. 1564–1565). New York, NY: Springer.

Yeager, D., Bryk, A., Muhich, J., Hausman, H., & Morales, L. (2013). *Practical measurement.* Palo Alto, CA: Carnegie Foundation for the Advancement of Teaching.

Contextualizing Improvement Science in Higher Education

CHAPTER FOUR

Crossing the Streams

Improvement Science, Educational Development and Systems Thinking in Higher Education

AMY B. CHAN HILTON
University of Southern Indiana

LAURA CRUZ
Penn State University

Abstract

Several factors are contributing to a profound shift in the mission of centers of teaching and learning (CTLs) across higher education in the United States: growing professionalization of the field, tightening budgets and decreasing resources and increasing attention to the significance of teaching and learning for maintaining an institution's strategic and/or competitive advantage (Beach, Sorcinelli, Austin, and Rivard, 2016). To meet these growing demands, educational developers are looking to expand their foundations to encompass new ways of thinking about their role in institutional change. Systems thinking, with its emphasis on interactions and interdependence over formal hierarchies, has the potential to be an insightful approach to bring order to the apparent chaos of higher education, but advocates will need to find ways to adapt and disseminate its principles effectively. Improvement science is predicated on a set of assumptions about what organizations look like and how they function, but also on the shifting of mental models toward a culture of sustained innovation. This chapter identifies and elucidates the critical intersections between three streams—educational development, improvement science and systems thinking. We focus on systems mapping, S-curves and organizational learning practices as tools for enabling educational developers to become highly effective agents of teaching and learning transformation.

Keywords

educational development, higher education, systems thinking, innovation, learning organization

Background

In the United States, the field of faculty development emerged in the 1960s to serve as a bridge between the research and practice of teaching and learning in higher education (Ortquist-Ahrens, 2016). This foundational role has evolved into a deep and abiding advocacy for the principle of evidence-based practice, both in the work that faculty developers do and the faculty they serve. Until recently, faculty developers had largely focused their transformational efforts at the level of the individual faculty member and/or the singular classroom. More recently, however, the field has found itself evolving in response to the broader challenges facing contemporary higher education (Cruz, 2018; Gibbs, 2013; Haras, Taylor, Sorcinelli, & van Hoene, 2017; Land, 2001). Several factors are contributing to a profound shift in the mission of centers of teaching and learning (CTLs) across the United States: growing professionalization of the field, tightening budgets and decreasing resources and increased attention to the significance of teaching and learning for maintaining an institution's strategic and/or competitive advantage (Beach et al., 2016).

In response, CTLs no longer see themselves as primarily support centers but rather as agents of organizational change (Schroeder, 2012), leading to a shift in nomenclature from faculty to educational development (Diamond, 2005; Leibowitz, 2014; Little, 2014).

In this new role, educational developers must increasingly connect not only evidence to practice but also both of these to institutional policy and procedures. Similarly, they have been increasingly called upon to document the impact of their work at new levels, extending from the programmatic to the institutional, and to ensure that efforts to transform teaching and learning are iterative and sustainable (Albon, Iqbal, & Pearson, 2016; Austin & Sorcinelli, 2013; Chism & Hollye, 2012). To meet these growing demands, educational developers are looking to expand their foundations to encompass new ways of thinking about cultural change, such as continuous improvement models (Hanson, 2001).

The latter has shown great promise in K–12 education and private industry, but efforts to import the approach into higher education have come up against the distinctive organizational and logistical challenges of academia, sometimes referred to by theorists as "organized anarchy" (Cohen & March, 1986). When compared to the K–12 context, most colleges and universities lack commensurate systems of accountability, and any form of accountability must address the appropriate balance of teaching commitments, research productivity and service activities. Until recently, these and many other differences between secondary and postsecondary education have largely been taken as a given (Clark, 1985), but there are an increasing number of conversations focusing on identifying and bridging divides across the K–16 levels, especially as public higher education comes to embrace its role in increasing access and student success. A significant part of the process of bridging these divides involves engaging faculty meaningfully in the process, a relational skill with which educational developers are highly adept.

And this skill is likely a necessary component of organizational change in higher education. When compared to corporate environments, institutions of higher education usually have fewer levers by which they can exercise centralized control or influence, including over a relatively large number of employees (faculty) with significant degrees of independence from the organization. In universities, decision-making is often fluid, contested and ambiguous, characterized by a constantly shifting set of priorities, methods and participants (Biancani, McFarland, & Dahlander, 2014; DiBella, 1992; March & Olsen, 1986; Ruscio, 2016). Rather than viewing such a state of affairs as chaotic, we see it as an opportunity for expanding our change management toolkit to encompass more flexible and adaptive tools.

Because of these social and cultural differences between universities and corporations, efforts to implement best practices drawn from business management into higher education have led to mixed results (Brewer, Brewer, & Hawksley, 2000; Davies, Douglas, & Douglas, 2007; Grant, Mergen, & Widrick, 2004; Owlia & Aspinwall, 1997; Roffe, 1998); universities have found themselves constrained in their ability to embrace the increasingly entrepreneurial mission of higher education (Slaughter & Leslie, 1997). This track record is compounded by the fact that a number of academics have mounted strong moral defenses against the incursion of strategies the primary aim of which is perceived to be profit (rather than learning), and their influence has held some sway (Prichard & Willmott, 1997; Ritzer, 1996). Despite these practical and philosophical divides, there is reason to believe compromise is possible, especially as the study of organizational development within higher education becomes increasingly robust and capable of producing models that seek to embrace, rather than sidestep or eradicate, the long-held idealism and often quirky culture of academia.

Systems thinking, with its emphasis on interactions and interdependence over formal hierarchies, has the potential to be an insightful approach to bring order to the apparent chaos of higher education; however, advocates will need to find ways to adapt and disseminate its principles effectively. From the K–12 world, improvement science, which integrates processes for continuous improvement, has the potential to provide institutions of higher education with the means to become more nimble in the face of change and to more readily embrace innovation, but universities often lack the formal structures needed to sustain these processes. Educational developers are seeking to embrace their new role as agents of organizational change and identify effective strategies for transforming institutions into flourishing teaching and learning communities (Felten, Kalish, Pingree, & Plank, 2007), but they lack a strong base of evidence with which to ground their work (Smyth, 2003). It seems possible that these two aspirations could become mutually reinforcing, with educational developers serving in the familiar role as the bridge between (systems and change) theory and (educational) practice.

It also is possible that bringing these streams together could prove to be dangerous, compounding the problems faced by each separately. In the movie *Ghostbusters* the team members, too, initially believed that crossing the streams would be dangerous. After a period of experimentation, they instead discovered that joining them together actually increased their power. Similarly, we argue that although the respective obstacles to each of these movements appear to be considerable, it may be possible for these streams to converge, thereby enhancing their collective ability to overcome challenges and provide new opportunities and perspectives. This chapter identifies and elucidates the critical intersections between three streams—educational development, improvement science and systems thinking—with the intention of building a toolkit for future research and practice in higher education. We selected three tools from the systems thinking toolkit—systems mapping, S-curves and organizational learning practices—as most readily applicable to the current constraints and opportunities within higher education. To illustrate their adaptability, we explore examples of how educational developers can wield these instruments in the service of changing hearts, minds and learning environments.

Systems Mapping

The shift from faculty development to educational and organizational development necessitates the facilitation of change and a better understanding of the interconnections and interdependencies between people, structures and activities. To effect this institutional change, educational developers "lead from the middle" and "cultivate a bird's-eye view of the institution, understanding its mission and major obstacles to achieving the mission"—in other words, take a systems thinking approach to consider how we might lead change to address complex issues such as student learning and success (Frerichs, Pace, & Rosier, 2011, p. 158).

Systems thinking is cultivating understanding of how organizational elements are interrelated and interdependent in service of a goal or issue, in the context of the overall complex system (such as a university); this is in contrast to reductionist perspectives in which the whole can be broken down into its parts and is the sum of its parts (Shaked & Schechter, 2017). For example, student retention is a complex system that involves numerous interrelated components, and the creation of a menu of supports and programs, functioning independently and in silos, likely will not serve the goal for the students as effectively as if these parts are purposely developed as connected pieces of the whole system. In improvement science, practitioners believe it is fundamental to gain deeper understanding of an issue before considering changes or solutions (Carnegie Foundation, n.d.; Kivel, 2015), and systems thinking tools can help provide ways to develop this understanding.

To develop a deeper understanding and identify the connections and interactions between components of a complex issue, the process of systems mapping can "provide an exploration of the system, communicate understanding, and allow for the identification of knowledge gaps, intervention points, and insights" (Acaroglu, 2017, para. 1). Systems mapping (see Figure 4.1) can help educational developers place their work in the context of a broader issue and identify opportunities for strengthening their efforts by leveraging and connecting with other system components. Systems mapping can be done individually, to stimulate learning and reflection about a complex issue, as well as collaboratively, to convene multiple perspectives around a goal in a systems-level context. Through the iterative process of systems mapping, we can create opportunities for stakeholders to have in-depth conversations and gain insights around a common goal or issue. Systems mapping also can help us to identify bottlenecks and future opportunities, informing the strategies around how we approach where we are headed next.

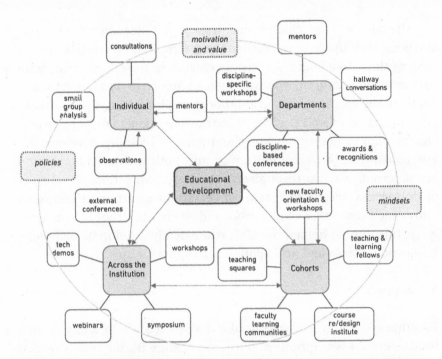

Figure 4.1. Example of a systems cluster map for a center for teaching and learning. Additional arrows between the boxes may be added to show connections between programs and services.

Systems mapping tools include cluster maps, connected circles causal loop diagrams (Acaroglu, 2017) and iceberg models (Northwest Earth Institute, n.d.). For example, the iceberg model can be used to examine the underlying reasons why faculty members do not participate in programs intended to help improve their teaching practice. At the tip of the iceberg (event level) is the observation of few faculty members coming to workshops. Below is the trend level, in which patterns are noted (e.g., trends of decreasing participation as the academic year progresses or faculty members have settled into their routines), and the underlying structures are beneath, in which reasons why the patterns are happening are identified (e.g., lack of time, competing priorities, no interest). The foundation of the iceberg, at the bottom, is formed by the mental models that include attitudes, beliefs and values that drive everything else above.

The collaborative cluster map process includes individual brain-storming of components related to the system written on sticky notes, posting them to a board, iteratively clustering the components with conversations along the way and then adding arrows to indicate connections and relationships. In another example of using systems mapping, members of a CTL advisory board were asked to draft a systems cluster map to identify existing and potential faculty development and educational development programs, both within its institution and externally such as through professional organizations. The intent of this process was to facilitate conversations about what programs and capacity existed, in what areas, and where the strengths and gaps were; this in turn helped the CTL strategically develop its programming and services and anticipate future opportunities.

S-Curves

To embrace systems thinking also entails a shift in some of our fundamental assumptions about what change is and how it works. Since the birth of the idea of progress in the 18th century, we have learned that the process of embracing new knowledge is not as steady, linear or unilateral as these philosophers thought it would be. Rather, organizational change tends to follow a trajectory that, when graphed, follows the shape of the letter *S* (see Figure 4.2), in which a slow start is followed by rapid implementation, which then levels off, reaching a steady state, also called the plateau of productivity, in which the change has been integrated into the culture.

Whether or not the term itself is widely used, the S-curve dynamic may be familiar to educational developers, as it mirrors the trajectory of the coaching process. When we consult with a faculty member, we agree on a set of changes, which are then slowly implemented, followed by period of intense investment of time and effort, culminating in the integration of the new practice in their permanent teaching toolkit (and, possibly, the desire to start the cycle over again and adopt a new set of practices). In systems thinking, this coaching dynamic applies not to an individual, but to the level of the organization, whether that is defined as a unit (such as a

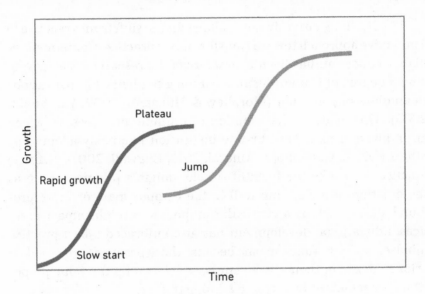

Figure 4.2. Example of S-curves for a center for teaching and learning.

CTL) or the institution as a whole. The visual representation of that dynamic, in the form of an S-curve, allows those implementing the change to monitor their progress and adjust their goals as needed, not unlike how coaches support their clients in reaching their goals.

Understanding the S-curve dynamic may also aid in how we plan for changes at the level of the organization, such as the adoption of new technologies. Unlike a business or a school, universities lack the leverage to implement changes across the board. Faculty have more autonomy than a typical employee, and they may choose to evaluate whether or how a proposed technology will enhance their work and, if not, they may ignore or discard it. This process leads to uneven adoption at the institutional level, and the question becomes how success is defined. Because we know that the S-curve will end in a plateau of productivity or impact (rather than continuing to increase), it can enable those implementing change to focus their time and energy on those faculty for whom the new technology will be beneficial, especially the early adopters and early majority, while not expending effort on those who either lag behind or may never come on board (Abrahams, 2010).

Finally, the S-curve dynamic allows for the shift from a reactive to a proactive approach toward transformative practice. Contemporary higher education has been characterized by researchers as having a high degree of isomorphism, meaning a tendency for institutions to emulate one another (Morphew & Huisman, 2002; Van Vught, 2008). This leads to the adoption of mimetic practices, in which an innovation pioneered by one institution is quickly adopted by others (Diogo, Carvalho, & Amaral, 2015; Engwall, 2007). Mimetic practices can take the form of simple, tangible practices, such as the erection of a climbing wall in the campus gym, or more profound shifts, such as a curricular emphasis on high-impact practices. Educational development has also embraced a best practice mindset as a core value, in part because these practices are based on prior evidence of their effectiveness, which can tip the value proposition for reluctant faculty and administrators.

There is much to commend in such an approach, but the downside of a best practice mentality is that it rewards adaptation over innovation. Because we know that a cycle of change will level off and a new S-curve will overcome the previous one, we can use that knowledge to anticipate future challenges and get prepared to meet them directly, rather than waiting to follow the lead of others. The period when two S-curves overlap is often one of disruption, but it also represents a window of opportunity to get ahead of the next curve, but we have to be prepared to do so. From this perspective, it would be wise to begin planning for the next change cycle simultaneously with the initial implementation of the current cycle (Christensen, Horn, Caldera, & Soares, 2011). In this way, change becomes expected rather than distrusted. The S-curve represents a big-picture, long-run view, in which educational developers partner with administrators to ensure that the institution has both the mindset and sustained capacity to respond to the evolving teaching and learning needs of higher education.

Organizational Learning

Institutions of higher education are organizations with learning as outcomes (primarily in the context of students), but the practices of a learning organization might not be part of the culture (Senge, 2000; Watkins, 2005). A symptom of an institution not embracing an organizational learning mindset is the inclination to jump to solutions before a problem is fully understood. These solutions may be based on untested hunches, anecdotal evidence or best practices applied in other contexts. Stepping back with a systems thinking mindset (by using system mapping and a proactive S-curve vision) allows us to shift toward more informed, strategic and sustained approaches to complex problem-solving. Because it takes place at the broader level of organizational culture, the model is also broadly collaborative, whereby educational developers work together with faculty members and administrators to test and refine problem-specific and learner-focused efforts to improve outcomes with iterative assessment feedback loops, which are familiar to educational developers and similar to Plan, Do, Study, Act (PDSA) cycles in improvement science.

The elements of organizational learning—systems thinking, mental models, shared vision, personal mastery and team learning (Senge, 2006)—align with the practice of improvement science and we can incorporate these into higher education settings as elements of our change management strategy (Kezar, 2018). By regularly taking the time to reflect and take a big picture view (systems thinking), while also considering the information available from past experiences to learn from mistakes and intentionally synthesize information from across the system (personal mastery and team learning), individuals and groups can integrate the practices of a learning organization (Gino & Staats, 2015). However, the higher education structures and cultures noted earlier may not be conducive to organizational learning and thus conditions, or antecedents, at the individual and organization levels need to exist to support an institution as it transforms into a learning organization (Bui & Baruch, 2010). Educational developers can act as catalysts (Bui & Baruch, 2010; Frerichs et al., 2011) who incorporate these practices into their work, model them for others and advocate for their value.

An example of how educational developers contribute to organizational learning within an institution is a CTL leading a group of faculty members in a yearlong project to explore student retention in lower level undergraduate mathematics and science courses (shared vision). The framework includes peer-to-peer learning through the shared exploration of initiatives within the institution, team learning through the development of a common evidence base (Cox, 2004) and generative practice through the iterative development of systems cluster maps which highlight bottlenecks to student retention. To support personal mastery and motivation, participants draw on their own curiosity to identify an individual research question, the resolution of which require interactions across disciplines and offices, and then disseminate their findings with and outside the group (Chan Hilton, 2018). The role of the educational developer in this example is to act as a conduit by facilitating organizational learning processes and propagating similar values and practices across the campus.

Discussion

Just as the field of educational development began by creating a bridge between the theory and practice of teaching, it now stands poised to serve as the conduit between systems theory and the practice of organizational change in higher education. As such, a major responsibility for practitioners in the field has been to legitimize the transition through the development of a body of evidence-based practice. In their prior role, educational developers were the consumers and facilitators of a body of research known as the scholarship of teaching and learning (SoTL), to the point where some advocates have argued that this has served as the signature pedagogy of the field (Felten & Chick, 2018). In their emerging roles as conduit, on the other hand, educational developers are increasingly becoming the consumers and producers of a body of research known as improvement science, which marries many of the long-term goals of SoTL (e.g., teaching transformation) with a set of tools, practices and perspectives associated with institutional change. Whereas SoTL focuses on the single classroom as the locus of change, improvement science expands the scale and scope to more broadly address the demands the learning revolution has placed not just on faculty and students but also universities and colleges as learning organizations.

This transition does not entail a change in practice but rather, perhaps more profoundly, a shift in mindset and culture as well. Improvement science is predicated on a set of assumptions about what organizations look like and how they function, but also on the shifting of mental models toward a culture of sustained innovation. In recent years, universities have been under heavy criticism for not being sufficiently nimble in their response to changing market conditions, resulting in a range of suboptimal outcomes, from a lag in research innovation to underprepared graduates. Recent efforts to spearhead change through administrative tools, such as policy, shifting rewards or public/private partnerships, could be enhanced through attention to the underlying cultural norms of the campus as a teaching and learning community, a perspective that educational developers, who work closely with faculty and staff from nearly all areas of university life, are in a distinctive position to influence.

The pressure for modern universities to transform what they are, who they serve and why they matter in order to adapt to the demands of the current and changing landscape is considerable; the stakes are high, with Harvard Business School professor Clayton Christensen notoriously predicting that half of the colleges and universities in the United States will close over the next 10 years (Seltzer, 2017). This dynamic has often led to increased friction within the conventional divisions that characterize much of the sociology of higher education; as administrators blame faculty reluctance to adopt change, faculty blame administrators for poor or unclear incentive structures, students struggle to find relevance in what and how they are learning and the public questions rising costs with diminishing returns (Brownell & Tanner, 2012; Chandler, 2013; Tagg, 2012). Systems thinking involves a fundamental reorientation that replaces this mental model of a university as a series of silos and extends a more global vision, one that emphasizes the constructive value of harnessing our interdependence. In the past, the tendency of educational developers to "cool the mark," or sidestep confrontation in favor of more conciliatory models, has been viewed as a potential weakness (Cruz, 2018), but in the context of intertwining the competing streams of higher education, improvement science and pedagogy, it becomes a strength. To paraphrase the movie *Ghostbusters* once again, perhaps it is time for others to step aside and let the educational developers come to the fore.

Key Concepts

Educational development
Learning organization
S-curve
Systems thinking
Systems mapping

Discussion Questions

1. What is the relationship between educational development, systems thinking and improvement science?
2. What are some applications of these tools (e.g., systems mapping, the concept of S-curves and learning organization practices) to your setting?
3. What are the challenges and opportunities associated with using systems thinking and improvement science in higher education?

References

Abrahams, D. A. (2010). Technology adoption in higher education: A framework for identifying and prioritizing issues and barriers to adoption of instructional technology. *Journal of Applied Research in Higher Education, 2*(2), 34–49.

Acaroglu, L. (2017). Tools for systems thinkers: Systems mapping, *Disruptive Design*. Available from https://medium.com/disruptive-design/tools-for-systems-thinkers-systems-mapping-2db5cf30ab3a

Albon, S. P., Iqbal, I., & Pearson, M. L. (2016). Strategic planning in an educational development centre: Motivation, management, and messiness. *Collected Essays on Learning and Teaching, 9*, 207–226.

Austin, A. E., & Sorcinelli, M. D. (2013). The future of faculty development: Where are we going? *New Directions for Teaching and Learning, 133*, 85–97.

Beach, A. L., Sorcinelli, M. D., Austin, A. E., & Rivard, J. K. (2016). *Faculty development in the age of evidence: Current practices, future imperatives.* Sterling, VA: Stylus.

Biancani, S., McFarland, D. A., & Dahlander, L. (2014). The semiformal organization. *Organization Science, 25*(5), 1306–1324.

Brewer, P. D., Brewer, V. L., & Hawksley, M. (2000). Strategic planning for continuous improvement in a college of business. *The Mid-Atlantic Journal of Business, 36*(2/3), 123.

Brownell, S. E., & Tanner, K. D. (2012). Barriers to faculty pedagogical change: Lack of training, time, incentives, and . . . tensions with professional identity? *CBE—Life Sciences Education, 11*(4), 339–346.

Bui, H., and Baruch, Y. (2010). Creating learning organizations in higher education: Applying a systems perspective. *The Learning Organization, 17*(3), 228–242.

Carnegie Foundation for the Advancement of Teaching. (n.d.). *The six core principles of improvement.* Available from https://www.carnegiefoun dation.org/our-ideas/six-core-principles-improvement/

Chan Hilton, A. B. (2018, June). Collaborating with faculty development in retention improvement. *Proceedings of the 2018 American Society for Engineering Education Conference & Exposition* (Salt Lake City, UT). Available from https://peer.asee.org/31276

Chandler, N. (2013). Braced for turbulence: Understanding and managing resistance to change in the higher education sector. *Management, 3*(5), 243–251.

Chism, N., & Hollye, M. (2012). Researching the impact of educational development: Basis for informed practice. In J. Groccia and L. Cruz (Eds.), *To Improve the Academy* (Vol. 31, pp. 129–145). San Francisco, CA: Jossey-Bass.

Christensen, C. M., Horn, M. B., Caldera, L., & Soares, L. (2011). Disrupting college: How disruptive innovation can deliver quality and affordability to postsecondary education. Washington, DC: Center for American Progress. Available from https://files.eric.ed.gov/fulltext/ED535182.pdf

Clark, B. (1985). *The school and the university*. Berkeley, CA: University of California Press.

Cohen, M. D., & March, J. G. (1986). Leadership in an organized anarchy. In M. C. Brown (Ed.), *Organization and governance in higher education* (pp. 16–35). Boston, MA: Pearson Custom Publishing.

Cox, M. D. (2004). Introduction to faculty learning communities. *New Directions for Teaching and Learning, 97*, 5–23.

Cruz, L. (2018). The idea of educational development: An historical perspective. *To Improve the Academy, 37*(1), 159–171.

Davies, J., Douglas, A., & Douglas, J. (2007). The effect of academic culture on the implementation of the EFQM Excellence Model in UK universities. *Quality Assurance in Education, 15*(4), 382–401.

Diamond, R. M. (2005). The institutional change agency: The expanding role of academic support centers. In S. Chadwick-Blossey (Ed.), *To Improve the Academy* (Vol. 23, pp. 24–37). Bolton, MA: Anker Publishing Company

DiBella, A. J. (1992). Planned change in an organized anarchy: Support for a postmodernist perspective. *Journal of Organizational Change Management, 5*(3), 55–65.

Diogo, S., Carvalho, T., & Amaral, A. (2015). Institutionalism and organizational change. In J. Huisman, H. de Boer, & D. D. Dill (Eds.), *The Palgrave international handbook of higher education policy and governance* (pp. 114–131). London, UK: Palgrave Macmillan.

Engwall, L. (2007). Universities, the state and the market. *Higher Education Management and Policy, 19*(3), 1–18.

Felten, P., & Chick, N. (2018). Is SoTL a signature pedagogy of educational development? *To Improve the Academy, 37*(1), 4–16.

Felten, P., Kalish, A., Pingree, A., & Plank, K. M. (2007). Toward a scholarship of teaching and learning in educational development. *To Improve the Academy, 25*, 93–108.

Frerichs, C., Pace, D. & Rosier, T. (2011). Leading from the middle, in C. Schroeder (Ed.), *Coming in from the Margins* (pp. 143–161). Sterling, VA: Stylus.

Gibbs, G. (2013). Reflections on the changing nature of educational development. *International Journal for Academic Development, 18*(1), 4–14.

Gino, F., & Staats, B. (2015, November). Why organizations don't learn. *Harvard Business Review.* 110-118. https://hbr.org/2015/11/why-organizations-dont-learn

Grant, D., Mergen, E., & Widrick, S. (2004). A comparative analysis of quality management in US and international universities. *Total Quality Management & Business Excellence, 15*(4), 423-438.

Haras, C., Taylor, S. C., Sorcinelli, M. D., & van Hoene, L. (2017). *Institutional commitment to teaching excellence: Assessing the impacts and outcomes of faculty development.* Washington, DC: American Council on Education.

Hanson, M. (2001). Institutional theory and educational change. *Educational Administration Quarterly, 37*(5), 637-661.

Kezar, A. (2018). Scaling improvement in STEM learning environments: The strategic role of a national organization. Available from https://www.aau.edu/strategic-role-national-organization

Kivel, L. (2015). *A lesson in system-wide change.* Available from https://www.carnegiefoundation.org/blog/a-lesson-in-system-wide-change/

Land, R. (2001). Agency, context and change in academic development. *International Journal for Academic Development, 6*(1), 4-20.

Leibowitz, B. (2014). Reflections on academic development: What is in a name? *International Journal for Academic Development, 19*(4), 357-360.

Little, D. (2014). Reflections on the state of the scholarship of educational development. *To Improve the Academy, 33*(1), 1-13.

March, J. G., & Olsen, J. P. (1986). Garbage can models of decision making in organizations. *Ambiguity and Command, 10,* 11-35.

Morphew, C. C., & Huisman, J. (2002). Using institutional theory to reframe research on academic drift. *Higher Education in Europe, 27*(4), 491-506.

Northwest Earth Institute. (n.d.). *A systems thinking model: The iceberg.* Available from https://www.nwei.org/iceberg/

Ortquist-Ahrens, L. (2016). Beyond survival: Educational development and the maturing of the POD Network. *To Improve the Academy, 35*(1), 1-34.

Owlia, M. S., & Aspinwall, E. M. (1997). TQM in higher education—A review. *International Journal of Quality & Reliability Management, 14*(5), 527-543.

Prichard, C., & Willmott, H. (1997). Just how managed is the McUniversity? *Organization Studies, 18*(2), 287-316.

Ritzer, G. (1996). McUniversity in the postmodern consumer society. *Quality in Higher Education, 2*(3), 185–199.

Roffe, I. M. (1998). Conceptual problems of continuous quality improvement and innovation in higher education. *Quality Assurance in Education, 6*(2), 74–82.

Ruscio, K. P. (2016). Leadership in organized anarchy. *Public Administration Review, 76*(2), 219–220.

Schroeder, C. (2012). *Coming in from the margins: Faculty development's emerging organizational development role in institutional change.* Sterling, VA: Stylus.

Seltzer, R. (2017). Days of reckoning. *Inside Higher Ed.* Available from https://www.insidehighered.com/news/2017/11/13/spate-recent-college-closures-has-some-seeing-long-predicted-consolidation-taking

Senge, P. M. (2000). The academy as learning community: Contradiction in terms or realizable future? In A. F. Lucas (Ed.), *Leading academic change: Essential roles for department chairs* (pp. 275–300). San Francisco, CA: Jossey-Bass.

Senge, P. M. (2006). *The Fifth Discipline: The art and practice of the learning organization* (2nd ed.). London, UK: Random House.

Shaked, H., & Schechter, C. (2017). *Systems thinking for school leaders.* Cham, Switzerland: Springer International Publishing.

Slaughter, S., & Leslie, L. L. (1997). *Academic capitalism: Politics, policies, and the entrepreneurial university.* Baltimore, MD: Johns Hopkins University Press.

Smyth, R. (2003). Concepts of change: Enhancing the practice of academic staff development in higher education. *International Journal for Academic Development, 8*(1–2), 51–60.

Tagg, J. (2012). Why does the faculty resist change? *Change: The Magazine of Higher Learning, 44*(1), 6–15.

Van Vught, F. (2008). Mission diversity and reputation in higher education. *Higher Education Policy, 21*(2), 151–174.

Watkins, K. E. (2005). What would be different if higher educational institutions were learning organizations? *Advances in Developing Human Resources, 7*(3), 414.

CHAPTER FIVE

Navigating the Improvement Journey with an Equity Compass

MANUELITO BIAG

The Carnegie Foundation for the Advancement of Teaching

Abstract

Calls for continuous improvement through the use of evidence and data are seen increasingly in federal and state policy guidelines, and in the education initiatives of prominent philanthropic organizations. Persistent disparities in learning outcomes among students from different racial, ethnic and socioeconomic groups have compelled an expanding number of leaders to turn to improvement science to remedy these long-standing inequities. Yet despite growing use of improvement methods, there remains little discussion on how leaders can more intentionally configure their practice at each stage of the improvement journey—from understanding the problem to scaling well-tested innovations—in service of equitable outcomes for marginalized children and youth. To address this gap, this chapter offers three guiding principles rooted in the essence of networked improvement science that can help leaders approach continuous improvement not merely as a technical enterprise utilizing iterative testing, but as a student-focused, multifaceted endeavor that demands deep understanding of systemic oppression and the ways it manifests and influences learning and development. For young people to receive a high-quality and equitable educational experience, improvement leaders must engage in a disciplined practice that critically interrogates system structures, processes and norms; brings diverse stakeholders together in meaningful ways; and maintains the cognitive, physical, social and emotional well-being of underserved students as the "true north" in all improvement journeys.

Keywords

educational equity, continuous improvement, improvement journey

Background

Across the United States, students from low-income, immigrant, linguistic- and ethnic-minority backgrounds continue to achieve at lower levels than their counterparts (Cardichon & Darling-Hammond, 2017; Duncan & Murnane, 2011; Isaacs, 2012; Rabinowitz, 2016). Compared to districts serving the fewest minority students, those serving high proportions of African American, Native American or Hispanic populations receive on average 13% less per student in state and local funding (Morgan & Amerikaner, 2018). Consequently, these students are less likely to have access to effective teachers, academic and social services and other supports that bolster their achievement (Darling-Hammond, 2007; Reform Support Network, 2015). Given continued disparities in learning outcomes among students from different racial, ethnic and socioeconomic groups, an expanding number of leaders have turned to improvement science to redress these long-standing inequities (Bryk, Gomez, Grunow, & LeMahieu, 2015; LeMahieu, Bryk, & Grunow, 2017; LeMahieu, Grunow, Baker, Nordstrum, & Gomez, 2017).

With its roots in management theory (Deming, 1993), improvement science employs disciplined inquiry, testing and iteration to solve complex problems of practice (Langley et al., 2009). The use of improvement science bloomed in healthcare during the 1990s and has spread quickly to other sectors, including education (Berwick, 1996; Lewis, 2015). For the past decade, the Carnegie Foundation for the Advancement of Teaching has been developing improvement science principles enacted through networked improvement communities, or NICs (Bryk et al., 2015; Russell et al., 2017). The foundation has been testing this approach through its own NICs as well as with a growing number of partners such as the Building a Teaching Effectiveness Network (Hannan, Russell, Takahashi, & Park, 2015) and the Carnegie Math Pathways (Huang, 2018). Positive outcomes from these and other similar networks continue to build confidence in NICs and improvement science as viable approaches to help marginalized students succeed in school. In fact, philanthropic organizations including the Gates Foundation have invested heavily in the spread of improvement networks (Festerwald & Freeberg, 2018).

Although the concept of continuous improvement has been in the lexicon of educational reforms for years, a deeper understanding of these ideas challenges educational leaders to engage their staffs effectively at all stages of the improvement journey—from identifying opportunities for improvement to testing and evaluating changes (Elgart, 2017). In addition, how leaders can apply an equity lens to organize their practice at each stage of the improvement process is less explored. To address these gaps, this chapter offers three principles to help leaders approach continuous improvement not merely as a technical enterprise but as a complex endeavor that demands keen attention to systemic oppression and the different ways it manifests and influences students' opportunities to learn and grow.

To inform these principles, I draw from the core tenets of networked improvement science (Bryk et al., 2015; LeMahieu, Grunow, et al., 2017); extant research in leadership for systemic improvement (e.g., Elmore, 2006; Mintrop, 2016); and transformational and culturally responsive leadership (e.g., Khalifa, Gooden, & Davis, 2016; Leithwood & Sun, 2012), as well as from studies investigating how educational environments shape students' development (e.g.,

Eccles & Roeser, 2010). Additionally, I draw from the work of the National Equity Project (NEP), a leadership development organization seeking to advance educational equity across the country.

The chapter is organized as follows: first, I provide an overview of key concepts and terms regarding equity and continuous improvement to clarify definitions and orient readers. Next, I describe some of the major activities and tools involved in the different stages of the improvement journey. Then, I outline three guiding principles on how school leaders can configure their efforts at each improvement stage in service of educational equity. Finally, I conclude the chapter by suggesting discussion questions that require further inquiry and debate among leaders, educators, researchers and policymakers who seek to understand the capacities necessary to direct and sustain equity-focused improvement work.

Defining Equity

Equity is a widely used term that nearly everyone understands at an intuitive level, although few people share the same definition. Yet having a clear definition (or at least a working one) is essential for leaders to galvanize others into action (Zuieback, 2012). For the purposes of this chapter, I borrow from the NEP (2016), which defines *educational equity* to mean that "each child receives what he or she needs to develop to his or her full academic and social potential" (p. 6). To achieve educational equity, NEP contends that students' race/ethnicity, gender, socioeconomic status and other characteristics must not predetermine their success in school. NEP's definition argues that for historically underserved students to achieve equal accomplishment, they must be provided with and have access to meaningful learning opportunities and supports. This characterization aligns with research on social justice and transformative leadership (e.g., Brown, 2004; Furman, 2012; Shields, 2010; Theoharis, 2007).

Unlike *equality*, which means all individuals are given the same resources despite their needs, working toward equity is identifying and interrupting the beliefs and assumptions that perpetuate unequal outcomes by virtue of unequal opportunities for students from nondominant and low-income backgrounds. NEP (2016) argues that "to become agents of change who make strategic and courageous decisions, we must learn to run a set of filters, or lenses, that shift our vantage point" (p. 9). As leaders set their vision and develop their staff's capacity to continuously improve their systems, seeing the world through this "equity lens" can help uncover institutional norms, patterns and behaviors that favor some students to the detriment of others (Leithwood & Riehl, 2003).

Attention to educational equity (as defined above) in contemporary leadership practices continues to grow. For example, working toward equity is represented in 4 of the 10 Professional Standards for Educational Leaders (National Policy Board for Educational Administration, 2015). Also, the Aspen Institute and the Council of Chief State School Officers (2017) released 10 leadership actions to promote equitable school improvement systems. Yet despite these standards, there remains little discussion on how leaders can craft their practice at each stage of the improvement process to more purposefully ensure that learning opportunities are equitable for all students.

An Ecological View of Schooling and Development

To develop heightened awareness of how marginalization affects students' learning and well-being, it is useful for leaders to adopt an ecological view of schooling and development (Bronfenbrenner & Morris, 1998; Eccles & Roeser, 2010). Schools are central contexts for the cognitive, physical, social and emotional development of young people (Meece & Schaefer, 2010). Not only do students' experiences in school influence how they acquire knowledge and skills, they can also shape their behaviors, relationships and beliefs (Battistich, 2010; Wentzel, 2012). The cumulative effects of schooling can also affect children's lives as adults such as influencing their job prospects, cognitive functioning and lifetime earnings (Heckman, 2006).

An ecological view of schools and the outcomes of schooling (Bronfenbrenner & Morris, 1998; Eccles & Roeser, 2010) encourages leaders to examine how the broader environment and the processes within it (e.g., organizational, interpersonal, instructional) shape students' development and performance in school (Eccles & Roeser, 2010). This view is particularly important given that students of color, as well as those who are economically disadvantaged, are more likely to face adversities at home and in their communities (e.g., food insecurity) and receive their education in poorly resourced schools (Darling-Hammond, 2007). Moreover, an ecological perspective allows leaders to look beyond grades and test scores and consider support of the "whole child" as critical to their improvement agenda. This orientation can have important implications for how leaders distribute the human, technical and financial resources in their systems.

Defining Continuous Improvement

To guide this chapter, I borrow from Park, Hironaka, Carver, and Lee (2012) and O'Day and Smith (2016), who characterize continuous improvement work as attending to

1. processes that influence outcomes for specific populations;
2. the learning derived from failures and variations in performance;
3. the system and how changes within it are necessary to effect change in students' outcomes;
4. how actors within the system use different types of evidence to support improvement work; and
5. the use of an organizing methodology (e.g., improvement science) to guide the identification and specification of high-leverage problems and testing of change ideas.

This definition illustrates the interconnected structures and processes leaders must consider to carry out improvement work such as developing user-friendly systems for data use; supporting the capabilities of teachers to engage in disciplined inquiry and experimentation; and creating coherence around shared strategies and goals (Bryk & Schneider, 2002; Bryk et al., 2010; Bryk et al., 2015; Fullan & Quinn, 2015; LeMahieu, Bryk, & Grunow, 2017). This definition also hints at the kinds of knowledge, skills and dispositions useful when conducting improvement efforts, such as being open to change and valuing others' perspectives (Lucas & Nacer, 2015; Toussaint & Ehrlich, 2017).

Although the improvement cycle of Plan, Do, Study, Act, and repeat (Langley et al., 2009) is widely understood, many leaders have found it difficult to enact in consistent and effective ways (Fullan & Quinn, 2015; Hough et al., 2017). Several obstacles can impede improvement work, including insufficient supports to build staff capabilities and difficulties prioritizing improvement efforts over other mandates (Hough et al., 2017). Without deliberate attention to the practice and conditions that enable continuous improvement, leaders run the risk of having their efforts devolve into a ritualized practice (Peurach, Penuel, & Russell, in press), where "schools and individuals may go through the motions of each step without understanding the deeper purpose that guides them" (Elgart, 2017, p. 3).

Stages in the Improvement Journey

The work of networked improvement communities (LeMahieu, Grunow, et al., 2017) is broadly organized around three overlapping phases. The chartering phase occurs when the network comes together and takes on a causal system analysis of the local problem(s) to be addressed and develops a working theory of improvement as well as a measurement system. The network learning phase is when evidence is collected from rapid test cycles to determine whether changes are in fact improvements. Lastly, in the spreading phase, effective changes are incorporated into the system and further tested in varied contexts.

Although the activities that occur within these phases are nonlinear and iterative in nature, they can be generally categorized as occurring in the following stages: (a) understand the problem and the system that produces it; (b) focus collective efforts; (c) generate ideas for change; (d) test and build evidence; and (e) spread and scale (Bryk et al., 2015). In what follows, I describe some of the tools and main pursuits involved in each of these stages.

Understand the Problem and the System That Produces It

Improvement teams often begin their journey by conducting an in-depth analysis of the problem and the driving forces behind it. Depending on what teams need to know, a range of processes and tools can be used such as fishbone diagrams to identify root causes of a problem; Pareto charts to indicate which causes play a more prominent role; and process maps to diagram steps in key workflows (Tague, 2005). User-centered design techniques such as empathy interviews (Portigal, 2013) and participant observations (DeWalt & DeWalt, 2011) can also help teams see the problem from the vantage point of those closest to it (Biag, 2017; Hanington & Martin, 2012). Investing adequate time to study the problem and system helps school leaders identify and target high-leverage causes and avoid wasting resources on ill-informed solutions (i.e., "solutionitis"; see Kivel, 2015).

Focus Collective Efforts

Once a clear understanding of the problem is established, improvement teams organize their efforts using a theory of practice improvement (often expressed as a driver diagram; see Bennett & Provost, 2015; Bryk et al., 2015). Collaboratively constructed and constantly evolving, a driver diagram has two parts: (a) an aim statement that represents the overarching goals of the effort and (b) a working theory of what changes need to be made to achieve the aim (Bennet & Provost, 2015).

Aim statements specify what is to be accomplished, with regard to what, for whom and by when. They can be written in inspirational ways to convey a sense of urgency and motivate others to take action. For instance, an early aim statement of the Carnegie Math Pathways was to "reclaim the mathematical lives of 10,000 college students by July 1, 2015" (Grunow & Park, 2014, p. 42). Without a clear aim statement, teams will have a tough time knowing whether substantive improvements have occurred (Langley et al., 2009).

Figure 5.1 depicts a sample driver diagram from the Early Literacy Network Campaign (ELNC). It shows four change processes that the network theorizes—based on their causal system analysis and review of research and practice—will facilitate communication and coordination among staff (e.g., huddles on student progress). ELNC posits that improving communication and coordination will strengthen supports for struggling students, and this, in turn, will help ensure that 80% of district students reach proficiency in third grade literacy by the year 2022.

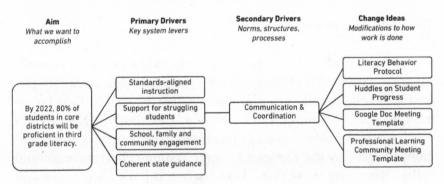

Figure 5.1. Sample driver diagram from the Early Literacy Network Campaign.

The practice of co-constructing an aim and a working theory of improvement as a team helps strengthen social ties, establish consensus on what will and will not be part of the endeavor and make explicit underlying assumptions about how drivers are linked to the intended aim.

Generate Ideas for Change

Teams can generate ideas for change based on their causal system analysis, reviews of scholarly research and benchmarking of similar organizations that have demonstrated improvement tackling the same problem (Bryk et al., 2015). To help formulate ideas, Langley and colleagues (2009) identify 72 change concepts—derived from Lean Six Sigma and typically applied in business and industry—which fall under nine overarching categories: (a) eliminating waste, (b) improving work flow, (c) optimizing inventory, (d) changing the work environment, (e) enhancing the consumer relationship, (f) managing time, (g) managing variation, (h) designing the system to avoid mistakes and (i) focusing on a product or service. These categories can spur the development of more specific actions. For example, the concept of managing variation may prompt teams to create a checklist protocol to ensure that work processes are performed to some agreed-upon standard.

Test and Build Evidence

To test the viability of change ideas, improvement teams conduct Plan, Do, Study, Act (PDSA) cycles: systematic processes for iteratively testing small cycles of change that can build into larger improvements (Deming, 1993; Langley et al., 2009). During each cycle, teams develop a strategy (with related hypotheses and rationale) to test specific changes to their system (Plan); execute and collect data from these tests (Do); analyze the results (Study); and determine the next course of action (Act).

Given the limited capacity of most schools, improvement teams may choose to start testing change ideas in a modest way (e.g., in one classroom). By doing so, they can build motivation and goodwill among important constituents and determine whether tested changes produce the results they desire. If these initial tests prove successful, teams can then expand to more settings with larger numbers of students and other stakeholders (Bryk et al., 2015).

Spread and Scale

In addition to PDSA cycles, teams must consider how to spread improvements to other parts of their system, so that they become standard practice and are scaled in ways that last and benefit more people (Langley et al., 2009; Mittman, 2014). Coburn (2003) conceives of scale as comprising four interrelated dimensions: (a) depth (change in classroom practice); (b) sustainability (maintaining the change over time); (c) spread (diffusion of the change to other settings); and (d) shift in ownership (teachers, schools and districts assume ownership of the change). These dimensions suggest different factors teams must account for when spreading and scaling improvements, including the staff's understanding of the costs and advantages of the change and the availability of technical assistance to help staff integrate the change into their routines (Mittman, 2014; Rogers, 2003).

Addressing Equity Concerns Through Improvement Science

As more leaders turn to NICs and improvement science methods and tools, it is critical that the manner in which the work is conducted at each stage of the journey addresses the causes of long-standing inequities. Educational equity does not happen by chance. Leaders and educators will need to develop their know-how and address both the in- and out-of-school factors that hinder the learning and development of disadvantaged children and youth. Adopting an equity lens and an ecological perspective on schooling can encourage leaders to care for the whole child and take on a system-wide approach in dismantling the marginalizing structures and practices that prevent young people from accessing important learning opportunities.

It stands to reason that without purposeful attention to educational equity, the improvement science process on its own will not combat the effects of bias and exclusion. Leaders will need to be intentional about how they convene and guide teams throughout the continuous improvement journey—so that mindsets and actions at each stage explicitly address the perceptions, practices and structures that keep young people from economically disadvantaged and nondominant backgrounds from achieving equitable outcomes.

To inform an improvement practice committed to equitable schooling, I describe below three principles, along with some illustrative examples of each, that can serve as guideposts along the improvement journey. I also provide in the Appendix some examples of equity-related questions leaders can use as they apply these principles in their improvement practice. As improvement science becomes more commonplace, my hope is that these principles can begin to promote a humble practice that encourages critical reflection, openness to multiple perspectives and an unwavering focus on the positive development of historically underserved students.

Principle 1: Practice Critical Reflection Through an Equity Lens

Brookfield (1995) describes critical reflection as focusing on three interrelated processes: (a) questioning widely held assumptions; (b) considering alternative perspectives on taken-for-granted ideas or forms of reasoning; and (c) recognizing the influence of dominant cultural values. From this perspective, a practice of critical reflection can mean self-inspection of one's position based on personal values, beliefs and assumptions; attending to interpersonal relationships and dynamics; recognizing the questions and issues that have been privileged over others—and by whom and for what reasons; and questioning how established ways of thinking influence practice. In what follows, I discuss how critical reflection through an equity lens can help leaders recognize harmful patterns of deficit thinking and better understand the system in which they occur.

Equity Traps and Deficit Constructions

McKenzie and Scheurich (2004) identify equity traps or "patterns of thinking and behavior that trap the possibilities for creating equitable schools for children of color" (p. 603). They include attributing low student achievement to internal deficits or cultural inadequacy (Valencia, 2010) and holding "paralogical beliefs" where decisions and actions are rationalized from false premises (e.g., teachers blaming students to justify their own negative behaviors such as using demeaning language; see McKenzie & Scheurich, 2004).

Studies investigating teacher bias demonstrate how equity traps can harm students' academic prospects. For instance, Gershenson,

Holt, and Papageorge (2016) find that non–African American teachers of African American students exhibit systematically lower educational expectations—especially for male students—than do African American teachers. Differential teacher expectations and treatments can also exacerbate the effects of stereotype threat (Shapiro & Aronson, 2013), whereby low expectations of the intellectual strengths of ethnic-minority students cause them to disengage with school. Teachers who hold negative biases about their students have been found to modify how they instruct, assess and advise them (Peterson, Rubie-Davies, Osborne, & Sibley, 2016), which, in effect, serves to institutionalize unjust practices (Brown, 2004).

Reframing how one perceives students, families and communities historically disadvantaged by their race/ethnicity or socioeconomic status is crucial to overcoming deficit thinking (Dudley-Marling, 2015; McKenzie & Scheurich, 2004). This is especially salient as the educator workforce remains mostly White (and female) despite increasing student diversity (Carver-Thomas, 2018; Goldring, Taie, & Riddles, 2014; Taie & Goldring, 2017). By engaging in a practice of critical reflection, improvement leaders can "identify and come to grips with their prejudices and assumptions arising from their cultural backgrounds" (Furman, 2012, p. 197). Practicing this kind of critical consciousness (McKenzie et al., 2008) can help leaders understand who they are, identify with the contexts in which they serve and critique the manner in which they engage in the improvement process (e.g., "In what ways does my identity influence how I see our problem?").

Seeing the System

Critical reflection and attention to equity is important in all stages of the improvement journey. For example, as leaders seek to understand system forces driving local problems, an equity lens can encourage investigation of privilege structures that deprive some students of opportunities to learn. One way to scan these structures is to inspect not only the "visible" aspects of the system (e.g., standard operations and processes) but also the "invisible" dimensions (e.g., quality of relationships) critical for bringing about sustained change (Bryk & Schneider, 2002; Zuieback, 2012). These include the organization's identity (e.g., the level of shared purpose among staff); relationship dynamics (e.g., the level of connectivity among people); and information exchange (e.g., the nature of how information is shared and used within the system).

Undoubtedly, access and active exchange of information is essential in all improvement efforts. Although most districts and schools collect a vast array of student data (e.g., attendance, dropout rates), information is often collected and housed in disparate systems that do not speak to one another (Means, Padilla, DeBarger, & Bakia, 2010). Therefore, improvement teams need to develop their capabilities in navigating and making diverse types of data actionable (Bryk et al., 2015; Grunow & Park, 2014; Norman & Chabran, 2018).

Since 2009, the Roble Unified School District's Equity and Access Team has utilized improvement science methods along with its data dashboard and School Quality Improvement Index to increase students' awareness of postsecondary choices and application to selective state colleges and universities (Aguilar, Nayfack, & Bush-Mecenas, 2017). Throughout their work, the team critically investigated how their traditional ways of thinking and working were contributing to the unsatisfactory outcomes they were observing. They also analyzed different data elements (e.g., the percentage of students who were on track to attend college the following term) and documented each PDSA cycle to monitor their failures and successes (Bryk, 2018). In all, Roble's efforts—which illustrate many improvement tenets including explicit concern for variability in performance and anchoring practice in disciplined inquiry (Bryk et al., 2015)—resulted in a 50% increase in the number of students applying to California public universities (Aguilar et al., 2017).

Principle 2: Promote Inclusion

In addition to a practice of critical reflection, engaging in ways that invite diverse perspectives and stakeholders is useful when pursuing equity-centered improvement work. The improvement principle of deeply understanding the problem, and the system in which it occurs, embeds participatory involvement across multiple perspectives (Bryk et al., 2015). Connecting with those who historically have had less access to, or who feel neglected by, the school system, can chip away at the structural marginalization that keeps young people of color and those who are economically disadvantaged from meaningful educational opportunities (Cardichon & Darling-Hammond, 2017; Darling-Hammond, 2007). By bringing stakeholders together across race/ethnicity and socioeconomic status lines, leaders can lay the groundwork for healing, community and positive relationships necessary to undo the harmful exclusion of underserved children, youth and families (McKenzie & Scheurich, 2004). Below, I describe how collaborative leadership models and user-centered approaches can help democratize the improvement process, where the privileged and less privileged develop a collective sense of ownership and responsibility for redressing educational inequities.

Collaborative Leadership

One way leaders can counter power dynamics that allow certain voices to count more than others is to employ a collaborative leadership model that seeks to create "governance structures and processes that empower staff and students, and encourage commitment, broad participation, and shared accountability for student learning" (Hallinger & Heck, 2010, p. 101). The shared governance structure of networked improvement communities, for instance, encourages collaborative working and inclusive innovation (Bryk et al., 2015). Other efforts to promote inclusion throughout the improvement journey might include promoting "courageous conversations" to investigate potential biases so that educators may modify their practices to address the needs of all students (Singleton, 2012); developing culturally responsive pedagogy (e.g., Gay, 2010) and culturally affirming school cultures (e.g., Dantley & Tillman, 2010) to elevate student voice and experiences; and organizing with families to better support their key needs and concerns (e.g., Ishimaru, 2013).

User-Centered Approaches

Improvement leaders can also employ tools from user-centered design to promote inclusion. User-centered design is premised on the notion that the people who face the problem day to day are the ones who hold the key to its answer (Biag, 2017). As the first principle of improvement (Bryk et al., 2015), making the work problem-specific and user-centered means engaging participants closest to the problem early and often, including in the process of formulating and prototyping change ideas. Educators who utilize user-centered design tools frequently immerse themselves in the lives of their users—interviewing, observing and consulting with them so that they can fully understand their viewpoints and experiences. Methods include directed storytelling, which allows teams to gather information about specific lived experiences (e.g., transitioning from middle school to high school); shadowing, in which teams collect insights through firsthand observations of daily life (e.g., *Shadow a Student Challenge*, n.d.); and think-aloud protocols that direct students to verbalize what they are doing and thinking as they complete a particular task (e.g., solving a math problem), to reveal aspects that warrant improvement or innovation (Hanington & Martin, 2012).

As part of their improvement efforts to increase third grade literacy, the Early Literacy Network Campaign (ELNC) conducted student journey mapping (Baron, 2017). Journey or story maps (Lichaw, 2016) break down the highs and lows of users' experiences through a particular journey—shedding light on where problems may exist. In this example, district leads were first tasked to identify and review the administrative file of a struggling third grade student. Next, interviews were conducted with the student's teachers and other instructors and then with the student to gain insight on their perceptions of reading (e.g., what they liked to read, how they perceived themselves as readers). Among other findings, the journey maps revealed that communication among teachers and intervention specialists was weak and resulted in misaligned expectations, and some students needed additional supports and materials to read at home. Districts in the network were encountering similar challenges (Baron, 2017).

Youth Leading the Way, a network of charter schools in San Diego County, also utilizes user-centered tools to gain insights into their students' learning experiences. For instance, in their Mathematical Agency Improvement Community, teams employed empathy interviews (Portigal, 2013) as part of their root cause problem analysis (Biag, Callier, Dawkins-Jackson, & Sharrock, 2018). They observed that many of their students struggled in math, were unable to understand its relevance in their lives and spent most of their class time memorizing procedures. As such, teachers were not confident that students were developing deep content knowledge and conceptual mastery.

Combining what they learned from scholarly research and analyses of their data, network members conducted interviews with students to understand where and why they struggled in math. Chief among their findings was that students felt intimidated to share and ask their peers questions in their small groups. In response to this, teachers introduced group norms and roles, as well as sentence starters, to establish classroom practices that encouraged all students to share their thinking. Teachers also initiated mindset interventions to help students rethink the role of mistakes in learning math and foster the notion that "being good in math" is the result of hard work and collaboration.

Both ELNC and Youth Leading the Way illustrate how problem-specific and user-centered improvement approaches can encourage inclusion and afford teams nuanced understanding of students' needs, challenges and aspirations. These approaches can also help inform change ideas on how teams can reconfigure school and classroom environments to better enable student learning and success, particularly for those most vulnerable.

Principle 3: Focus on the Whole Child

Improvement projects that are oriented toward student performance or outcomes need to consider the whole child in defining the problem and potential solutions. Research affirms that when students are physically and emotionally healthy, they are more likely to attend school, avoid risky behaviors (e.g., substance use) and receive better grades (Basch, 2011). Yet far too many students are growing up in circumstances that undermine their ability to do well in school (Darling-Hammond, 2007). Many live with a wide range of adversities such as community violence, crime and unstable housing, which can contribute to chronic stress that negatively impacts their readiness to learn (Duncan & Murnane, 2011).

Improvement leaders recognize they must attend not only to students' academic needs but also their physical, social and emotional well-being—given that each of these domains develops alongside others and cannot be separated (Blank & Berg, 2006). As leaders work toward educational equity, their efforts must necessarily address the out-of-school factors (e.g., poverty) that bear upon students' learning and healthy development (Duncan & Murnane, 2011). In what follows, I discuss how leaders can consider the scholarly knowledge on community schools and positive youth development as helpful organizing models to inform their improvement efforts in addressing the whole-child needs of their students.

The Community Schools Approach

Community schools present an evidence-based strategy that can help leaders attend to the multiple factors that influence students' positive growth (Dryfoos, 2005; Oakes, Maier, & Daniel, 2017). With the school serving as the hub, community schools provide students and their families a range of wraparound services such as medical care, after-school tutoring and parenting classes (Blank, Jacobson, & Melaville, 2012). By providing supports year-round at the school site, community schools seek to remove barriers that impede learning and encourage collaborative work among educators and community partners, including social service agencies and youth service providers (Blank & Berg, 2006; Dryfoos & Quinn, 2007).

In their review of the empirical literature on community schools, Oakes and her colleagues (2017) conclude that "the evidence base provides a strong warrant for using community schools to meet the needs of low-achieving students in high-poverty schools and to help close opportunity and achievement gaps for students from low-income families, students of color, English learners, and students with disabilities" (p. 105). They also found that successful community schools share four "pillars" (or features) whose combined effect can "increase the odds that young people in low-income and under-resourced communities will be in educational environments with meaningful learning opportunities, high-quality teaching, well-used resources, additional supports, and a culture of high expectations, trust, and shared responsibility" (p. 13). These four pillars are (a) expanded and enriched learning time and opportunities; (b) collaborative leadership and practices; (c) active family and community engagement; and (d) integrated student supports (Oakes et al., 2017). Improvement teams may consider these pillars as they work to determine the high-leverage system changes that can better support the cognitive, physical, social and emotional development of their students.

Features of Positive Developmental Settings

Another research-based model that can organize improvement efforts to educate the whole child comes from the National Research Council and Institute of Medicine, which similarly identifies environmental features that promote positive youth development (Eccles & Gootman, 2002). The eight factors are

1. physical and physiological safety (e.g., classroom practices that increase safe peer group interactions);
2. appropriate structure (e.g., consistently-enforced school rules);
3. supportive relationships (e.g., caring student-teacher relationships);
4. opportunities to belong (e.g., school clubs that are inclusive of students from a variety of backgrounds);
5. positive social norms (e.g., staff members model respectful interactions);
6. support for efficacy and mattering (e.g., programs that encourage student leadership);
7. opportunities for skill building (e.g., student participation in college and career fairs); and

8. integration of family, school, and community efforts (e.g., providing workshops to teachers on how to connect families to community providers). (pp. 90–91)

As improvement leaders find ways to support the achievement and optimal development of their students, they may consider how to establish structures, routines and practices that enable these features in their schools and classrooms. As teams study their context and problems closely, identify key levers and refine working theories of improvement, consideration of these features may address some of the root causes contributing to inequitable student outcomes. For example, leaders seeking to improve middle school math achievement may take into account physical and psychological safety as a primary driver in order to establish stability in classrooms and afford teachers more time for teaching and learning.

The features and conditions outlined above can also guide the development of specific change ideas. Examples might include sending families suggestions via text messages to help them to engage in math discourse with their child at home (i.e., integration of family, school and community efforts); creating advisory periods to increase student-teacher interactions (i.e., supportive relationships); and developing project-based curriculum designed around real-life experiences (i.e., opportunities for skill building). In all, consideration and integration of scholarly knowledge with local improvement and practical expertise, at each stage of the improvement journey, can help leaders enhance the whole-child focus and equity character of their improvement practices.

Discussion

Although the concept of continuous improvement continues to appear more and more in discussions of educational reform, greater clarity is needed regarding how leaders can apply it in consistent and effective ways to improve students' educational outcomes. More understanding is also needed about how leaders can discipline their mindsets, strategies and work at each stage of the improvement journey to help reduce the marginalization of young people from economically disadvantaged and nondominant backgrounds.

This chapter describes three principles that encourage improvement leaders to practice critical reflection, promote inclusion and focus on the needs of the whole child. These principles seek to help leaders treat continuous improvement not only as a technical enterprise composed of testing and iteration but as a multifaceted endeavor that demands deep understanding of systemic oppression and the different ways it manifests and shapes students' learning and healthy development. This chapter also discusses how these principles relate to the improvement process and suggest ways in which they can be embedded within it to more intentionally address equity concerns.

As increasing numbers of leaders turn to NICs and improvement science to better serve their students, my hope is that these principles, while not exhaustive, can expand conversations that might otherwise narrowly focus on leaders' ability to employ process maps, Pareto charts and other quality improvement tools. Although I am not contesting the importance of technical improvement expertise, I argue that for students to receive a high-quality and equitable educational experience, improvement leaders will need to engage in a disciplined practice that critically interrogates routines, culture and other system forces through an equity lens; brings diverse stakeholders together in decision-making; and maintains the cognitive, physical, social and emotional well-being of vulnerable students as the "true north" in all improvement journeys.

Leaders will not reverse educational inequities overnight, but they can develop the capacity to think, engage and act at each stage of the improvement journey in ways that support equity for all young people regardless of their backgrounds (NEP, 2016). Without interrupting the structures, norms and processes that make it difficult for underserved groups to access opportunities and experiences, improvement science will fall short in addressing the deep-rooted issues that allow educational inequities to persist and grow.

Discussion Questions

1. How might we redesign leadership preparation and pedagogy to more effectively support a critical practice that integrates equity and continuous improvement?
2. What are the dispositions that enable equity-centered, continuous improvement work? How might leaders foster these dispositions among their staff? What types of structures, activities, rituals and supports might be useful?
3. How might leaders engage students, families and community members to play a greater role in supporting continuous improvement? What types of opportunities might leaders design and provide to build their improvement capacity and, at the same time, leverage their unique strengths and assets?

Key Concepts

Educational equity
Ecological perspective
Continuous improvement
Equity traps
User-centered approaches

References

Aguilar, J., Nayfack, M., & Bush-Mecenas, S. (2017). *Exploring improvement science in education: Promoting college access in Fresno Unified School District*. Stanford, CA: Policy Analysis for California Education. Available from http://www.edpolicyinca.org/sites/default/files/FUSD-continuous-improvement.pdf

Aspen Institute Education and Society Program & Council of Chief State School Officers. (2017). *Leading for equity: Opportunities for state education chiefs*. Washington DC. Available from https://ccsso.org/sites/default/files/2018-01/Leading%20for%20Equity_011618.pdf

Barron, K. (2017). Journey mapping a path to early literacy in Tennessee [Blog post]. Available from https://www.carnegiefoundation.org/blog/journey-mapping-a-path-to-early-literacy- in-tennessee/

Basch, C. E. (2011). Healthier students are better learners: High-quality, strategically planned, and effectively coordinated school health programs must be a fundamental mission of schools to help close the achievement gap. *Journal of School Health, 81*(10), 650–662.

Battistich, V. (2010). School contexts that promote students' positive development. In J. L. Meece & J. S. Eccles (Eds.), *Handbook of research on schools, schooling, and human development* (pp. 111–128). New York, NY: Routledge.

Bennett, B., & Provost, L. (2015). What's YOUR Theory? *Quality Progress, 48*(7), 36.

Berwick, D. M. (1996). A primer on leading the improvement of systems. *BMJ: British Medical Journal, 312*(7031), 619–622.

Biag, M. (2017). Improvement is a team sport [Blog post]. Available from https://www.carnegiefoundation.org/blog/improvement-is-a-team-sport/

Biag, M., Callier, S., Dawkins-Jackson, P., & Sharrock, D. (2018, April 4). *Understanding the user experience: Empathy tools and techniques.* Lecture conducted at the 2018 Carnegie Summit on Improvement in Education, San Francisco, CA.

Blank, M., & Berg, A. (2006). *All together now: Sharing responsibility for the whole child.* (Association for Supervision and Curriculum Development Report). Washington DC: Coalition for Community Schools at the Institute for Educational Leadership. Available from http://www.csun.edu/~SB4310/601%20files/sharingresponsibility.pdf

Blank, M., Jacobson, R., & Melaville, A. (2012). *Achieving results through community school partnerships.* Washington DC: Center for American Progress. Available from http://community-wealth.org/sites/clone.community-wealth.org/files/downloads/paper-blank-et-al. pdf

Bronfrenbrenner, U., & Morris, P. A. (1998). The ecology of developmental processes. In R. Lerner (Vol. Ed.), *Handbook of child psychology: Theoretical models of human development.* (5th ed., Vol. 1, pp. 993–1028). New York, NY: Wiley.

Brookfield, S. D. (1995). *Becoming a critically reflective teacher.* San Francisco, CA: Jossey-Bass.

Brown, K. M. (2004). Leadership for social justice and equity: Weaving a transformative framework and pedagogy. *Educational Administration Quarterly, 40*(1), 79–110.

Bryk, A. S. (April 3, 2018). *Advancing quality in continuous improvement.* Keynote lecture at the 2018 Carnegie Summit on Improvement in Education, San Francisco, CA. Available from https://www.carn egiefoundation.org/wp-content/uploads/2018/06/Carnegie_Bryk_ Summit_2018_Keynote.pdf

Bryk, A. S., Gomez, L. M., Grunow, A., & LeMahieu, P. G. (2015). *Learning to improve: How America's schools can get better at getting better.* Cambridge, MA: Harvard Education Press.

Bryk, A. S., & Schneider, B. (2002). *Trust in schools: A core resource for improvement.* New York, NY: Russell Sage Foundation.

Bryk, A. S., Sebring, P. B., Allensworth, E., Easton, J. Q., & Luppescu, S. (2010). *Organizing schools for improvement: Lessons from Chicago.* Chicago, IL: University of Chicago Press.

Cardichon, J., & Darling-Hammond, L. (2017). *Advancing educational equity for underserved youth: How new state accountability systems can support school inclusion and student success.* Palo Alto, CA: Learning Policy Institute. Available from https://learningpolicy institute.org/sites/default/files/product-files/Advancing_Educational_ Equity_Underserved_Youth_REPORT.pdf

Carver-Thomas, D. (2018). *Diversifying the teaching profession: How to recruit and retain teachers of color.* Palo Alto, CA: Learning Policy Institute. Available from: https://learningpolicyinstitute.org/sites/default/files/ product-files/Diversifying_Teaching_Profession_REPORT_0.pdf

Coburn, C. E. (2003). Rethinking scale: Moving beyond numbers to deep and lasting change. *Educational Researcher, 32*(6), 3–12.

Dantley, M. E., & Tillman, L. C. (2010). Social justice and moral transformative leadership. In C. Marshall & M. Olivia (Eds.), *Leadership for social justice* (2nd ed., pp. 19–34). Boston, MA: Allyn & Bacon.

Darling-Hammond, L. (2007). Race, inequality and educational accountability: The irony of "No Child Left Behind." *Race Ethnicity and Education, 10*(3), 245–260.

Deming, W. E. (1993). *The new economics.* Cambridge, MA: Massachusetts Institute of Technology, Center for Advanced Engineering Study.

DeWalt, K. M., & DeWalt, B. R. (2011). *Participant observation: A guide for fieldworkers.* Plymouth, UK: Rowman Altamira.

Dryfoos, J. G. (2005). Full-service community schools: A strategy—not a program. *New Directions for Youth Development, 107,* 7–16.

Dryfoos, J., & Quinn, J. (2007). *Community schools: A strategy for integrating youth development and school reform.* San Francisco, CA: Jossey-Bass.

Dudley-Marling, C. (2015). The resilience of deficit thinking. *Journal of Teaching and Learning, 10*(1), 1–12.

Duncan, G., & Murnane, R. (2011). *Whither opportunity? Rising inequality, schools, and children's life chances.* New York, NY: Russell Sage Foundation.

Eccles, J. S., & Gootman, J. A. (Eds.). (2002). *Community programs to promote youth development* (Committee on Community-Level Programs for Youth Report). Washington DC: National Academy Press.

Eccles, J. S., & Roeser, R. W. (2010). An ecological view of schools and development. In J. L. Meece & J. S. Eccles (Eds.), *Handbook of research on schools, schooling, and human development* (pp. 6–22). New York, NY: Routledge.

Elgart, M. A. (2017). Can schools meet the promise of continuous improvement? *Phi Delta Kappan, 99*(4), 54–59.

Elmore, R. F. (2006, July). International perspectives on school leadership for systemic improvement. *Politics,* 1–28.

Festerwald, J., & Freeberg, L. (2018, August 28). Gates Foundation's new school initiative awards big grants to California nonprofits. *EdSource.* Available from https://edsource.org/2018/gates-foundations-new-school-initiative-awards-big-grants-to-california-nonprofits/601664

Fullan, M., & Quinn, J. (2015). *Coherence: The right drivers in action for schools, districts, and systems.* Thousand Oaks, CA: Corwin Press.

Furman, G. (2012). Social justice leadership as praxis: Developing capacities through preparation programs. *Educational Administration Quarterly, 48*(2), 191–229.

Gay, G. (2010). *Culturally responsive teaching: Theory, research, and practice* (2nd ed.). New York, NY: Teachers College Press.

Gershenson, S., Holt, S. B., & Papageorge, N. W. (2016). Who believes in me? The effect of student–teacher demographic match on teacher expectations. *Economics of Education Review, 52,* 209–224.

Goldring, R., Taie, S., & Riddles, M. (2014). *Teacher attrition and mobility: Results from the 2012-13 Teacher Follow-Up Survey* (National Center for Education Statistics Report). Available from https://files.eric. ed.gov/fulltext/ED546773.pdf

Grunow, A., & Park, S. (September 4, 2014). *Learning to improve: Collective learning systems.* Lecture conducted at the Society for Research on Educational Effectiveness (SREE), Washington, DC.

Hallinger, P., & Heck, R. H. (2010). Collaborative leadership and school improvement: Understanding the impact on school capacity and student learning. *School Leadership & Management, 30*(2), 95–110.

Hanington, B., & Martin, B. (2012). *Universal methods of design: 100 ways to research complex problems, develop innovative ideas, and design effective solutions.* Beverly, MA: Rockport.

Hannan, M., Russell, J. L., Takahashi, S., & Park, S. (2015). Using improvement science to better support beginning teachers: The case of the building a teaching effectiveness network. *Journal of Teacher Education, 66*(5), 494–508.

Heckman, J. J. (2006). Skill formation and the economics of investing in disadvantaged children. *Science, 312*(5782), 1900–1902.

Hough, H., Willis, J., Grunow, A., Krausen, K., Kwon, S., Mulfinger, L., & Park, S. (2017). *Continuous improvement in practice.* Stanford, CA: Policy Analysis for California Education. Available from https://ed policyinca.org/sites/default/files/CI%20in%20Pratice.pdf

Huang, M. (2018). *2016-2017 impact report: Six years of results from the Carnegie Math Pathways.* San Francisco, CA: WestEd. Available from https://www.carnegiefoundation.org/wp-content/uploads/2018/04/ Pathways_Descriptive_Report_201802.pdf

Isaacs, J. B. (2012, March). *Starting school at a disadvantage: The school readiness of poor children.* Washington DC: Brookings Institution. Available from https://www.brookings.edu/wp-content/uploads/2016/06/0319_ school_disadvantage_isaacs.pdf

Ishimaru, A. M. (2013). From heroes to organizers: Principals and education organizing in urban school reform. *Educational Administration Quarterly, 49*(1), 3–51.

Khalifa, M. A., Gooden, M. A., & Davis, J. E. (2016). Culturally responsive school leadership: A synthesis of the literature. *Review of Educational Research, 86*(4), 1272–1311.

Kivel, L. (2015, May 18). The problem with solutions [Blog post]. Available from https://www.carnegiefoundation.org/blog/the-problem-with-solutions/

Langley, G. J., Moen, R. D., Nolan, K. M., Nolan, T. W., Norman, C. L., & Provost, L. P. (2009). *The improvement guide: A practical approach to enhancing organizational performance* (2nd ed.). San Francisco, CA: Jossey-Bass.

Leithwood, K. A., & Riehl, C. (2003). *What we know about successful school leadership*. Philadelphia, PA: Temple University Press.

Leithwood, K., & Sun, J. (2012). The nature and effects of transformational school leadership: A meta-analytic review of unpublished research. *Educational Administration Quarterly, 48*(3), 387–423.

LeMahieu, P. G., Bryk, A. S., & Grunow, A. (2017). Working to improve: Seven approaches to improvement science in education. *Quality Assurance in Education, 25*(1), 1–5.

LeMahieu, P. G., Grunow, A., Baker, L., Nordstrum, L. E., & Gomez, L. M. (2017). Networked improvement communities: The discipline of improvement science meets the power of networks. *Quality Assurance in Education, 25*(1), 5–25.

Lewis, C. (2015). What is improvement science? Do we need it in education? *Educational Researcher, 44*(1), 54–61.

Lichaw, D. (2016). *The user's journey: Storymapping products that people love*. Brooklyn, NY: Rosenfeld.

Lucas, B., & Nacer, H. (2015). *The habits of an improver*. London, UK: Health Foundation. Available from https://www.health.org.uk/publication/habits-improver

McKenzie, K. B., Christman, D. E., Hernandez, F., Fierro, E., Capper, C. A., Dantley, M., . . . Scheurich, J. J. (2008). From the field: A proposal for educating leaders for social justice. *Educational Administration Quarterly, 44*, 111–138.

McKenzie, K. B., & Scheurich, J. J. (2004). Equity traps: A useful construct for preparing principals to lead schools that are successful with racially diverse students. *Educational Administration Quarterly, 40*(5), 601–632.

Means, B., Padilla, C., DeBarger, A., & Bakia, M. (2010). *Implementing data-informed decision-making in schools—Teacher access, supports and use*. Washington DC: U.S. Department of Education Office of Planning, Evaluation and Policy Development. Available from https://files.eric.ed.gov/fulltext/ED504191.pdf

Meece, J. L., & Schaefer, V. A. (2010). Schools as contexts of human development. In J. L. Meece & J. S. Eccles (Eds.), *Handbook of research on schools, schooling, and human development* (pp. 3–5). New York, NY: Routledge.

Mintrop, R. (2016). *Design-based school improvement: A practical guide for education leaders.* Cambridge, MA: Harvard Education Press.

Mittman, B. (2014, January 29). Factors that influence the scale up and spread of innovations [Blog post]. Available from https://innovations. ahrq.gov/perspectives/factors-influence-scale-and-spread-innovations

Morgan, I., & Amerikaner, A. (2018). *Funding gaps 2018: Too many students do not get their fair share of education funding.* Available from https://edtrust.org/resource/funding-gaps-2018/

National Equity Project. (2016). *Leading for equity in complex systems.* Oakland, CA: National Equity Project.

National Policy Board for Educational Administration. (2015). *Professional standards for educational leaders.* Reston, VA: Author. Available from http://npbea.org/wp-content/uploads/2017/06/Professional-Standards-for-Educational-Leaders_2015.pdf

Norman, J., & Chabran, M. (2018, April 4). *Measurement for improvement.* Lecture conducted at the 2018 Carnegie Summit on Improvement in Education, San Francisco, CA. Available from http://summit.carnegiefoundation.org/session_materials/C1.%20Measurement%20for%20Improvement/C1_JNorman_MeasurementforImprovementPPT.pdf

Oakes, J., Maier, A., & Daniel, J. (2017). *Community schools: An evidence-based strategy for equitable school improvement.* Palo Alto, CA: Learning Policy Institute. Available from https://learningpolicyinstitute.org/sites/default/files/product-files/Community_Schools_Effective_REPORT.pdf

O'Day, J. A., & Smith, M. S. (2016). Quality and equality in American education: Systemic problems, systemic solutions. In I. Kirsch, H. Braun (Eds.), *The dynamics of opportunity in America* (pp. 297–358). Princeton, NJ: Educational Testing Service.

Park, S., Hironaka, S., Carver, C., & Lee, N. (2012). *Continuous improvement in education.* Stanford, CA: Carnegie Foundation for the Advancement of Teaching. Available from https://www.carnegiefoundation.org/wp-content/uploads/2014/09/carnegie-foundation_continuous-improvement_2013.05.pdf

Peterson, E. R., Rubie-Davies, C., Osborne, D., & Sibley, C. (2016). Teachers' explicit expectations and implicit prejudiced attitudes to educational achievement: Relations with student achievement and the ethnic achievement gap. *Learning and Instruction, 42*, 123–140.

Peurach, D. J., Penuel, W. R., and Russell, J. L. (in press). Beyond ritualized rationality: Organizational dynamics of instructionally-focused continuous improvement. In C. James, D. E. Spicer, M. Connolly, & S. D. Kruse (Eds.), *The Sage handbook of school organization*. Thousand Oaks, CA: Sage.

Portigal, S. (2013). *Interviewing users: How to uncover compelling insights*. Brooklyn, NY: Rosenfeld.

Rabinowitz, J. (2016, April 29). Local education inequities across U.S. revealed in new Stanford data set [Press release]. Available from https://news.stanford.edu/2016/04/29/local-education-inequities-across-u-s-revealed-new-stanford-data-set/

Reform Support Network. (2015, February). *Promoting more equitable access to effective teachers: Strategic options for states to improve placement and movement*. Available from https://www2.ed.gov/about/inits/ed/implementation-support-unit/tech-assist/equitableaccess toeffectiveteachersstrategicoptions.pdf

Rogers, E. (2003). *Diffusion of innovation* (5th ed.). New York, NY: The Free Press.

Russell, J. L., Bryk, A. S., Dolle, J., Gomez, L. M., LeMahieu, P., & Grunow, A. (2017). A framework for the initiation of networked improvement communities. *Teachers College Record, 119*(5), 1–36.

Shadow a student challenge. (n.d.). Available from https://www.shadow astudent.org/

Shapiro, J. R., & Aronson, J. (2013). Stereotype threat. In C. Stangor & C. Crandall (Eds.), *Stereotyping and prejudice* (pp. 107–130). New York, NY: Psychology Press.

Shields, C. M. (2010). Transformative leadership: Working for equity in diverse contexts. *Educational Administration Quarterly, 46*(4), 558–589.

Singleton, G. E. (2012). *More courageous conversations about race*. Thousand Oaks, CA: Corwin Press.

Tague, N. R. (2005). *The quality toolbox* (Vol. 600). Milwaukee, WI: ASQ Quality Press.

Taie, S., & Goldring, R. (2017). *Characteristics of public elementary and secondary school teachers in the United States: Results from the 2015–16 National Teacher and Principal Survey First Look* (NCES 2017-072rev, U.S. Department of Education). Washington, DC: National Center for Education Statistics. Available from http://nces.ed.gov/pubsearch/pubsinfo.ap?pubid=2017072rev

Theoharis, G. (2007). Social justice educational leaders and resistance: Toward a theory of social justice leadership. *Educational Administration Quarterly, 43*(2), 221–258.

Toussaint, J. S., & Ehrlich, S. P. (2017). *Five changes great leaders make to develop an improvement culture.* Available from https://catalyst.nejm.org/five-changes-great-leaders-improvement-culture/

Valencia, R. R. (2010). *Dismantling contemporary deficit thinking: Educational thought and practice.* New York, NY: Routledge.

Wallace Foundation. (2012, January). *The school principal as leader: Guiding schools to better teaching and learning.* New York, NY: Author. Available at www. wallacefoundation.org/knowledge-center/school-leadership/effective-principal-leadership/Pages/The-School-Principal-asLeader-Guiding-Schools-to-Better-Teaching-and-Learning.aspx

Wentzel, K. R. (2012). Teacher–student relationships and adolescent competence at school. In T. Wubbels, P. den Brok, J. van Tartwijk, & J. Levy (Eds.), *Advances in learning environments research,* Vol. 3: *Interpersonal relationships in education* (pp. 19–35). Rotterdam, Netherlands: Sense Publishers.

Zuieback, S. (2012). *Leadership practices for challenging times: Principles, skills and processes that work.* Ukiah, CA: Synectics.

Appendix. Example Equity-Related Questions, by Guiding Principle and Improvement Stage

Improvement Stage	Practice Critical Reflection Through an Equity Lens	Promote Inclusion	Focus on the Whole Child
Understand the problem and the system that produces it	In what ways does my identity and experiences influence how I see this problem? Because of who I am, how might I excel but fall short in solving this problem?	Which individuals and communities are burdened most by this problem? How might we reach out to these stakeholders to develop a shared understanding of the problem and the forces driving it?	In what ways does our understanding of the problem keep the needs of our most vulnerable students at the center of our improvement efforts?
Focus collective efforts	To what degree are we in agreement about what equitable outcomes and opportunities look like in our context? What are the agreed-upon indicators and measures of success? To what extent do my beliefs, values and assumptions drive our working theory of improvement?	In what ways • have we reached out to and incorporated the ideas, viewpoints and experiences of diverse groups (e.g., families, students) in our aim and working theory of improvement? • does our aim and working theory of improvement promote inclusion of diverse communities and groups? • do our improvement plans help empower students and families to change the system to improve learning?	How does our current aim and working theory of improvement • take into account factors that shape the cognitive, physical, social and emotional development of students? • attend to the learning conditions in schools and classrooms that support positive youth development (e.g., physical and psychological safety)?

Improvement Stage	Practice Critical Reflection Through an Equity Lens	Promote Inclusion	Focus on the Whole Child
Generate ideas for change	To what extent do our change ideas only reflect my beliefs, values and assumptions? Could there be other ideas I have overlooked because of who I am and how I view the world? Which ideas do I feel more strongly about and why? What assumptions am I making about these ideas?	Which individuals bear the most responsibility for the implementation of change ideas and why? Which individuals have the least responsibility and why? In what ways have we created opportunities for diverse groups to contribute ideas for change? To what extent do these groups feel a sense of ownership and responsibility for the implementation and success of these ideas?	To what extent do our change ideas • take into account factors that shape the cognitive, physical, social and emotional development of students? • interrupt practices that limit the opportunity of students from nondominant backgrounds? • help create meaningful opportunities to engage all youth? • create settings that promote positive youth development?

Improvement Stage	Practice Critical Reflection Through an Equity Lens	Promote Inclusion	Focus on the Whole Child
Test and build evidence	What do I count as valid evidence? Might there be other sources of evidence I have overlooked? What types of data are we collecting and to what extent do they provide us with knowledge about the students we serve and the community in which we work? In what ways may I have perpetuated inequities in building evidence for these change ideas?	In what ways have we • created opportunities for diverse groups to take part in the testing and analysis of these change ideas? • communicated with diverse constituents our learning from the testing of these change ideas?	How does our analysis of the data keep the needs of marginalized students at the center of our improvement efforts? To what extent have we examined variations in results based on socioeconomic status, race/ethnicity, gender and other student characteristics?
Spread and scale	In what ways may I be using my identity, power and privilege in exclusionary ways to scale and spread improvements? How might I correct for this?	In what ways • have we created opportunities for diverse groups to help scale and spread new system improvements and innovations? • does our plan to scale and spread system improvements reproduce inequitable practices and structures?	To what extent do system improvements and innovations disrupt historical and current forms of oppression that hinder students' learning and development?

CHAPTER SIX

The UCEA's Program Design Network

Roles and Opportunities for Professional Learning Using Improvement Science

KATHLEEN M. W. CUNNINGHAM
University of South Carolina
MICHELLE D. YOUNG
University of Virginia, University Council for Educational Administration
DAVID EDDY SPICER
University of Virginia

This chapter describes the University Council for Educational Administration's Program Design Network (UCEA-PDN). We describe how the faculty, facilitator, knowledge partner and hub roles within the UCEA-PDN are designed for knowledge development and improvement efforts of participating educational leadership preparation programs and share some emergent successes and challenges. Four distinct roles help organize the UCEA-PDN. The *program faculty* are stakeholders from educational leadership preparation programs who are interested in improving their program and learning in cross-institutional groups. The *facilitators* are the leaders of each networked improvement community (NIC). They guide and support program faculty and serve as a liaison to the *hub* (UCEA Headquarters). *Knowledge partners* are graduate students who serve as participant observers and synthesizers for PD-NIC. As the *hub*, UCEA Headquarters supports PD-NIC efforts and helps build professional capacity. Strengths of the UCEA-PDN include selecting problems of practice for PD-NIC focus, increasing capacity in improvement science and organizing learning opportunities (e.g., study visits). Challenges we have faced include coordinating meetings, predicting pacing, shifting from sensemaking to small tests of change and meeting the varying levels of familiarity in improvement science. An array of reports and initiatives over the past decade has highlighted the need for innovation and improvement in university leadership preparation programs. The UCEA-PDN is a response to programs' goals of improvement and supports cross-institutional learning for leadership preparation faculty.

Keywords

educational leadership, faculty, educational leadership preparation programming, improvement science, NIC development, hub capacity, facilitator capacity, cross-institutional learning

Setting/Background

Never has it been more important to have well-prepared educational leaders who understand teaching and learning; who are able to support their school staffs, student bodies, and school communities; and who are willing to question structures and norms in their efforts to meet the needs of those they lead. (Young & Crow, 2017, p. 1)

School administrators who are equipped to address problems of practice and target areas of improvement will likely be successful leaders for students, teachers and the school community. To this end, the University Council for Educational Administration (UCEA) aims to assist programs in building their preparation programs for developing successful educational leaders through research, resources and supportive initiatives. This chapter explores the design and implementation of one such initiative: UCEA's Program Design Network (UCEA-PDN). Beginning in 2016, this initiative supports cross-institutional learning for leadership preparation faculty and program changes. The overarching goal of this chapter is to describe how the different roles within the UCEA-PDN catalyze the knowledge development and program improvement efforts of engaged faculty concerning program quality, design and improvement science.

New standards for educational leaders are emphasizing continuous improvement (NPBEA, 2017) while the use of paradigms such as improvement science engage leaders supporting successes for their teachers and students. In order to meet these standards for educational leaders, supporting the learning of educational leadership faculty is therefore essential. UCEA, serving as the hub in this initiative, plays a critical role in assisting the learning of faculty to support improvement science approaches for their programs and their own work.

We begin by describing the critical role of the school leader, which provides a rationale for why improvement is a focus in programs where educational leadership candidates enroll. We then offer an argument highlighting the importance of educational leadership faculty in the development of successful school leaders. Next, we introduce readers to the UCEA-PDN initiative, its purpose and the different roles participants hold. Using our perspective of working in or directly with UCEA Headquarters, we dedicate particular attention in this chapter to the role of the hub (housed at UCEA Headquarters). We then connect the UCEA-PDN efforts to concepts or frameworks that inform its design: continuous improvement, improvement science and collaboration. Finally, we describe some successes and barriers revealed over the course of the initiative.

The Critical Role of the School Leader

Across years, research shows the importance of leadership in schools. Whether in the interpretation and implementation of policy (e.g., Fullan, 2001), cultivating a positive school culture and climate (e.g., Hitt & Tucker, 2016), demanding a socially just educational experience for all learners (e.g., Theoharis, 2009) or indirectly impacting student learning by directly influencing teacher practices (e.g.,

Leithwood et al., 2010), the school leader plays a critical role in the education of all children. Indeed, this responsibility and influence serve as evidence that the selection and preparation of school leaders is no small endeavor. We argue school leaders should be trained in rigorous, high-quality programs that honor the important nature of the position and help prepare individuals for the job's myriad responsibilities.

Those Who Prepare School Leaders

Since we know (a) educational leadership preparation matters in supporting and developing future school leaders (e.g., Fuller, Young, & Baker, 2011) and (b) aspiring school leaders typically enroll in a university-based leadership preparation program (NAESP, 2018), faculty members are positioned to shape and influence how future leaders will evaluate problems of practice and subsequent decision-making. Educational leadership programs are responsible for training principal candidates to effectively and equitably lead a school. Although research on educational leadership preparation has grown in recent years, there is still a dearth of literature examining the professional learning of faculty members and their development processes, supports and advancements (McCarthy, Hackmann, & Malin, 2017). The lack of literature centered on educational leadership faculty learning does not imply faculty members are not interested in continuous improvement for themselves or their programs. Rather, examples of UCEA faculty demonstrating their valuing of continuous improvement are seen through the dedication to the UCEA-PDN, where a commitment to engage in efforts to purposefully design programs to fully prepare their graduates is the cornerstone. Studying the role of educational leadership faculty is an important focus since there is evidence (e.g., Darling-Hammond, LaPointe, Meyerson, & Orr, 2007; Jackson & Kelley, 2002; Leithwood, Jantzi, Coffin, & Wilson, 1996; Orphanos & Orr, 2013; Orr & Orphanos, 2011) that preparation programming influences the level of leadership success of their program graduates.

When working to improve leadership preparation programs, faculty members need to deepen their own learning and skills for the purposes of designing and implementing their leadership programs. McCarthy and colleagues (2017) point out that for purposes of addressing relevant needs of the profession and honing instructional and research skills, "continuing professional development is an essential component for novice and veteran educational leadership faculty" (p. 130). We predict that engagement in the UCEA-PDN and using improvement science cultivates an opportunity for faculty members to do this.

Implementing and Testing the Change

Program Design Network Description

The UCEA-PDN supports collective engagement in educational leadership preparation design, redesign and improvement. In line with adult learning theory (Knowles, 1988) and using principles of design thinking and improvement science (Bryk, Gomez, & Grunow, 2010; Bryk, Gomez, Grunow, & LeMahieu, 2015; Langley et al., 2009; Russell, 2016), the initiative engages faculty in facilitated learning groups focused on bettering specific program design elements centered on the outcome of offering leadership candidates high-quality preparation. It builds on UCEA's research and development work as well as its success in fostering collaborative networks by supporting focused collective action around continuous program improvement and fostering engagement in leadership preparation design, redesign and improvement processes.

The organization of the UCEA-PDN is structured in such a way so that four different roles work together to help support leadership preparation programs. The roles require differing engagement and responsibilities and include program design networked improvement community (PD-NIC) members, PD-NIC facilitators, PD-NIC knowledge partners and the UCEA-PDN hub (see Figure 6.1).

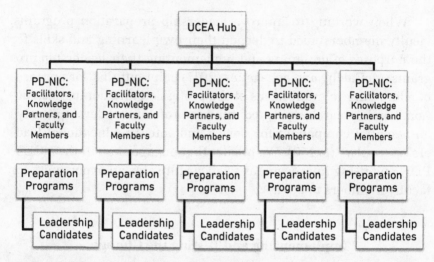

Figure 6.1. The organization of the UCEA-PDN.

Role: PD-NICs and PD-NIC Members

The UCEA-PDN utilizes a type of collaborative learning group—specifically, *networked improvement communities* (NICs). A NIC is commonly associated with the paradigm of improvement science. NICs are focused on "getting better at getting better" and as a group, members learn and gather data incrementally and systematically (Bryk, Gomez, & Grunow, 2011). PD-NICs, like other NICs working in an improvement science paradigm, often focus on three key questions: "First, what problem(s) are we trying to solve? Second, whose expertise is needed to solve these problems? And third, what are the social arrangements that will enable this work?" (Bryk et al., 2011, p. 4).

At the heart of each of the five PD-NICs is a problem of practice—areas linked to quality preparation outcomes within the research literature—and include:

1. Preparation Partnerships,
2. Candidate Recruitment, Selection & Evaluation,
3. Mentorship & Coaching,
4. Curriculum, Instruction & Coherence,
5. Powerful Learning Experiences (with an emphasis on equity).

The problem of practice anchors PD-NIC activity and stimulates the collective action of participants toward program improvement in their focus area. UCEA members who are interested in participating in the UCEA-PDN indicated which areas they wanted to focus efforts and then were placed in an aligned PD-NIC. Each has around four to six UCEA universities from across the United States.

After faculty joined the PD-NIC, they began to meet. Most meetings are held in virtual spaces, due to the cross-institutional membership. Two face-to-face meeting opportunities take place annually in conjunction with professional conferences. PD-NIC members participate in facilitated collaborative meetings designed to support faculty understanding and use of improvement science/continuous improvement and design thinking strategies targeted at participating programs' priority area of redesign (e.g., curriculum, partnerships, etc.). Together, PD-NIC members explore research and best practice, use tools of improvement science (e.g., fishbone diagrams) and develop implementation plans (such as Plan, Do, Study, Act, or PDSA, cycles) to examine and improve elements of their preparation program, share and develop new resources, and provide other PD-NIC members feedback and support.

Role: PD-NIC Facilitator

Each PD-NIC has a facilitator who serves as an organizer as well as a liaison linking the PD-NIC and the hub. The facilitator is responsible for several elements such as:

- Foster the development of PD-NIC identity through cultivating group norms and culture
- Train PD-NIC participants in the improvement science paradigm
- Manage and organize resources for the PD-NIC and the UCEA-PDN (UCEA, n.d.).

The facilitators have much experience in leading groups but have varying levels of experience with the improvement science approach. The facilitators play a critical role in communication and sensemaking both within their PD-NIC and across the initiative.

Role: PD-NIC Knowledge Partner

Each of the five PD-NICs also has a knowledge partner. Knowledge partners are doctoral students or candidates whose primary responsibility is to attend each meeting and serve as participant-observers. Knowledge partners take meeting notes, synthesize learning and progress and subsequently assist the facilitator with debriefing meetings and designing future meetings.

Role: Hub

UCEA Headquarters serves as the hub for the PD-NIC. Like the facilitator group, at the hub level there are varying degrees of experience with improvement science. Thus, the hub is working to build its capacity alongside others in different roles. The hub is organized to help build the capacity for improvement work initiative-wide. As Bryk and colleagues (2015) write:

> The hub is responsible for detailing the problem to be solved and for developing and maintaining the coherence of the evolving framework that guides efforts among many different participants. It establishes the processes and norms governing how individuals and groups work together and the evidentiary standards for warranting claims. The hub also provides technical resources and supports the open communication mechanisms necessary to accelerate learning networkwide (p. 12).

The hub organizes meetings with facilitators, and knowledge partners to check-in and helps organize learning opportunities such as attending the Carnegie Summit on Improvement, coordinating study visits and cultivating resources.

As the hub, UCEA aims to stimulate and outline a process and structure that fosters the development of faculty knowledge and skills in their own continuous improvement in design thinking (while also working to support program improvement efforts among its membership writ large).

Faculty Collaborative Learning for Continuous Improvement

For the purposes of meeting the present and future needs of educational leadership students, partner districts and the students they serve, opportunities for faculty members to learn and develop in collaborative spaces may foster the work. We anticipate positive outcomes associated with UCEA-PDN participation due to prior research that demonstrates faculty members (and their programs) can benefit from opportunities to engage in collaborate initiatives (e.g., Wenger, 2008). Based upon the literature in collaborative learning at both the PK–12 and higher education levels, some potential benefits faculty may experience when working within a collaborative learning community include (a) a positive change in institutional culture (e.g., Ferren, 1989); (b) improvements in instruction (e.g., Cox, 2004; MacConnell & Caillier, 2016); (c) higher student achievement (e.g., Vescio, Ross, & Adams, 2008); and/or (d) support from external stakeholders (e.g., Marks & Nance, 2007). These benefits shown in the existing literature espouses potential for faculty learning within the UCEA-PDN work and provides guidance when planning the next steps of this initiative.

Collaboration aligns with those theories of learning that privilege social interactions as a means through which to expand one's knowledge (Wenger, 2008). Faculty can work in learning communities, such as the UCEA-PDN, to tackle individual, programmatic or other organizational problems of practice. Participation in structured and collaborative redesign efforts may advance their own professional learning and development. Faculty members can benefit from opportunities to engage in professional development and improvement, which, in turn, may enhance their programs' and graduates' successes.

Within the UCEA-PDN, program faculty support cross-organizational thinking and sharing on common problems of practice that are in distinctly different contexts. "A network organizational approach can surface and test new insights and enable more fluid exchanges across contexts and traditional institutional boundaries—thus holding potential to enhance designing for scale" (Bryk et al., 2010, p. 6). Indeed, the ability to scale improvement practices emerges as an increasingly important attribute and principle element of NICs (Martin & Gobstein, 2015).

Lessons Learned Thus Far

The inaugural UCEA-PDN initiative has enjoyed wins as well as faced challenges of working within the improvement science structure. Below, we offer four of each as related to the hub's role.

Wins

The hub (a) selected problems of practices that resonated with the constituency of the UCEA membership as there was quite a lot of interest not only in the opportunity to engage in cross-institutional collaborative groups for program improvement purposes but also to focus on a priority area that aligned with their programmatic goals. The hub has (b) served as a catalyst to leverage the PD-NICs, highlighting the need for continuous improvement to be an organizational focus of higher education institutions. This is notable since continuous improvement has garnered less attention in higher education than it has in the PK–12 setting. The hub (c) has helped facilitators professionally learn by attending the Carnegie 2017 Summit on Improvement in Education as a team. This opportunity supported the group in not only learning more about the nuances of improvement science but also offered the team the occasion to work face-to-face to reflect upon, process, connect and plan next steps for the initiative. The hub (d) organized opportunities for each PD-NIC to travel to an exemplary leadership preparation program that is strong in their area of focus to learn from that program's faculty, learn from others in their PD-NIC and learn from others in their own program (see Table 6.1). In particular, the study visit experience invites participants to engage in the way Bryk and colleagues (2015) describe as a benefit to improvement science, for while "embracing Improvement Science, educators are able to draw upon a well-established set of tools and deep practical experiences"

(p. 7). This is precisely what the visits aimed to do: to provide educational leadership faculty the opportunity to learn from colleagues in other programs.

Table 6.1. Study Visit

PD-NIC	Exemplary Program Visited	Month of Visit
Powerful Learning Experiences	University of Texas at San Antonio	October 2017
Mentoring & Coaching	University of Washington	January 2018
Recruitment & Selection	North Carolina State University	January 2018
Curriculum, Instruction & Coherence	University of Illinois at Chicago	March 2018
Preparation Partnerships	University of Denver	September 2018

Representatives from each PD-NIC visited a leadership preparation program recognized as effective in the problem of practice of focus for the PD-NIC (see Table 6.1). Visit agendas included opportunities to learn from those in the roles of faculty members, students and practicing leaders. The Powerful Learning Experiences PD-NIC's visit to the University of Texas at San Antonio (UTSA) illustrated through conversations with numerous stakeholders how they engage their leadership candidates in a variety of powerful learning experiences including a community engagement project and developing one's autoethnography, an exercise that spans each semester of the program. The visit to the University of Washington (UW) helped the Mentoring and Coaching PD-NIC understand how UW leadership candidates are supported during their clinical internship experience through teams, how the clinical experiences and course experiences are blended together and how their program selects and then professionally develops advocates/mentors to support candidates and novice leaders. The site visit experience with the North Carolina State University (NCSU) faculty engaged the Recruitment and Selection PD-NIC by having the PD-NIC discuss recruitment and selection artifacts as well as having the PD-NIC members participate in the program's annual Candidate Assessment Day. The Curriculum, Instruction, and Coherence PD-NIC visited the University of Illinois at Chicago (UIC) and saw how the program incorporates cycles of inquiry as a leadership framework for their candidates and how the faculty themselves use cycles of inquiry for the continuous improvement of the program. PD-NIC visitors learned how UIC faculty reconstructed their curriculum to be vertically aligned and used key learning experiences to anchor the program. University of Denver (DU) hosted the Preparation Partnerships PD-NIC. Participants on this visit were able to learn from DU faculty, representatives from Denver Public Schools and practicing school leaders about the relationships DU has and the impact of the program and how this relationship has shaped program decisions.

During each visit there was opportunity for the PD-NIC members to reflect and think collectively about their experiences and how they might move forward as a program and as a NIC to develop and test previously unused strategies. From the anecdotal feedback we have received thus far, these two-day study visits seem to have been successful experiences. Participants have indicated the value of learning from and generating new ideas to bring back to then try and collect data within in their own contexts.

Challenges

Working through a new initiative, time constraints and varying levels of experience in improvement science are notable challenges. First, because this is a new initiative, many adjustments have been made. For example, the calendar the hub first proposed was too ambitious and the timing of things were adjusted accordingly. Second, time—in both the amount of time and the availability of time—is challenging. We have seen that it is difficult for PD-NICs to have consistent meeting times that engage the entire PD-NIC due to the busy schedules of faculty members. It is not uncommon that facilitators hold multiple meetings or one-on-one meetings with PD-NIC members. This poses a challenge as it takes up time for the facilitators to engage in this level of connection and it also does not easily allow for PD-NIC development or collaborative work to be leveraged. Similarly, it has been challenging for the hub to schedule consistent times to meet with facilitators and knowledge partners. Our third challenge pertains to the levels of familiarity and experience using improvement science of those in the hub and the facilitators. Meetings have revealed the different interpretations stakeholders have had about various improvement science structural components, rhythms or tools (e.g., driver diagrams or improvement aim). The group has heavily tapped one member of the facilitator team to help navigate and better understand improvement science components. The fourth challenge has emerged as PD-NICs have started to move from a sensemaking stage toward designing and using rapid tests of change to gather data, like PDSA cycles. The challenge here lies in determining the types of rapid cycles to try because many of the pressing problems the PD-NICs are addressing are temporally situated in a higher education context and calendar. For example, institutions taking deliberate steps to improve their recruitment and selection process are constrained by the timing of the school year as tasks pertaining to recruitment and selection of principal candidates into their program ebbs and flows. Navigating and making sense of this timeline has proven challenging. In addition, for projects that involve large or complex systems, leading improvement can be a challenge. This is true for the UCEA-PDN since there are multiple universities, located across the country, each with its own organizational culture, aspirations, resources and set of norms that need to coalesce in the focus of the PD-NIC.

Conclusion

Improvement science intends to be a good fit for the complex organizational system that is the reality of education today and:

> Improvement Science addresses this reality by focusing on the specific tasks people do, the processes and tools they use, and how prevailing policies, organizational structures, and norms affect this. Applying Improvement Science to education would direct greater attention to how better to design and fit together the many elements that shape the way schools work. The latter is key to making our educational institutions more effective, efficient, and personally engaging. (Bryk et al., 2015, p. 8)

Although not a new approach to problem solving, but because it is relatively new to education, there is likely preparation, sensemaking and "catching up" to do as a field holistically. Given current interest in continuous improvement and the prevalence of rigorous methodologies such as improvement science, educational leadership faculty are well positioned to facilitate learning for pre-service leaders to develop skills and understanding of continuous improvement during preparation coursework. Those who are preparing our future educational leaders are crucial linchpins in in this growing movement. Educational leadership faculty members are charged with the responsibility of providing development and training to educational leadership candidates that are not only grounded in research and best practices but also consider professional contexts and realities, candidates' needs and the needs of the school districts with whom they partner. If educational leadership faculty are familiar with and utilize improvement science themselves in their higher education context, then they could be key actors in helping forward this approach to their leadership students, thus encouraging the use of improvement science to become a framework from which to address PK–12 problems of practice in schools. School leaders are critical stakeholders in shaping the culture and operational core of schools. If principals are trained in programs that draw upon the tenets of improvement science, then they can feasibly use improvement science with their teachers as a way to collectively learn and address problems to make their school more effective in educating each student.

Bryk and colleagues (2015) write, "Individual educators and institutions are learning much every day" (p. 11). It is our hope that the UCEA-PDN work will help "organize, refine, and build on these lessons" (p. 11). Continuous improvement in higher education has not received the same attention as it has in the PK–12 setting. Networked improvement science can be a powerful tool for leveraging continuous improvement due to the emphasis on interorganizational learning through networks. In this new initiative, the UCEA hub, facilitators, knowledge partners and PD-NIC members are all learning, not only about their programs, how to improve their programs and how the improvement science approach works but also how an initiative of this nature is implemented.

Participation in the UCEA-PDN has multiple benefits including the opportunity to improve or redesign elements of educational leadership preparation programs in collaboration with a team and with the support of colleagues in the UCEA network. In addition, through active engagement, UCEA program faculty have the opportunity to partake in high-quality professional learning experiences that will build their skills and understanding in the use of improvement science and design thinking. The impact, however, is unlikely to be relegated to higher education faculty and the programs they design; rather, as UCEA program faculty's knowledge and expertise in these areas increase, they will be better prepared to incorporate improvement practices within courses they instruct to pre-service or in-service educational leaders. Thus, the benefits of participation can extend well beyond the individuals and programs involved in the initiative.

Key Concepts

Continuous improvement: A perspective that assumes there are always places in a process, system or organization that can be refined or made more effective, and therefore it is important for stakeholders to be consistently working to improve their context in systematic ways

Educational leadership faculty: Faculty members who teach and/or research the role of educational leadership and administration

Facilitator: The leader of the NIC

Hub: A centralized group who supports the NICs and the initiative holistically

Improvement science: A perspective focused on "getting better at getting better" and using small tests of change to help inform improvement steps

Networked improvement community: A type of collaborative learning group that is focused on an improvement aim

Problems of practice: Areas in a field that are both common and integral to the effectiveness of an organization or context

Discussion Questions

1. What preparation is necessary for facilitators or hub members who are interested in starting a NIC?
2. In many professors' realities, there are competing priorities. What realistic expectations should be made for those who are voluntarily taking on the work that accompanies NIC participation? How should this be communicated?
3. How should the NICs approach rapid cycles of improvement in the areas that are calendar-based. In other words, how should faculty engage in cycles of improvement during the "off season"?
4. What NIC would you like to see exist in your professional circle? What roles and planning would you engage in to organize the NIC?
5. The participants in the UCEA-PDN are primarily individuals who make up a coalition of the willing. What are the benefits and challenges in initiatives that might accompany this characteristic?

Class Activities

1. One of the challenges faced by the UCEA-PDN is working on implementing something as a faculty that is relevant for that time period. For example, selecting candidates only happens at particular times of year. List improvement ideas that can be rapidly tested for a focus area that may be calendar-dependent.
2. Identify an area of improvement that either the UCEA-PDN is focused upon or choose your own. Then construct either a fishbone or a driver diagram for your own context. Be prepared to explain why you chose the tool you did and what you learned from engaging in this exercise.
3. Identify an area of improvement that either the UCEA-PDN is focused upon or choose your own. Then (a) outline the different roles and responsibilities needed for your NIC; (b) determine who should help plan the NIC development (and why); (c) consider who should be part of the NIC (and why); and (d) make a communication plan for recruitment into the initiative.

References

Bryk, A. S., Gomez L. M., & Grunow, A. (2010). *Getting ideas into action: Building networked improvement communities in education.* Stanford, CA: Carnegie Foundation for the Advancement of Teaching. Retrieved from https://www.carnegiefoundation.org/resources/publications/getting-ideas-action-building-networked-improvement-communities-education/

Bryk, A. S., Gomez, L. M., & Grunow, A. (2011). Getting Ideas into Action: Building Networked Improvement Communities in Education. *Frontiers in Sociology of Education*, 42. https://doi.org/10.1007/978-94-007-1576-9

Bryk, A. S., Gomez L. M., Grunow A., & LeMahieu, P. G. (2015). *Learning to improve: How America's schools can get better at getting better.* Cambridge, MA: Harvard Education Press.

Cox, M. D. (2004). Introduction to faculty learning communities. *New Directions for Teaching and Learning*, 5–23. doi:10.1002/tl.129

Darling-Hammond, L., LaPointe, M., Meyerson, D., & Orr, M. (2007). *Preparing school leaders for a changing world: Executive summary.* Stanford, CA: Stanford University, Stanford Educational Leadership Institute. Retrieved from http://www.wallacefoundation.org/knowl edge-center/pages/preparing-school-leaders.aspx

Ferren, A. S. (1989). Faculty development can change the culture of a college. *Professional and Organizational Development Network in Higher Education,* 8, 101–116. https://doi.org/10.1002/j.2334-4822 .1989.tb00149.x

Fullan, M. (2001). *Leading in a culture of change.* San Francisco, CA: Jossey-Bass.

Fuller, E., Young, M., & Baker, B. D. (2011). Do principal preparation programs influence student achievement through the building of teacher-team qualifications by the principal? An exploratory analysis. *Educational Administration Quarterly,* 47, 173-216. doi:10.1177/ 0011000010378613

Hitt, D. H., & Tucker, P. D. (2016). Systematic review of key leader practices found to influence student achievement: A unified framework. *Review of Educational Research,* 86, 531–569. https://doi.org/10.3102/ 0034654315614911

Jackson, B. L., & Kelley, C. (2002). Exceptional and innovative programs in educational leadership. *Educational Administration Quarterly,* 38, 192–212. doi:10.1177/0013161X02382005

Knowles, M. S. (1988). *The modern practice of adult education: From pedagogy to andragogy.* Englewood Cliffs, NJ: Prentice Hall Regents.

Langley, G. J., Moen, R. D., Nolan, K. M., Nolan, T. W., Norman, C. L., & Provost, L. P. (2009). *The improvement guide* (2nd ed.). San Francisco, CA: Jossey-Bass.

Leithwood, K., Jantzi, D., Coffin, G., & Wilson, P. (1996). Preparing school leaders: What works? *Journal of School Leadership,* 6, 316–342. Retrieved from https://files.eric.ed.gov/fulltext/ED384963.pdf

Leithwood, K. A., Seashore Louis, K., Wahlstrom, K., Anderson, S., Mascall, B., & Gordon, M. (2010). How successful leadership influences student learning: The second installment of a longer story. *Second International Handbook of Educational Change.* https://doi. org/10.1007/978-90-481-2660-6_35

MacConnell, K., & Caillier, S. (2016). Getting better together. *Phi Delta Kappan, 98*, 16–22. https://doi.org/10.1177/0031721716677257

Marks, H. M., & Nance, J. P. (2007). Contexts of accountability under systemic reform: Implications for principal influence on instruction and supervision. *Educational Administration Quarterly, 43*, 3–37. https://doi.org/10.1177/0013161x06291414

Martin, W.G., & Gobstein, H. (2015). Generating a networked improvement community to improve secondary mathematics teacher preparation. *Journal of Teacher Education, 66*, 482–493. https://doi.org/10.1177/0022487115602312

McCarthy, M. M., Hackmann, D. G., & Malin, J. R. (2017). What we know about those who prepare educational leaders. In M. D. Young & G. M. Crow (Eds.), *Handbook of research on the education of school leaders* (2nd ed., pp. 118–147). New York, NY: Routledge.

NAESP (National Association of Elementary School Principals). (2018). *The pre-K–8 school leader in 2018: A 10-year study*. Retrieved from https://www.naesp.org/sites/default/files/NAESP%2010-YEAR%20REPORT_2018.pdf

NPBEA (National Policy Board for Educational Administration). (2017). *Professional standards for educational leaders 2015*. Reston, VA: Author. Retrieved from http://npbea.org/wp-content/uploads/2017/06/Professional-Standards-for-Educational-Leaders_2015.pdf

Orphanos, S., & Orr, M. T. (2013). Learning leadership matters: The influence of innovative school leadership preparation on teachers' experiences and outcomes. *Educational Management Administration & Leadership, 42*, 680–700. doi:10.1177/1741143213502187

Orr, M. T., & Orphanos, S. (2011). How graduate-level preparation influences the effectiveness of school leaders: A comparison of the outcomes of exemplary and conventional leadership preparation programs for principals. *Educational Administration Quarterly, 47*, 18–70. doi:10.1177/0011000010378610

Russell, J. (2016, January 13). How to launch a productive network (Web log). Retrieved from: https://www.carnegiefoundation.org/blog/how-to-launch-a-productive-network/

Theoharis, G. (2009). *School leaders our children deserve*. New York, NY: Teachers College Press.

UCEA (University Council for Educational Administration). (n.d.) Program Design Network (PDN). Retrieved from http://www.ucea.org/initiatives/program-design-network-pdn/

Vescio, V., Ross, D., & Adams, A. (2008). A review of research on the impact of professional learning communities on teaching practice and student learning. *Teaching and Teacher Education, 24*(1), 80–91. https://doi.org/10.1016/j.tate.2007.01.004

Wenger, E. (2008). *Communities of Practice: Learning, Meaning, and Identity.* New York, NY: Cambridge University Press.

Young, M. D. & Crow, G. (2017). Introduction. In M. Young and G. Crow (Eds.), *The Handbook of Research on the Education of School Leaders, 2nd Edition.* New York: Routledge.

CHAPTER SEVEN

Developing Stewards of the Practice

Understanding the Role of Improvement Science in EdD Programs

JILL A. PERRY

Executive Director, Carnegie Project on the Education Doctorate
University of Pittsburgh

DEBBY ZAMBO

Associate Director, Carnegie Project on the Education Doctorate

Abstract

In recent years, new inquiry approaches that utilize the wisdom of individuals facing a problem and rapid testing of an intervention have emerged and show promise for education doctorate (EdD) programs. This chapter offers faculty teaching in EdD programs discussion questions and activities to help them better understand why improvement science can be a signature pedagogy in preparing educational professionals to become scholarly practitioners and agents of change in their practice. Our idea of teaching improvement science in EdD programs is nested in Golde's (2006) notion of developing "stewards of the practice," professional caretakers who conserve, generate and transform their knowledge and their field. Stewards generate research usable for practice, conserve the professional wisdom they possess, merge what they know with the theories and inquiry skills they learn and transform their practice through improvement that is user-centered and empirical.

Keywords

Faculty development, education doctorate, signature pedagogy, CPED, scholarly practice, stewardship

Background

Historically, doctoral students in education have been prepared in the same way whether they wanted to enter into academia as tenure-track faculty or return to practice as educational leaders, resulting in poor preparation for both professions. Since 2007, however, the Carnegie Project on the Education Doctorate (CPED), a consortium of 100+ graduate schools of education, has worked to distinguish the education doctorate as the professional practice degree that prepares educational leaders to impact their practice by applying knowledge and theory to generate improvement. To do this, the consortium developed a framework (© 2018) to guide the redesign of education doctoral degrees (EdD), one that would allow for flexibility to meet student and institutional needs and maintain consistency across members. This framework comprises six grounding principles, six design concepts and a new definition of the EdD. The new definition states, "The professional doctorate in education prepares educators for the application of appropriate and specific practices, the generation of new knowledge, and for the stewardship of the profession" (CPED, 2009, par. 3). The notion of stewardship was a founding idea within CPED and is further described in the sixth principle: "The professional doctorate in education emphasizes the generation, transformation, and use of professional knowledge and practice" (CPED, 2009). Given these ideas, what does *stewardship* mean in professional practice and how might it guide the need for distinct research and inquiry preparation for the professional doctorate?

Chris Golde (2006) made the distinction between stewards of the discipline, those whose work seeks to further the knowledge of a field, and stewards of the practice, those whose work furthers the improvement of practice. According to Golde (2006), "stewardship establishes the purpose of doctoral education" (p. 9). She describes stewardship as the ability "to inculcate those we educate with the highest levels of competency and integrity" (p. 9). She further suggests that a steward is "a caretaker who trains a critical eye to look forward and must be willing to take risks, to move the [field] forward" (p. 13) through the generation, conservation and transformation of knowledge (Golde, 2006). As the professional doctorate in education, the EdD seeks to prepare stewards of the practice as the caregivers of the profession by teaching them to generate new understanding, conserve professional knowledge and transform practice through the application of research and inquiry to the problems they face daily (Perry & Abruzzo, in press). In doing so, practitioners become scholarly practitioners able to "blend practical wisdom with professional skills and knowledge to name, frame, and solve problems of practice" (CPED, 2011, para. 5) and produce improved educational contexts.

Considering Improvement Science in EdD Programs

As the members of CPED have considered ways to prepare scholarly practitioners to be stewards, it has become clear that applied inquiry methods are primary skills that these practitioners need to be able to impact their practice. The CPED design concept, *inquiry as practice*, defines this need as "the ability to use data to understand the effects of innovation" (CPED, 2011). Improvement science, a disciplined inquiry process collaboratively performed by those closest to a problem (Bryk, Gomez, & Grunow, 2011) offers a promising means to provide these skills to professional practitioners. Improvement science melds pragmatism and science and builds knowledge that can sustain and spread (Bryk, 2015; Bryk et al., 2011). Its learning-by-doing design focuses on systems and uses theories developed from the ground up, providing practitioners with the skills to become scholarly practitioners and the means to be stewards of the practice.

In this chapter, we explain how teaching improvement science in EdD programs offers scholarly practitioners the opportunity to do inquiry as practice to improve the persistent and perplexing problems they face and, as a result, generate new understanding for the profession, conserve their professional knowledge and transform their practice and their profession. To further understanding among those who teach in EdD programs of the value of improvement science as an applied inquiry methodology and potential signature pedagogy, the chapter offers activities and discussion questions faculty considering new ways to prepare professional practitioners in EdD programs can use.

Generation

Research training is a central component of doctoral study and should prepare a steward to "conduct investigation according to accepted standards of rigor and quality" (Golde, 2006, p. 10). For traditionalists, this definition has a fixed meaning akin to PhD research training. As professional practitioners, however, those in EdD programs are intimately connected to problems and conduct research "at a depth that traditional forms of research might well not be capable of, precisely because they are practitioners" (Jarvis, 1999, p. 24). Therefore, developing these students into stewards of the practice requires a different kind of research preparation that is equally rigorous and maintains scholarly levels of quality. As faculty, we need to redesign traditional methods to be more applied and impactful so that the graduates of these programs can generate useful, practical knowledge that is grounded in disciplined inquiry.

How does the preparation of scholarly practitioners differ from PhD training and what skills do they need to become stewards of the practice? What research abilities do EdD students need to generate rigorous, quality research that impacts practice and generates improvement? To address questions like these CPED developed the concept of *inquiry as practice*, the process of posing significant questions that focus on complex problems of practice and using data to understand the effects of a solution tried to address a problem. As such, inquiry as practice requires practitioners to address a problem and then gather, organize, judge and analyze the data they collect about it with a critical lens (CPED, 2011). Hochbein and Perry (2013) further outline the need for practitioners to be able to decipher existing knowledge and the validity of this knowledge, debate the need and design of reforms using practical evidence and design studies that create understanding about ways to confront daily problems in education. This type of training should contain methods and scholarship "suited to the context of practice" (Willis, Inman, & Valenti, 2010, p. 25) and be mediated by intellectual understanding and reflection (Green & Powell, 2005; Perry, 2013).

Traditional research preparation conducts research *on* practice, bringing discipline and rigor to understanding practice from the outside and generating information that is meant to be applied to all types of educational situations. The questions that traditional researchers ask, however, are often of little interest to practitioners. Furthermore, practitioners know that what works in one context does not always work in another. Large samples and randomized clinical trials lack clear understanding of the true nature of the problem, erase variability and fail to specify what works for whom and why. The quick implementation of improvement or change ideas coupled with slow learning about impacts leaves frontline practitioners continually searching for ways to make problems better (Berwick, 2008; Bryk, 2017).

In contrast to traditional research, improvement science changes the target and process of inquiry. Instead of focusing on researcher-generated questions that get answered at the end of an intervention, improvement science uses Plan, Do, Study, Act (PDSA) cycles aimed at answering the following questions:

1. What problem(s) are we trying to solve?
2. What change can we make that will lead to an improvement?
3. Why do we think this change will be an improvement?
4. How will we know that a change is an improvement?

Individuals closest to the problem work together collaboratively to answer these questions with tools and processes that help them take a systems perspective, operationalize a working theory of improvement, develop and implement improvements based on their own theory and gather data practically, quickly and often. In such a process, data gathering is embedded into, rather than added onto, the day-to-day work of practitioners and the analysis of data gathered is collaborative and ongoing (Bryk, Gomez, Grunow, & LeMahieu, 2015b). Traditional psychometric measures (e.g., qualitative, quantitative and mixed) are used to measure change to problems of practice and are gathered on systems, progress or performances. Such measurement for improvement focuses on a small number of concepts that can be used to guide actions (Bryk, Yeager, Muhich, Hausman, & Morales, 2013). Training to use traditional psychometric measures is framed in an improvement process and teaches EdD students how to answer the questions above by gathering evidence that provides a variety of measures:

1. *Outcomes.* How is the overall system performing? What is the result?
2. *Primary drivers.* Is progress being made on the drivers of the aim?
3. *Processes.* Are the processes, norms and structures of the system performing reliably?
4. *Balance.* What is happening to the parts of the system not being focused on?

As improvers, students will quickly learn how to use practical data to learn quickly if an intervention is working or if it has failed. From there, they can change their approach and apply the process all over, rather than wait months or years to see an impact.

This "learn fast and fail fast" approach is often not done alone and offers students the opportunity to collaborate with their workplace colleagues or with other students in the program. Collaboration in professional preparation makes sense. Practitioners do not work alone in general. Educational settings are collaborative; therefore, it makes sense to think of ways to engage the workplace as a laboratory of practice, or "settings where the intersection of theory, inquiry, and practice can be implemented, measured, and analyzed for the impact made and that facilitate transformative and generative learning" (CPED, 2011, para. 8). Improvement science is best performed in a networked improvement community (NIC), an intentionally designed social organization with a distinct problem-solving focus and specific roles, responsibilities and norms (Bryk et al., 2011). A NIC is marked by four characteristics:

1. Focused on a well-specified aim
2. Guided by a deep understanding of the problem, the system that produces it and a shared working theory of improvement
3. Disciplined by methods of improvement research to develop, test and refine improvement efforts
4. Organized to accelerate diffusion into the field and integration into practice (LeMahieu, 2015)

Performing improvement science in an NIC offers practitioners more practical and meaningful ways to apply theory to practice for the generation of useful knowledge by engaging stakeholder needs and understanding.

We believe improvement science should be the signature pedagogy in EdD programs that prepares scholarly practitioners to generate understanding through applied inquiry settings that impact their practice. This way of thinking about research training in doctoral programs may be radically different from how EdD program faculty have been prepared in their own doctoral programs. Faculty who teach in EdD programs need to first understand the distinction between research *on* practice and research *as* practice before they can consider ways to redesign and teach the inquiry training in their programs. Within CPED, we have seen early redesign strategies that seek to change faculty mindsets center on structured conversations about change ideas. To facilitate change we offer Activity 1 in the Activities section below. Activity 1 contains reflection questions and a comparison chart faculty can use to rethink the purpose of inquiry in their EdD programs.

Conservation

Bryk (2015) notes that, as a field, we have a tendency toward "solutionitis." That is, we "undervalue the importance of systematic and organized methods to improve" (p. 468). In this process of solutionitis, we frequently disregard input from practitioners and disregard their knowledge and understanding of the problems they face. CPED would argue that bringing practitioner understanding into the learning process is essential to making them better problem-solvers. In EdD programs, we have the opportunity to both honor this practitioner knowledge and enhance it with better ways of teaching practitioners how to improve their practice through signature pedagogies.

According to CPED and building on the work of Lee Shulman, a signature pedagogy in EdD programs is the pervasive set of practices used to prepare scholarly practitioners for all aspects of their professional work: "to think, to perform, and to act with integrity" (Shulman, 2005, p. 52). Improvement science is a disciplined inquiry process that is guided by principles and offers hands-on tools that systematically teaches practitioners how to think about problems, perform inquiry skills to solve those problems and to do so with the highest aim of improving the lives of students and families. As a signature pedagogy, improvement science can be taught in a professional preparation program with deliberate, pervasive and persistent teaching practices. Its epistemological underpinnings are grounded in theory and research with the goal of improving problems of practice. It also teaches students to develop a critical and professional stance as they apply disciplined inquiry tools to professional settings where students and communities are impacted. As a signature pedagogy, improvement science has the potential to distinguish professional practitioners as scholarly practitioners and provide them with the means to become stewards of educational practice where their disciplined application of theory to practice will allow them to generate new solutions to problems, conserve the role that professional knowledge should have in solving problems and transform the ways improvement in education happens in a faster, more effective way.

Improvement science is guided by six principles that seemingly marry practice with theory as a means for improvement. These six principles (see Table 7.2 later in chapter) can help faculty understand the theory behind this methodology as well as outline the ways to consider incorporating the improvement science process into their programs.

We recognize, however, that faculty struggle with this new methodology and that changing our behaviors and ideas about what the research process is can be difficult. In our work with and research on faculty (Perry, 2013; Perry, Zambo, & Wunder, 2015) we have found the most prominent challenges faculty face when it comes to changing programs and courses are lack of time and resources for learning new ways of teaching and mentoring, difficulty grappling with uncertainty and possible failure of implementing new ideas, and struggling to let go of comfortable ways of doing. When it comes to improvement science, we have also found that faculty question its legitimacy as a rigorous research methodology. If we are able to put the needs of practitioners at the front and center in our practitioner-oriented doctoral programs, then we have begun to meet these challenges.

To facilitate this, CPED membership developed six guiding principles for program (re)design to support members as they consider distinguishing their EdD as a professional practice doctorate. The Carnegie Foundation for the Advancement of Teaching (2017) also developed six Core Principles of Improvement that guide the work of educational improvement within and across networked communities. Combined, both sets of principles offer faculty an opportunity to reflect on what an EdD should be and how improvement science might serve as a signature pedagogy for inquiry and research training, and how it might guide dissertation work EdD students do. Activity 2 provides a crosswalk of each set of principles and offers questions to facilitate structured conversations for faculty thinking about, or engaged in, program (re)design efforts.

Transformation

Golde (2006) defined transformation as the way in which stewards apply "knowledge, skills, findings, and insights" (p. 12). Her definition aligns with ideas posed by the Council of Graduate Schools' (2005) *Task Force on the Professional Doctorate*, which defined the professional doctorate as preparation for the "potential transformation for that field of professional practice" (p. 7). CPED contends that transformation of the field lies in the impact graduates make on problems of practice, defined as "a persistent, contextualized, and specific issue embedded in the work of a professional practitioner, the addressing of which has the potential to result in improved understanding, experience, and outcomes" (CPED, 2011, para. 10). Further, CPED views the greatest area of this impact will come from the student's Dissertation in Practice, or scholarly endeavor that impacts a complex problem of practice. (CPED, 2010). A *dissertation in practice* does four things that make it transformational:

1. Exhibits the doctoral candidate's ability "to think, to perform, and to act with integrity" (Shulman, 2005, p. 52)
2. Demonstrates how the candidate's research has addressed and impacted a complex problem of practice
3. Serves as the launching pad for practitioners to be change agents in their practice just as the traditional dissertation serves as the launching pad for publication for newly minted PhDs
4. Benefits a larger community of stakeholders (i.e., the candidate's organization, community or profession)

Dissertation work that is focused on improvement provides new ways of identifying and solving problems with tools that practitioners can learn and use over and over to solve future problems. For example, a *fishbone diagram* tool (Langley et al., 2009) produces a visual representation of a group's analysis of the root causes of a problem. A *systems map* (Bryk, Gomez, Grunow, &

LeMahieu, 2015b) is an analytic tool used to diagram the essential features of an organizational system and identify where improvement is needed and takes place throughout the improvement process. Analyzing problems with tools like these makes EdD students think deeply and wisely about the problems they face and how those problems extend deeply throughout an organization. They encourage students to avoid "solutionitis" and work to find root causes of problems and how they are manifested. Furthermore, applying the improvement science process to a dissertation in practice provides a framework to follow. For faculty, this process can shape program content and understanding how to teach improvement science. For students, this process guides not only the dissertation in practice, but also offers a process for how to tackle future problems in practice. In Figure 7.1, we demonstrate how the improvement science process can map onto a dissertation in practice model and provide understanding for faculty and guidance for students.

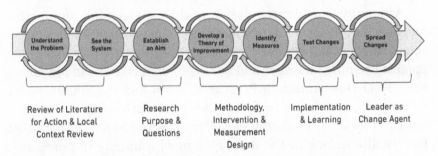

Figure 7.1. Mapping improvement science onto the dissertation in practice.

Networked Improvement Communities

In practice, problems are rarely solved by one individual alone. What does that mean for dissertation work that is traditionally done solo? CPED Principle 3 suggests that scholarly practitioners should learn how to collaborate with diverse communities to improve the problems they face. How might we consider improvement science as a means to provide better preparation for Principle

3? The Carnegie Foundation for the Advancement of Teaching suggests that networked improvement communities are the way to engage more practitioners in the scientific process of using evidence to improve problems (Bryk, 2015). Having more people involved also allows for the identification and testing of multiple change ideas (Donovan, 2013). If we think of an EdD program as the place where practitioners learn and try out new skills on a small scale, then we can consider a few ways that NICs might be tried out with the dissertation in practice. The first way would be for the doctoral student to engage their workplace stakeholders in the use of improvement as they embark on an improvement science dissertation in practice. The second might be to organize groups of EdD students to address a single problem of practice in a group dissertation. In both scenarios, students develop stronger leadership capabilities (often a programmatic goal in EdD programs) as they try out ways to address problems by engaging multiple perspectives.

As faculty consider the design of their dissertation in practice and how that final product demonstrates their students' ability to be scholarly practitioners, we suggest considering two tools that guide applied learning and rigor and quality in dissertations in practice— the CPED Dissertation in Practice Criteria and the Standards for QUality Improvement Reporting Excellence EDU (QSEN Institute, n.d.). In the Activities section we offer Activity 3 as a way to support faculty discussions in the development of a quality improvement science dissertation in practice.

Discussion

The Council of Graduate Schools' (2007) *Task Force on the Professional Doctorate* argued, "Graduate colleges should not use one-size-fits all standards that simply ask why a professional doctorate is not just like a PhD" (p. 3). In terms of the education doctorate (EdD), this statement means that we can no longer redesign EdD programs by shuffling around PhD courses, reducing the number of research credits or lowering our expectations for practitioner dissertations. It means that we need to completely rethink, from start to finish, what the goals, outcomes, program components and skills of our faculty are to be able to create a program that will develop scholarly practitioners who can generate understanding about problems in practice, conserve their practitioner knowledge as they enhance it through professional preparation and transform their practice through inquiry as practice. In doing so, they will become stewards of the practice and will advance the educational profession while improving educational practice. CPED offers means to create such programs and, in partnership with the Carnegie Foundation for the Advancement of Teaching, suggests that improvement science be considered a signature pedagogy within these programs.

Activities

Rethinking the Purpose of the EdD Inquiry Sequence: Activity 1

Table 7.1 can be used to engage faculty in conversations about research *on* practice and research *as* practice and what that difference means to their EdD programs. Utilizing Table 7.1, faculty might discuss these questions:

1. What commonalities and differences do you see?
2. Why might students in EdD programs be better served if they learn to conduct research *as* practice as opposed to research *on* practice?
3. How will teaching research *as* practice require our doctoral programs to change?
4. How could this work generate and spread new usable knowledge?

Table 7.1. Differences Between Research on Practice
and Research for Practice

Research *on* Practice	Research *for* Practice
Conducted by academics—outsiders with autonomy.	Conducted by insiders closest to the problem working together collaboratively. Best performed in network improvement communities (NICs).
Aims to understand what works globally. Examines whether a particular intervention in a specified setting has a specific measureable effect and addresses questions concerning safety, feasibility, side-effects and appropriate level of use.	Aims to articulate local problems and the systems surrounding them. Strives to deliver meaningful and scientifically rigorous effectiveness research on improvement in practice.
Focuses on implementing a researcher/theory-developed intervention. Aims for control. Tries to determine how to make an intervention work for everyone, everywhere.	Focuses on understanding variability (what worked, how, for whom and under what conditions).
Implemented with fidelity fast and scaled wide regardless of unintended consequences	Rapid tests of change through Plan, Do, Study, Act cycles that guide development and tuning of tools, processes, roles and relationships. Learn fast to implement well.
Guided by theoretical perspectives.	Melds pragmatism and science. Guided by literature, practical knowledge and experience.
Data analysis performed by researcher(s)—sophisticated; trends, comparisons, relationships; objective/unbiased/valid/reliable and generalizable. What is found must get translated into knowledge for practice.	Data gathered to understand variability in performance—timely and sophisticated.
Findings get published in journals, become mandates or get incentivized to scale widely. Manuscripts often take a long time to get published and practitioners often do not have access to them.	Rapid reporting and sharing in a low-stakes, safe environment. Builds a professional knowledge base that can spread and sustain.

After you have engaged in a substantial discussion about the differences, next steps include creating an action plan to learn more about (and possibly begin to teach) improvement science. To learn more about improvement science go to the website of the Carnegie Foundation for Advancement of Teaching (https://carnegiefoundation. org/). To learn more about improvement science implementation in EdD programs, go to the Carnegie Project on the Education Doctorate website (http://cpedinitiative.org). Once there go to the Our Work tab and find the link to CPED's Improvement Science Interest Group.

Understanding the Theory Behind Improvement Science: Activity 2

CPED membership has developed six guiding principles for program (re)design and the Carnegie Foundation for the Advancement of Teaching has developed six Core Principles of Improvement to guide the work of educational improvement within and across networked communities. Table 7.2 contains both of these side by side and can be used to perform a crosswalk of both sets of principles. Using Table 7.2, faculty might engage in conversation with the following questions:

1. In comparing the two sets of principles, what commonalities and differences do you see? What are the implications of this comparison for your EdD program?
2. How would both sets of principles support students in merging their professional knowledge with the theory and tools of inquiry?
3. How might your students benefit from infusing the six Core Principles of Improvement into your EdD program?
4. How might the six Core Principles of Improvement be used to (re)design your research courses and dissertation in practice experience?
5. Examining CPED's definition of the EdD (below) and Guiding Principles for Program Design, discuss how your EdD programs can use these to identify and design your program's signature pedagogy. How do the six Core Principles of Improvement fit with your thinking?

The professional doctorate in education prepares educators for the application of appropriate and specific practices, the generation of new knowledge, and for the stewardship of the profession. (CPED, 2011)

Table 7.2. CPED's Guiding Principles and Carnegie Foundation's Core Principles

CPED's Guiding Principles for Program Design	The Six Core Principles of Improvement
The professional doctorate in education	1. Make the work problem-specific and user-centered.
1. Is framed around questions of equity, ethics and social justice to bring about solutions to complex problems of practice.	*It starts with a single question: "What specifically is the problem we are trying to solve?" It enlivens a co-development orientation: It engages key participants early and often.*
2. Prepares leaders who can construct and apply knowledge to make a positive difference in the lives of individuals, families, organizations and communities.	2. Variation in performance is the core problem to address. *The critical issue is not what works, but rather what works, for whom and under what set of conditions. Aim to advance efficacy reliably at scale.*
3. Provides opportunities for candidates to develop and demonstrate collaboration and communication skills to work with diverse communities and to build partnerships.	3. See the system that produces the current outcomes. *It is hard to improve what you do not fully understand. Go and see how local conditions shape work processes. Make your hypotheses for change public and clear.*
4. Provides field-based opportunities to analyze problems of practice and use multiple frames to develop meaningful solutions.	4. We cannot improve at scale what we cannot measure. *Embed measures of key outcomes and processes to track if change is an improvement. We intervene in complex organizations. Anticipate unintended consequences and measure these too.*

CPED's Guiding Principles for Program Design	The Six Core Principles of Improvement
5. Is grounded in and develops a professional knowledge base that integrates both practical and research knowledge, that links theory with systemic and systematic inquiry.	5. Anchor practice improvement in disciplined inquiry. *Engage rapid cycles of Plan, Do, Study, Act (PDSA) to learn fast, fail fast and improve quickly. That failures may occur is not the problem; that we fail to learn from them is.*
6. Emphasizes the generation, transformation and use of professional knowledge and practice.	6. Accelerate improvements through networked communities. *Embrace the wisdom of crowds. We can accomplish more together than even the best of us can accomplish alone.*

After completing this exercise, consider the following implications for program (re)design. Programs and courses with both sets of principles can develop the leaders our educational system needs—individuals who work for social justice, see variation as the problem to be solved, use data as an everyday process and work collaboratively and incrementally to make lasting improvements. Improvement science brings analytic discipline to design development efforts and encourages EdD students to act as translational researchers who blend the vast amount of wisdom they have with the scholarly/theoretical knowledge they learn in their courses. As such, improvement science taught deliberately, persistently and pervasively prepares scholarly practitioners "to think, to perform, and to act with integrity" (Shulman, 2005, p. 52) and provides them with the tools to be stewards of the practice.

The Dissertation in Practice as Training for Improvement: Activity 3

Dissertations written for improvement must meet the expectations of the university, the program, the dissertation chair and the dissertation committee, as well as the stakeholders who are part of the context in which the dissertation work occurs. This means dissertations in practice must be judged for quality, rigor and impact. Below we offer two resources to do this, the CPED Dissertation in Practice Award Evaluation Criteria and the Standards for QUality Improvement Reporting Excellence EDU (QSEN Institute, n.d.) that can serve as guides for ensuring quality, rigor and impact.

CPED Dissertation in Practice Award Evaluation Criteria

1. Identifies a researchable, complex problem of practice
2. Demonstrates the integration of theory and practice to advance professional knowledge
3. Demonstrates use of rigorous and appropriate methods of critical inquiry to address the identified complex problem of practice
4. Demonstrates potential for positive impact on the identified complex problem of practice and establishes reciprocity with the field
5. Demonstrates the integration of both theory and practice to advance professional knowledge and to impact the field
6. Demonstrates rigorous, appropriate and ethical methods of inquiry
7. Demonstrates the scholarly practitioner's ability to communicate effectively to an appropriate audience to advance professional knowledge and impact the field
8. Demonstrates the goals of the problem-based thesis as involving decisions, changed practices, better organizational performances and application of a theory of change
9. Engages in creative, innovative or interdisciplinary inquiry
10. Experiments with distinctive designs or alternatives to traditional doctoral dissertation format or product (e.g., alternatives to five chapters; additional reflective elements relating to personal reflections on the learning journey, how the student's or field partner's ideas have changed)
11. Demonstrates potential for positive impact or contribution to practice beyond the DiP itself

12.Communicates effectively to advance professional knowledge and practice

Standards for QUality Improvement Reporting Excellence: SQUIRE-EDU

The SQUIRE-EDU standards are a set of guidelines intended to increase the completeness, transparency and replicability of published reports that describe systematic efforts to improve QSEN Institute (n.d.). The guidelines encourage a description of the process and context of educational change, description of iterative cycles and description of the change. They frame this research around four questions:

1. Why was the improvement started? (problem, available knowledge, rationale, aims);
2. What was done? (context, interventions, approach, measures, analysis, ethics);
3. What was discovered? (results); and
4. What does it mean? (summary, interpretation, limitations, conclusions). QSEN Institute, (n.d.)

Have faculty review both the CPED Dissertation in Practice Award Evaluation Criteria and the SQUIRE-EDU standards. Together compare these two sets of criteria and discuss the following questions:

1. What commonalities and differences do you see between these two?
2. What do you like or not like about these and what might you be willing to consider using in your EdD program?
3. How do each of these criteria compare to the measures by which your institution currently discerns quality dissertations?
4. How might both of these be used during your program to give students guides to writing quality dissertations in practice?

As these discussions progress, contemplate the role of a practitioner dissertation as one that should be transformative for their local educational context and for the field of education—research as practice. Additionally, consider how this type of work can still meet the high standards of dissertations to which academics are accustomed.

References

Berwick, D. M. (2008). The science of improvement. *The Journal of the American Medical Association, 299*, 1182–1184.

Bryk, A. S. (2015). Accelerating how we learn to improve. *Educational Researcher, 44*(9), 467–477.

Bryk, A. S. (2017, March 27). Redressing Inequities: An Aspiration in Search of a Method. Speech presented at Fourth Annual Carnegie Foundation Summit on Improvement in Education in California (CA), San Francisco.

Bryk, A.S, Gomez, L.M., & Grunow, A. (2011). *Getting ideas into action: Building networked improvement communities in education.* Available from http://www.carnegiefoundation.org/spotlight/webinar-bryk-gomez-building-netowrked-imporvement-communities-in-education

Bryk, A. S., Gomez, L. M., Grunow, A., & LeMahieu, P. G. (2015a). Breaking the cycle of failed school reforms: Using networked improvement communities to learn fast and implement well. *Harvard Education Letter, 31*(1), 1–3.

Bryk, A. S., Gomez, L. M., Grunow, A., & LeMahieu, P. G. (2015b). *Learning to improve: How America's schools can get better at getting better.* Cambridge, MA, Harvard Education Press.

Bryk, A. S., Yeager, D., Muhich, J., Hausman, H., & Morales, L. (2013). *Practical measurement.* Available from:https://www.carnegiefoundation.org/resources/publications/practical-measurement/

Carnegie Foundation for the Advancement of Teaching. (2017). The six core principles of improvement. Available from https://www.carnegiefoundation.org/our-ideas/six-core-principles-improvement/

Carnegie Project on the Education Doctorate. (2009). *Working principles for the professional practice doctorate in education.* (np).

Carnegie Project on the Education Doctorate. (2011). *Design Concept Definitions.* (np).

Council of Graduate Schools. (2007). *Task force on the professional doctor-ate.* Washington DC: Author.

Donovan, M. S. (2013). Generating improvement through research and development in education systems. *Science, 204,* 317–319.

Golde, C. M. (2006). Preparing stewards of the discipline. In C. M. Golde & G. E. Walker (Eds.), *Envisioning the future of doctoral education* (pp. 3–23). San Francisco, CA: Jossey-Bass.

Green, H., & Powell, S., (2005). *Doctoral study in contemporary higher education.* Maidenhead, UK: The Society for Research Into Higher Education/Open University Press/McGraw-Hill Education.

Hochbein, C., & Perry, J. A. (2013). The role of research in the professional doctorate. *Planning and Changing Journal, 44*(3/4), 181.

Hoffer, T. B., Hess, M., Welch, V. Jr., & Williams, K. (2007). *Doctorate recip-ients from United States universities: Summary report 2006.* Chicago, IL: National Opinion Research Center.

Jarvis, P. (1999). *The practitioner-researcher: Developing theory from prac-tice.* San Francisco, CA: Jossey-Bass.

Langley, G. J., Moen, R. D., Nolan, K. M., Nolan, T. W., Norman, C. L., & Provost, L. P. (2009). *The improvement guide: A practical approach to enhancing organizational performance* (2nd ed.). San Francisco, CA: Jossey-Bass.

LeMahieu, P. (2015). *Why a NIC?* Available from https://www.carnegie foundation.org/blog/why-a-nic/

Perry, J. A. (2013). Developing stewards of practice. In J. A. Perry & D. L. Carlson (Eds.), *In their own words: A journey to the stewardship of the practice in education.* Charlotte, NC: Information Age.

Perry, J. A. & Abruzzo, E. (in press). Preparing the scholarly practitioner: The importance of socialization in CPED-influenced Ed.D. programs. In J. C. Weidman & L. DeAngelo, *Socialization in higher education and the early career: Theory, research and application.* New York, NY: Springer.

Perry, J. A., & Imig, D. G. (2008). A stewardship of practice in education. *Change: The Magazine of Higher Learning, 40*(6), 42–49.

Perry, J. A., Zambo, D. & Wunder, S. (2015, Winter). Understanding how schools of education have redesigned the doctorate of education. *Journal of School Public Relations, 36.*

QSEN Institute. (n.d.) *SQUIRE-EDU v. 0.9*. Available from http://qsen.org/squire-edu-v0-9/

Shulman, L. S. (2005). Signature pedagogies in the professions. *Daedalus*, *134*(3), 52–59.

Willis, J. W., Inman, D., & Valenti, R. (2010). *Completing a professional practice dissertation: A guide for doctoral students and faculty*. Charlotte, NC: Information Age.

CHAPTER EIGHT

Preparing School Leaders to Effectively Lead School Improvement Efforts

Improvement Science

DEBORAH S. PETERSON AND SUSAN P. CARLILE

Portland State University

Abstract

How best to improve our educational system is the subject of intense national discussion with numerous legislative and philosophical strategies fueling the national debate. One response to school improvement, a response adapted from the healthcare and auto industries, is improvement science (IS). Although promising, design-based school improvement efforts may be seen by some as inconsequential in the educational world due to their origins in the health and automotive industries. However, key underlying concepts of IS are not new and are not a fad; rather, they build upon foundational concepts of esteemed educational philosophers John Dewey (1990) and Paolo Freire (1993), as well as respected educators such as Roland Barth (1990) and Michael Fullan (2011, 2013).

This chapter will conceptually describe how improvement science is a match for educators who believe in the work of Freire and Dewey, followed by a case study of how one principal preparation university is applying the concepts of improvement science in a program that values school leadership for equity, reducing educational disparities and context-based change leadership. The chapter concludes with implications for principal preparation programs desiring to increase the ability of their graduates to reduce educational disparities through the use of improvement science.

Keywords

improvement science, equity, school leadership, change leadership, principal preparation programs, K–12 school leadership

Background

Lucinda State University is an urban public university serving over 20,000 students, known for its innovations in many fields. The School of Education prepares the largest numbers of teachers and school leaders in the state and is known for its focus on equity and excellence. Its graduates earn a high number of state and national awards, with dozens of its graduates receiving significant awards in the last decade alone. The LSU faculty is sought after to consult on issues of equity in schools and to provide technical assistance supporting change initiatives in schools. LSU publicly commits to diversity and equity with a strong social justice orientation reflected in all its strategic plans, vision and mission work. The faculty for school leadership preparation are all experienced practitioners who have been recognized as effective leaders during their tenure as public school leaders. As a public university, funds for program improvement are generally quite limited and LSU depends on faculty volunteering for additional responsibilities to improve programming. In this case, all the faculty who engaged in improvement science in the principal preparation program volunteered additional time to engage in improvement science efforts with none of the usual university incentives of "course buyouts," where professors do not teach for a term, or extended contracts or other forms of compensation that increase faculty salary.

Need for Improvement

The LSU principal preparation program explicitly states that its goal is to prepare strong leaders for equity, leaders who resist the urge to blame teachers or students or families when initiatives fail to create success for all students in our schools. Rather, LSU prepares its graduates to experience firsthand how ecological, context-based and community-driven solutions, guided by the foundational concepts of improvement science, contribute to the success of each child in our schools.

Initiative overload and the current public discourse indicate a propensity to embrace authoritarian solutions that disregard the expertise of our families, students and teachers and the funds of knowledge they bring to our schools. These factors contribute to a sense of hopelessness in many schools. By engaging our teachers in school improvement solutions, and by ensuring empowerment of our students, families and teachers, we are contributing to the sustainability of public education and are honoring the heroes who have chosen to serve our students and our democracy. Although we are in the initial stages of implementing IS in our principal preparation institution, we are encouraged by our students' initial enthusiastic embrace of this promising school improvement strategy.

Why Improvement Science?

Improvement science is a type of "design-based" school improvement, an improvement strategy linked to "design thinking" (Mintrop, 2016). Although promising, design-based school improvement efforts may be seen by some as the newest fad (Lahey, 2017). Further, given that IS heralds from the business and healthcare fields, many might assume that the foundational philosophy of IS could not possibly be of benefit to educational systems. However, key underlying concepts of IS provide tools for implementation of the concepts of John Dewey (1990) and Paolo Freire (1993), Roland Barth (1990) and Michael Fullan (2011, 2013).

To understand the lineage of improvement science in education, we will start with the field of healthcare. The healthcare journey into the world of quality improvement began in the mid-1980s when professionals came to understand that a "reliance on inspection to improve" and "quality assurance" were insufficient approaches to quality care. In the words of one professional, "Few of us were systems thinkers and fewer had any theoretically grounded approach to improvement of care beyond inspection and accountability" (Langley et al., 2009, p. xii). Since that time, change efforts of medical leaders have been grounded by Deming's (1994) "system of profound knowledge" (knowledge of systems, knowledge of variation, theory of knowledge and knowledge of psychology). Knowledge and application of these four interrelated parts have informed practice in national and international healthcare.

No example is more informative to understanding how improvement science has improved healthcare practices over time than the work in 2010 of one asthmatic control team in Cincinnati, Ohio (Center for the Study of Social Policy, 2016). The team initiated changes in the practice of 150 pediatricians to achieve better outcomes for children with asthma in multiple hospital units. The goal was to reduce readmission rates for poor children and disparities in healthcare across the geographical area. The sustained, coordinated efforts included learning how to change the system so better outcomes would result, understanding variation across healthcare units, spreading effectiveness across multiple sites, creating purpose and understanding the human variables, including variables among patients, families and healthcare providers (Bryk, Gomez, Grunow, & LeMahieu, 2015).

There is no doubt that quality of improvement in healthcare is a matter of organizational survival, jobs and quality of life. As President Barack Obama (2016) shared in *United States Health Care Reform: Progress to Date and Next Steps,* "Health care costs affect the economy, the federal budget, and virtually every American family's financial well-being" (p .2). Aside from the impact on our pocketbooks and significant influence on our communities, quality healthcare is also very often a matter of life and death.

One could argue that the history of improvement science in businesses such as the auto industry, though perhaps less critical than that of healthcare to our longevity and quality of life, is nonetheless informative about organizational change. Important to note at the outset is that the work of Deming was also integral to the integration of improvement science concepts in business. Quality improvement in performance excellence, customer satisfaction and loyalty, accompanied by sustainable profitability—concepts foundational to sound business practices, are grounded in Deming's theory of profound knowledge. As we can see from results produced in Japan's automaking industries, such as at Toyota, where management practices focused on continuous improvement and adaptation, systems thinking, understanding of variation, knowledge of the products and understanding of human psychology made a difference. As an example, Ford Motor Company, upon examining a preference of customers to buy models with Japanese transmissions, discovered that though the American-made car parts were within specified tolerance levels, the Japanese car parts were virtually identical to each other. Thus, the Japanese parts ran more smoothly and customers experienced fewer problems (Rother, 2009). Similar efforts to make improvements in quality and productivity have included manufacturing plants, trucking firms, construction companies, law offices, governmental agencies, landscape architecture firms and industry associations (Langley et al., 2009).

Adapting Improvement Science to Education

Improvement science was thus developed as a method of improvement to ensure businesses would survive their competitors' advancements (Langley, Nolan, Nolan, Norman, & Provost, 1996). Although improving our educational system has an altruistic rather than financial aim, that of ensuring all students have access to and success in the benefits of our democracy, IS and other educational improvement efforts have certain commonalities. Dewey (1990) believed that the aim of education is to further our democracy and that a constructivist education—or meaning-making by those closest to the learning—will best serve that aim. Freire (1993) posited that freedom is obtained through contextualized, action-oriented and collaborative actions that enhance the humanity of individuals and the community. Barth (1990) proposed strategies in alignment with IS to promote shared leadership and to ensure that teachers' and principals' "extraordinary idealism, vision, and energy" are utilized to improve schools from within (p. 47). Strategies have included articulating goals, ensuring that teachers were empowered to identify solutions and implement them, creating a safe place to fail as well as succeed and developing leadership in all roles within the school. Fullan (2013) shared eight components of "change knowledge" that he believes will dramatically contribute to our ability to solve problems in education: focus, innovation, empathy, capacity-building, contagion, transparency, elimination of nonessentials and leadership, with "learning as we go" a key guiding concept (p. 67). The concepts described above are also foundational components of IS. Rather than imposing top-down, system-wide, large-scale, mandated solutions to problems of practice in education, as many educational initiatives of the early part of this century have done, IS specifically supports an organic, democratic and ecological approach to educational interventions, with short cycles of improvement tested and measured for their impact (Bryk et al., 2015).

In IS, teachers serve as the main players in identifying the educational problem, developing goals, testing any interventions and collecting data on the impact of the changes on students. Researchers and other support personnel add perspective; however, teachers are the main influence (Eagon, 2016). In other words, IS processes adhere to research indicating that teachers are the top influence on student achievement (Leithwood, Louis, Anderson, & Wahlstrom, 2004), that the context of the school impacts improvement efforts (Heifetz & Linsky, 2007) and the unique characteristics of each learner (Gay, 2010) guide curricular decisions. Further, IS tests and measures the impact of small-scale changes prior to complete knowledge and exploration of all potential solutions, asking *why* the intervention works or does not work, not just *whether* the intervention works (Peterson, 2016). Further, IS ensures we learn quickly and inexpensively what works in our context and what does not. Langley and colleagues (1996) note that "extensive study of the problem before a change or trial is attempted" can lead "to paralysis" (p. 3).

Many successful school improvement efforts, such as professional learning communities (DuFour, Eaker, & Many, 2006); culturally proficient schools (Lindsey, Robins, & Terrell, 2009); and positive behavior intervention support (OSEP Technical Assistance Center, 2017), present tools and processes that guide improvement efforts. When the tools and processes of these initiatives fail to result in student success, a common leadership response is to increase accountability measures, demand consistency of meeting agendas or protocols, or to otherwise blame the teachers or school leaders for the failure. A significant departure in IS, however, is that the teachers identify the goal, investigate potential interventions, collect and interpret data on their interventions and determine whether to continue the intervention or adjust it based on their particular context. When a solution is not working, the variability of context is considered as a potential reason for failure (Lewis, 2015), rather than placing blame on the failures of teachers and school leaders.

Although IS does respect the ability of teachers and leaders to understand the complexity of improvement in a particular context, it also places increasing responsibility on teachers and school leaders for reform. In that regard, one area for further development of IS is ensuring that our teachers and school leaders, most of whom are White, middle class and native English-speaking, do not perpetuate educational inequities by implementing interventions that reflect the biases of the dominant culture. Extensive school-wide professional development in culturally responsive practices is crucial for ensuring IS contributes to equity efforts. Despite this area of concern regarding IS, those committed to an educational system that seeks to increase freedom, expand democratic principles, reduce educational disparities and contribute to sustainable solutions that enhance the human dignity of students, families and colleagues must consider the potential of employing IS in schools.

Our Faculty Exploration of Improvement Science

Our principal preparation program prepares a significant number of our state's future leaders, and at the time of our initial exploration of IS, three full-time professors prepared two cohorts of future leaders and an expert policy professor provided continuing education for seated administrators. Two adjunct professors prepared two additional cohorts. Because of the time required for any major curricular change, the three full-time professors engaged in the initial exploration of IS, a two-year process leading to a pilot implementation in the third year.

Although our policy professor, dean and university president had explored the use of networked improvement communities several years earlier as a part of our statewide collective impact efforts, our exploration of the use of IS for principal preparation began in earnest when our dean inquired about our knowledge of IS and our curiosity regarding its use in schools. Our program coordinator, expert policy professor and department chair, all known for their intellectual curiosity and willingness to continually improve our curriculum, indicated their interest. With our dean's support and encouragement, our chair and policy professor then attended a Carnegie Foundation summit on IS and reported back to our team. Soon thereafter, our program coordinator (who also leads a cohort) and one additional cohort professor began independently reading about IS. Within a year, we each engaged in several additional activities: our program coordinator and chair attended the next Carnegie Foundation summit on IS and reported back to our team; our policy professor began working with a local school leader to implement IS; and our chair, program coordinator and policy professor joined bimonthly meetings in a Carnegie Foundation for the Advancement of Teaching networked improvement community for higher education institutions. Within 18 months, our two principal preparation cohort leaders took a four-credit university course from an expert in IS in public health with the goal of adapting the process of learning about IS to our principal preparation courses. In the following six months, these professors adapted existing curriculum to include IS.

Next, the dean led phone conferences with Carnegie Foundation for the Advancement of Teaching vice president Paul LeMahieu, our program coordinator, chair and a prominent education advocacy group. The dean then convened a meeting comprising LeMahieu, teachers and administrators from several school districts employing IS, the statewide education advocacy group Chalkboard, and our chair, program coordinator and principal preparation professors. Within weeks our two cohort professors, newly appointed third cohort professor and chair attended a Carnegie Project on the Education Doctorate conference on IS. Our program coordinator and one cohort professor then joined the University Council on Education Administration networked improvement community, with one cohort professor also attending the University Council on Education Administration conference sessions on this topic.

Thus, within two years, our small group of three professors, with the guidance and support of our dean and chair, had engaged in numerous activities, individually selected based on our interests and available time, to develop a strategy for preparing future school leaders to reduce educational disparities in our schools through IS.

Testing and Implementing the Change: Improvement Science in a Principal Preparation Program

LSU's principal preparation institution is known for its focus on preparing leaders who impact educational disparities in their schools, with culturally responsive leadership at its core. Further, the LSU program reflects the work around Gordon's (2012) "third way" of preparing leaders for equity, a focus on "awareness, care, critique, expertise, community, and accountability, with relationships at the model's center" (Peterson, Petti, & Carlile, 2013, citing Gordon, 2012, p. 3). Similar to other university preparation programs, we used a problem-based learning (PBL) project. This culminating term project was aligned with national and state leadership standards and included an equity audit with school-based data. In addition, future leaders solicited input from stakeholders, examined research-based practices and used local contractual and budgetary requirements for implementation planning. In addition, the project required students to explore school-specific, context-driven practices that must be considered. Although a separate yearlong educational leadership project (ELP) did include implementation requirements, the PBL project did not. Many districts did adopt the PBL plan, however, a testament to the strength of these projects.

When three of the five cohort professors decided to pilot IS as a school improvement strategy, we discontinued the PBL project and ELP. The most important characteristics of the ELP and PBL were folded into IS: alignment with state and national leaderships standards, equity audits, school-based data, stakeholder input, research-based practices and local contractual and budgetary requirements. As discussed earlier, IS believes responsibility for identifying problems, solutions, measurement and evaluation of effectiveness of the intervention should be situated among those impacted by the problem and those working to address the problem—in this case, by the students, families, community members and teachers. What we explicitly infused into IS was an equity focus and culturally responsive practices. Because we are a traditional institution with three terms per academic year, we divided the IS curriculum into three terms (Table 8.1).

Table 8.1. Teaching Improvement Science Over Three Terms

Term	Focus of Instruction
Term 1	School district presents how they use IS, why IS, how teachers are embracing IS Students read articles on IS Students do personal improvement project using IS Students reflect on how to use IS to lead for equity
Term 2	Students form groups to examine similar problems of practice Groups conduct fishbone, driver diagrams, root cause analyses
Term 3	Students lead equity improvement efforts in schools using IS Several Plan, Do, Study, Act cycles are completed Students reflect on implications for leading for equity using IS

In the first term, we introduced our students to the concepts of IS by having a local school district team present to our students on how they use IS, why they chose IS and the impact of the IS process on teachers. These practitioners believed that teachers were reengaged and energized in addressing problems of practice in their schools because of an organic process respectful of teachers. Next, we asked students to read multiple articles about the history of IS in the field of business and potential applications in educational leadership. Students then engaged in a personal improvement project, with most students choosing a health-related improvement goal. Students completed several cycles of improvement. Finally, students reflected on what they learned and how they could adapt IS as a future school leader for equity. Although many students understood that they were to revise their strategy for improvement in their next inquiry cycle if their data did not show improvement, most students simply "tried harder" to make the intervention work. Our learning was that this "try harder" concept is precisely what has happened when educators implement a new program or model for improvement: we focus on "fidelity to model" or "accountability systems." Failed efforts are interpreted as failures of the teachers rather than a failure to adapt an intervention to meet the needs of a particular context. IS, in contrast, notes that the intervention is not successful due to variation in the context—that is, the student characteristics, teaching conditions, teachers, the community or school leaders.

Our plan for winter term was for students to work in teams on a problem of practice that is common in their different schools and settings. They will lead teachers in a fishbone diagramming exercise in which the causes of a problem are explored (American Society for Quality, n.d.); driver diagrams in which participants examine what contributes to the problem and what change idea they can test (Institute for Healthcare improvement, n.d.a); and a root cause analysis to examine how problems are happening and why problems are occurring (Institute for Healthcare improvement, n.d.b). In addition, students examine the research on their chosen problem of practice. Previously, the work completed in this term would have been called a literature review and it would have included students examining research published only in peer-reviewed journals. Although this literature review has traditionally been the most highly regarded source of ideas for school improvement, much of the research has failed to consider variability within conditions of the context, a strength of IS.

In the third and final term of their principal preparation program, our future leaders lead an improvement effort in their own schools with a team of volunteer teachers or family members who want to work on a school-based problem of practice. Students will complete fishbone and driver diagrams, explore potential solutions with an equity lens and then will lead Plan, Do, Study, Act cycles in their schools. The goal will be for our future leaders to have the tools, the skills and practical experience guiding improvement cycles when they assume their roles as vice principals, principals or central office administrators.

Discussion

Our goal is for the graduates of our principal preparation program to become strong leaders for equity, leaders who resist the urge to blame teachers or students or families when initiatives fail to create success for all students in our schools. Rather, we hope our graduates have experienced firsthand how ecological, context-based and community-driven solutions, guided by the foundational concepts of improvement science, contribute to the success of each child in our schools. Initiative overload and the current public discourse indicate a propensity to embrace authoritarian solutions that disregard the expertise of our families, students and teachers and the funds of knowledge they bring to our schools. These factors contribute to a sense of hopelessness in many schools. By engaging our teachers in school improvement solutions and by ensuring empowerment of our students, families and teachers, we are contributing to the sustainability of public education and are honoring the heroes who have chosen to serve our students and our democracy (Peterson, 2014). While we are in the initial stages of implementing IS in our principal preparation institution, we are encouraged by our students' initial enthusiastic embrace of this promising school improvement strategy.

While engaging in the change process of including improvement science in any organization, it will be important to consider many factors. Does the culture of this organization allow for faculty to opt in and opt out according to their own individual professional goals? If so, be prepared to share publicly why some professors are included and others are not. Many will assume that those who are not participating were not "chosen." In our case, faculty have the contractual right to not participate in curriculum changes they do not approve of or simply choose not to engage in. Next, consider the time that faculty will need to get up to speed in the initiative, to test it and to fine-tune it. Supervisors may need to consider reducing other expectations of these faculty so as to not overload the early adopters or risk-takers during a fragile time of change. Further, supervisors should be prepared for an "implementation dip" in case course evaluations, reflecting the ups and downs of implementation cycles. Faculty cannot be penalized while taking the risks associated with curricular change initiatives. Another consideration is including school district leaders in the curricular changes. In our case, several school districts were clamoring for our support in the form of coteaching with us, partnering with us on their change initiatives using improvement science or through supporting their doctoral students who were exploring improvement science. Choosing one district over another or one practitioner over another will potentially cause conflict should the decision not be communicated widely and thoughtfully. Further, a plan should be made for taking improvement science to scale with partner districts and all teacher education courses, not just school leadership courses. Whereas these factors may be seen as limiting factors and discourage other organizations from exploring the use of improvement science, we experienced them as factors that were mitigated by our strong relationships with schools and districts and our reputation among practitioners.

Discussion Questions

1. When embarking on this change process, what considerations must be examined to ensure the process is not derailed prior to

beginning? Consider political, structural, budgetary, contractual or employee issues that are unique to your setting.

2. What strategies have been successful in the past to ensure that this change initiative is given the supports needed and in the areas needed in your particular context?

3. What group of students are you hurting if your organization chooses to not engage in an improvement method that tests changes quickly, adjusts changes based on data and takes changes to scale when they work in context? Use your local data to identify by race, ethnicity, home language, ability or other grouping students who are currently underserved.

4. What do you envision as the best possible outcome of implementing improvement science in your setting?

Class Activities

1. Engage in a small-scale personal improvement project that can be done within four weeks to practice the tools and theories of improvement science. This project can be as straightforward as "I'm going to drink more water" or as complicated as "I'm going to lose weight."

2. Identify two or three change efforts that worked in one school or district that did NOT work in another. Identify all the potential contextual reasons for why the change did not work in another context. What are the implications for your use of improvement science?

References

American Society for Quality. (n.d.). *Learn about quality.* Available from http://asq.org/learn-about-quality/

Barth, R. (1990). *Improving schools from within.* San Francisco, CA: Jossey-Bass.

Bryk, A., Gomez, L., Grunow, A., & LeMahieu, P. (2015). *Learning to improve: How America's schools can get better at getting better.* Cambridge, MA: Harvard Education Publishing Group.

Center for the Study of Social Policy. (2016). *Asthma improvement collab-orative: Case study*. Washington DC: Author. Available from https://www.cssp.org/policy/body/Asthma-Improvement-Collaborative.pdf

Deming, W. E. (1994). *The new economics* (2nd edition). Cambridge, MA; Center for Advanced Educational Services, Massachusetts Institute of Technology.

Dewey, J. (1990). *The school and society and the child and the curriculum*. Chicago, IL: University of Chicago Press.

DuFour, R., Eaker, R., & Many, T. (2006). *Learning by doing: A handbook for professional learning communities at work*. Bloomington, IN: Solution Tree.

Eagon, E. (2016). *Get educated on educator engagement*. Available from http://pie-network.org/article/get-educated-on-educator-engagement/

Freire, P. (1993). *Pedagogy of the oppressed*. New York, NY: The Continuum International Publishing Group.

Fullan, M. (2011). *Motion leadership: The skinny on being change savvy*. Thousand Oaks, CA: Corwin Press.

Fullan, M. (2013). *Stratosphere: Integrating technology, pedagogy, and change knowledge*. Toronto, ON: Pearson Canada.

Gay, G. (2010). *Culturally responsive teaching: Theory, research, and practice*. New York, NY: Teachers College Press.

Gordon, S. (2012). *Beyond convention, beyond critique: Toward a Third Way of preparing educational leaders to promote equity and social justice* (Pt. 2). Available from http://cnx.org/content/m43705/1.6/

Heifetz, R. A., & Linsky, M. (2007). *When leadership spells danger: Leading meaningful change in education takes courage, commitment, and politi-cal savvy*. Available from http://www.ode.state.or.us/search/default.aspx

Institute for Healthcare Improvement. (n.d.a) *Driver diagram*. Available from http://www.ihi.org/resources/Pages/Tools/Driver-Diagram.aspx

Institute for Healthcare Improvement. (n.d.b). *RCA2: Improving root cause analyses and actions to prevent harm*. Available from http://www.ihi.org/resources/Pages/Tools/RCA2-Improving-Root-Cause-Analyses-and-Actions-to-Prevent-Harm.aspx

Lahey, J. (2017, Jan. 4). How design thinking became a buzzword at school. *The Atlantic*. Available from https://www.theatlantic.com/education/archive/2017/01/how-design-thinking-became-a-buzz-word-at-school/512150/

Langley, G. J., Moen, R. D., Nolan, K. M., Nolan, T. W., Norman, C. L., & Provost, L. P. (2009). *The improvement guide: A practical approach to enhancing organizational performance*. Charlottesville, VA: Wiley.

Langley, G., Nolan, K., Nolan, T., Norman, C., & Provost, L. (1996). *The improvement guide: A practical approach to enhancing organizational performance*. San Francisco, CA: Jossey-Bass.

Leithwood, K., Louis, K. S., Anderson, S. R., & Wahlstrom, K. (2004). *How leadership influences student learning*. New York, NY: The Wallace Foundation and the University of Minnesota Center for Applied Research and Educational Improvement.

Lewis, C. (2015). What is improvement science? Do we need it in education? *Educational Researcher, 44*(1), 54–61.

Lindsey, R., Robins, K. N., & Terrell, R. (2009). *Cultural proficiency: A manual for school leaders*. Thousand Oaks, CA: Corwin Press.

Mintrop, R. (2016). *Design-based school improvement: A practical guide for education leaders*. Cambridge, MA: Harvard Education Press.

Obama, B. (2016). *United States health care reform: Progress to date and next steps*. Washington DC: The White House.

OSEP Technical Assistance Center on Positive Behavioral Interventions and Supports. (2017). *Positive behavioral interventions & supports* [Website]. Available from https://www.pbis.org/

Peterson, A. (2016). Getting 'what works' working: Building blocks for the integration of experimental and improvement science. *International Journal of Research & Method in Education, 39*(3), 299–313.

Peterson, D. S. (2014). A missing piece in the sustainability movement: The human spirit. *Sustainability: The Journal of Record, 7*(2), 74–77.

Peterson, D. S., Petti, A., & Carlile, S. (2013). Preparing future school leaders to ensure racial, ethnic, linguistic, and socio-economic equity in education: The "third way." [Special Issue]. *Education Leadership Review*, 88–95.

Rother, M. (2009). *Toyota Kata: Managing people for improvement, adaptiveness and superior results*. New York, NY: McGraw-Hill Professional.

CHAPTER NINE

Leveraging Improvement Science to Include Cultural Shift

RICHARD J. CORMAN
Asheville–Buncombe Technical Community College

Abstract

This chapter will focus on department chairs within a large academic division at Western Technical Community College (WTCC), who are using improvement science (IS) as a strategy for problem identification and problem-solving (Carnegie Foundation, 2018). Over the last 10–15 years all community college faculty across the nation have continually been asked to do more with less. This has caused many at WTCC to feel overwhelmed and stagnate in their role. As is the case with many individuals who feel overwhelmed, the faculty simply try to resolve problems as they arise—in a reactionary fashion, which leads to the phenomenon called "solutionitis" (LeMahieu, Bryk, Grunow, & Gomez, 2017), where problems are dealt with on the surface, but root causes are not explored. Solutionitis exists at WTCC and this chapter documents Dean Akeem's efforts to shift the problem-solving culture by teaching improvement science to midlevel managers and using improvement science to evaluate his efforts.

The process of creating this cultural shift utilized several IS tools such as the Plan, Do, Study, Act (PDSA) cycle, as well as fishbone and driver diagrams (Langley et al., 2009). The department chairs served as champions of IS problem-solving and have been able to implement the tools leveraged above in their own training and problem-solving environments.

Keywords

community, college, culture, faculty, improvement science, fishbone, driver, five whys

Setting/Background

Western Technical Community College (WTCC) is one of the largest community colleges in its state, with over 7,000 curriculum students (degree-seeking) enrolled annually and another 6,000–7,000 students enrolled as continuing education students (non-degree-seeking). Within WTCC a traditional leadership and organizational structure exists, with a board of trustees at the top, followed by a college president and vice presidents for various large divisions of the college; deans oversee subsections of divisions, and program chairs oversee individual programs, full-time faculty and finally adjunct faculty. WTCC has almost 200 full-time faculty and just under 500 adjunct faculty as of 2016. Many of the faculty and staff retire at WTCC with over 20 years of experience at the college. The average age of full-time faculty is nearly 50 years old, which makes finding employment difficult within the institution because so few jobs become available each year.

For a period between the late 1970s and the early 2000s, WTCC saw significant growth in enrollment and programs development to support local industries moving to the area. For the last 10–15 years there have been several sustainable new programs created, yet enrollment has been decreasing by about 2% each year since a peak in 2008/2009. Between the 1970s through the early 2000s the college had two individuals who held the office of president; however, over the last 10 years there have been three different individuals holding this same position. Current college leadership has been steady in their approach and have helped bring stability to a volatile relationship between faculty and administration that formed over 10 years previously when the first of the three latest presidents took on the leadership role. During this volatile time, faculty were pushed to extremes regarding work hours, production and expectations. From these rigorous work conditions employees began problem-solving as issues came up, instead of deciphering the root cause of problems. This approach to dealing with problems as they arise became the norm and has continued through today.

Need for Improvement

Even with leadership stability there is always room for continuous improvement. According to an internal survey performed biannually, one of the primary frustrations faculty have is their limited time for improvement initiatives due to their reactive problem-solving culture. This frustration was fairly evident throughout the college as many faculty and staff felt excited on days when they could progress in their primary responsibilities such as grading, advising and program planning. Faculty and staff would also voice frustration with being asked to take on more job responsibilities with no extra time off, and sometimes with no extra pay.

Treading water is how many faculty and staff described their ability to keep up with mounting workloads. This frustration with not being able to have the time or energy to improve course content or develop new programs for the department helped create a culture of resignation among small groups of employees. These faculty felt that decisions within certain offices would always yield a negative result (from the faculty perspective); thus the faculty would give up before even trying to attempt a change. This resignation mentality and problem-solving culture allowed for individuals to only do just enough to make the current issue go away. Alas, problem-solving this way only allows for the core issue to pop up again in a different manifestation.

Perhaps a better way to truly deal with our problems is not through seeking quick fixes, or as Albert Einstein once said, "if I were given one hour to save the planet, I would spend 59 minutes defining the problem and one minute resolving it" (quoted by Spradlin, 2012). Einstein illustrates the importance of truly understanding the core problem before attempting to solve said issue. I certainly would not want to get on an airplane and have the pilot take their best guess at where Atlanta is located, so why are we so willing to take our best guess at solving problems without truly knowing what is at the root of the issue?

Testing the Change

Cultural shifts of any kind can be difficult to navigate given the inherit change associated with doing something different. Within the culture at WTCC problems have been addressed in a reactionary or emotional manner. In order to change the mentality in which problems are addressed, Dean Akeem asked for volunteers from department chairs to participate in a pilot project regarding problem-solving. After sending the invitation to eight chairs, four volunteered, representing business, computers, cosmetology and brewing.

During the initial meeting Dean Akeem explained that the purpose of the group was to test a new approach to problem-solving. Dean Akeem explained to the program chairs that during their time together he would serve as a moderator, not a supervisor. He then explained the theory behind IS, going through problem identification (five whys), the fishbone diagram, the driver diagram, and ultimately the PDSA cycle with the improvement initiative (Langley et al., 2009). Each meeting consisted of a PDSA (see Figure 9.1), where Dean Akeem studied the participation of each member and the progress of each individual step during the process to determine the effectiveness of the meeting.

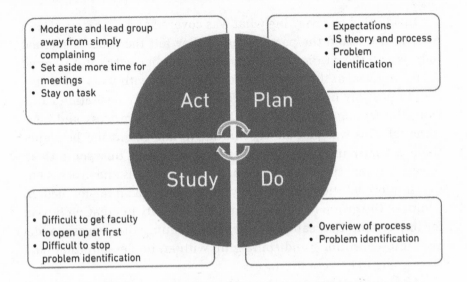

Figure 9.1. Plan, Do, Study, Act (PDSA) cycle. This figure reviews the initial PDSA cycle prior to the first group meeting.

The first meeting lasted almost two hours, with the group going over expectations and the IS process, and then starting problem identification. A few of the main points found after the first meeting included the introduction of the IS system and how/why we are approaching the various stages, which went over well with the chairs. After 20 minutes of reviewing the process Dean Akeem asked for the group to start problem identification by asking the group what they thought were the main problems within the division, or overall at the WTCC. Slowly the faculty started listing items while Dean Akeem simply wrote and focused on facilitating the progress of the meeting to avoid placing bias into the group. After over an hour of listing problems on a whiteboard, Dean Akeem helped pull the group to find commonality on some of the items on the board. This process took 5–10 minutes and the group did agree on two main topics: "lack of communication" and "lack of accountability." At this point Dean Akeem decided to wrap up the meeting by reviewing what they had accomplished that day and looked forward to next steps with a meeting date one week after the initial meeting.

In addition to reviewing what was covered and next steps, Dean Akeem also asked the participants if they felt the process seemed to be worth their time and effort. Each member felt that it seemed promising, and at the very least provided them with tools and a process to possibly utilize at a future time. The only hesitation came from the feeling that although this was a good process and idea, some felt this was just another initiative and might not be something actually used beyond the meetings. From this point Dean Akeem felt that the chairs had bought into the tools and process but that implementation in their daily roles seemed a bit far-fetched. In addition, the group felt there would be difficulty in creating buy-in for implementation campus-wide. Streamlining the process to feel less time-consuming and coming up with an implementation plan were going to be keys to success.

After the first meeting Dean Akeem reflected on what went well and how he could be more effective in facilitating the group. The PDSA cycle in Figure 9.1 showed that the dean needed to lead the group through the next series of steps more efficiently. In order to be more efficient with the time the group had together Dean Akeem decided to recommend only prioritizing one key term or problem area (either lack of communication or lack of accountability) from the previous meeting instead of going into both problems.

The second meeting started with Dean Akeem reviewing progress that was made during the previous meeting and asking if the group would like to only focus on one key term or problem area in order to be more efficient with their limited time together. Once all agreed, the dean began to ask the group a series of questions. He asked the team why the lack of communication was an important problem to address. Once the group came to consensus on an answer, he then asked why the answer they gave was important. He did this several times over in order to drill down into the root problem versus what the group started with (lack of communication). This process of asking "why?" multiple times over allows the moderator and group to see the surface problem and then drill down into what is really the issue at hand. In Figure 9.2, you can see what the group came up with after being asked why the answer they provided was of significance.

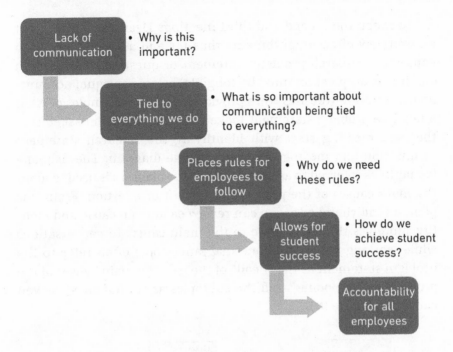

Figure 9.2. The Five Whys. This is how the group drilled down to what was truly a source of frustration during the initial meeting.

From the figure, you can see we started with lack of communication being the problem and quickly found our way to the feeling among the chairs of a lack of equal accountability for all employees throughout the college. Although another series of five whys could have been implemented for what the chairs saw as equal accountability, Dean Akeem felt in the moment that the chairs had drilled down as far as they could. This meeting lasted just over an hour with full participation from the group. Prior to the group leaving, the dean asked if anyone felt their voice had not been heard on anything. With no one offering an opinion, Dean Akeem asked if everyone felt like they had a personal investment or connection to the problem and process. All agreed to having a vested interest in determining how they could better implement an improvement plan to have equal accountability across the college. The next meeting was scheduled for three weeks later due to scheduling conflicts.

Between the second and third meetings Dean Akeem sent out an overview of accomplishments thus far and asked the group to consider a research problem statement or question (the research statement or question must be tangible) related to equal accountability. Links to websites were provided that gave examples of what a tangible problem statement looked like. Dean Akeem asked that the next meeting start with identifying the research statement or question and moving into the fishbone diagram. The fishbone (sometimes referred to as a causal analysis) diagram is used to identify main causes of the problem statement or question. From this point an individual or group can review each main cause and identify subtopics that contribute to the main cause. In conversations while working with a fishbone diagram people often refer to the problem statement as the "head" of the fish, the main causes of the problem as "big bones" and the subtopics as "little bones," as you can see in Figure 9.3.

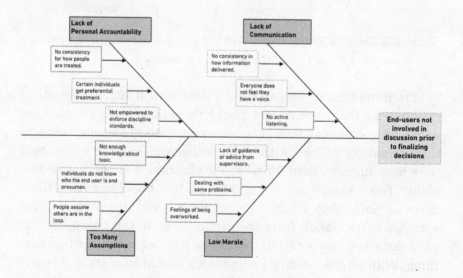

Figure 9.3. Fishbone diagram with problem statement.

Three weeks after the second meeting the group came together and met for two hours regarding the research statement or question they wanted to investigate. A problem statement was agreed on: "The College does not communicate with end users prior to finalizing decisions." From this point a fishbone diagram was created in about 30 minutes with four "big bones" and three "little bones" under each main cause. At this point the group identified the assumption of others being in the loop as the primary reason they wanted to explore for the next step. This was the stopping point for the meeting, and Dean Akeem again checked in with the chairs regarding the process. Remarkably, the chairs found themselves wanting to work on this during their free time and each member felt empowered. Remarks such as "I'm proud to work in this division once again" or "I can't wait to work on this when I get home" seemed to signal that the cultural shift and buy-in for this new approach to problem-solving was occurring.

The group met once more about two weeks after the third meeting and worked through the driver diagram. This diagram showcased a method to provide improvement ideas on solving the problem. During this meeting the chairs were highly engaged and said that they felt empowered and for the first time in a long time that their voice was being heard. Ultimately, the group decided to implement a pilot program that incorporated checks and balance. This implementation required that anytime a curriculum change or new curriculum program comes about, the department chairs must seek end user input and show proof of this by attaching meeting notes to curriculum changes. An end users was identified as anyone who will have to instruct, oversee or provide data entry. Dean Akeem would do the same to ensure equal accountability. At the end of the fourth meeting which lasted an hour and a half, the group felt that their voices were heard, that plenty of time was given to work through all steps, the process was clear and made sense and above all they wanted to spread this process for solving complex problems to others across the division and campus.

Ideas for improvement were to spend less time on the initial step of asking what issues each chair saw across campus. They also would have liked to have utilized a shared drive to work on documents in between meetings.

Implementation

With the assistance of the pilot group's success Dean Akeem was able to speak to the director of training and professional development at WTCC. To better implement this new way of problem-solving the dean suggested the chairs within the pilot group be champions of this process and help provide training to small groups. After meeting with the director of training and professional development the dean was told that this type of training is exactly what the college has been needing and looking for. The director of training and professional development along with Dean Akeem have set plans to meet with college administration regarding the IS process being the showcase piece at the next professional development day. In the interim, Dean Akeem and the department chair champions of IS are working with small groups (four to six people) to continue to spread the IS tools and process. This also helps perfect the length of time needed for training and how information is presented to groups.

If the small group trainings continue to go well and the executive leadership of the college are on board, the full implementation of IS should go into effect within the next year.

Discussion

The faculty and staff at WTCC have traditionally worked with certain of the same problems over and over again in various manifestations since the core issues have never been truly addressed. This has caused individuals to work longer hours and fight the feeling of being overwhelmed. The tools and process of IS have helped many across campus view and solve core issues on a more consistent basis. Through the use of drilling down with the five whys, employees are better able to identify the core problem before moving forward toward a resolution. Using other tools such as the fishbone and driver diagrams, the employees better identify causes of the core issue and create various improvement initiatives to be tested through PDSA cycles.

This cultural change in how problem-solving is performed has improved morale and empowered individuals to tackle problems with a new level of confidence. However, a cultural change is slow and requires champions to consistently speak about the change and answer questions.

Leaders looking to implement a cultural shift toward IS can expect skepticism and a general reluctance to learn a new process. One of the main lessons learned is how important it is to ensure individuals that this is not just another initiative. In addition, the time commitment for individuals learning the process is lengthy and many who already feel overwhelmed do not always see the benefit of adding another training session to their agenda. Explaining research that has shown how IS helps save time in the long run and/or adding a personal story on how IS has helped you solve a complex (or simple) problem can help ease concerns.

Key Concepts

Improvement science: Deploys rapid tests of change to guide the development, revision, and continued fine-tuning of new tools, processes, work roles and relationships

Fishbone diagram: Identifies many possible causes for an effect or problem

Driver diagram: Defines the range of actions or interventions that you may want to undertake in order to solve a problem of practice

Five whys: Process of drilling down to the root cause of a problem by asking "why?" five times

PDSA cycle: Systematic process for gaining valuable learning and knowledge for the continual improvement of a product, process or service

Cultural shift: A shift of belief, thought or behaviors for an individual or across a large group of individuals

Discussion Questions

1. How would you go about changing the cultural dynamics of your organization using improvement science?
2. Given the cyclical nature of a PDSA diagram, how long would you wait to perform an additional PDSA for a given problem?
3. What is an example of a problem you have within your organization, and how would you leverage improvement science to find a resolution?

Class Activities

1. In groups discuss problems within individual organizations and utilize the improvement science step of the five whys to find the core problem of one problem the group agrees upon. It would be helpful to identify someone to write the initial problems on a whiteboard (or piece of paper, depending on the size of the group) and to act as timekeeper.
2. Review a case study on cultural change and identify where IS could have been leveraged to improve the outcome.
3. Review this chapter and determine in a group how IS could have been leveraged in a better way.
4. Forecast how IS could play a role in bringing the executive leadership team on board with IS and how you would implement IS across the organization.

References

Carnegie Foundation. (2018). *Our ideas: Using improvement science to accelerate learning and address problems of practice.* Available from https://www.carnegiefoundation.org/our-ideas/

Langley, G. J., Moen, R. D., Nolan, K. M., Nolan, T. W., Norman, C. L., & Provost, L. P. (2009). *The improvement guide: A practical approach to enhancing organizational performance.* Charlottesville, VA: Wiley.

LeMahieu, P. G., Bryk, A. S., Grunow, A., & Gomez, L. M. (2017). Working to improve: Seven approaches to improvement science in education. *Quality Assurance in Education, 25*(1), 2–4.

Spradlin, D. (2012, September). Are you solving the right problem? *Harvard Business Review.* Available from https://hbr.org/2012/09/are-you-solving-the-right-problem

CHAPTER TEN

Improvement Science in Equity-Based Administrative Practicum Redesign

SUSAN P. CARLILE AND DEBORAH S. PETERSON

Portland State University

Abstract

School leaders need to understand how variations in context impact a change they want to make to the system. They must lead change efforts quickly and in collaboration with others. To prepare principal preparation graduates who are strong leaders for equity, leaders must resist the urge to blame teachers, students, the district, the community or families when initiatives fail to create success for all students in our schools. Thus, the graduates of our principal preparation program embody the following characteristics through their work with improvement science:

- Understand variations in the context
- Facilitate effective collective action
- Employ rapid learning cycles, fast feedback, continual reflection and ongoing coaching
- Experience firsthand ecological, context-based and community data-driven solutions guided by the foundational concepts of improvement science

- Embrace solutions that regard the expertise of our families, students and teachers and the funds of knowledge they bring to our schools

Educational disparities based on race, ethnicity and socioeconomic status persist in this nation, to the detriment of our democracy and the future of public education. To increase the effectiveness of school improvement efforts, improvement science provides a model for meaningful, sustainable, democratic improvement efforts that include student and teacher voice and enhance the dignity of our students and teachers while positively impacting our schools (Byrk, Gomez, Grunow, & LeMahieu, 2015). Additionally, field-based practicum experiences where leaders directly apply new knowledge to their practice increase student achievement (Chandler, Chan, & Jiang, 2013).

This chapter examines the process and lessons learned in our school administrator leadership program as we developed our capacity to deepen and broaden use of improvement science concentrating on preparation of effective, equity-focused leaders. Our cultural context included starting small, piloting IS in one initial administrative program and participating regularly in the Higher Education Network (HEN), a network sponsored by the Carnegie Foundation. The article will describe the evolution of our program as we, the higher education network, collaborated with one local education agency in the Improvement Leadership Education and Development (iLEAD) initiative sponsored by the Carnegie Foundation. The iLEAD work allowed increased face-to-face collaboration with other institutions of higher education (IHEs) and the Carnegie Foundation on problems of practice embedded in the work of educational leadership preparation. Collaboration between the local education agency and IHE and daily practice within each system were also strengthened. The chapter further describes the IHE and LEA collaborative focus on a well-specified common aim guided by a mutually developed understanding of the problem disciplined by the rigor of improvement science and coordinated to accelerate rapid diffusion into the field in varied educational contexts. Specifically, the chapter describes the expansion of equity-based, improvement science methodology from initial integration into the initial administrative curriculum to include the 30-hour, field-based practicum experience of currently practicing and experienced administrative school leaders.

Keywords

Educational disparities, administrative licensure redesign, school-based administrative practicum, change leadership, networked improvement community (NIC), university and district/school partnership

The Setting

Woodland State University (WSU) is an urban, public university serving 25,000 students situated in the downtown area of a major urban center. Recognized nationally for its innovation (https://www.usnews.com/best-colleges/rankings/national-universities/innovative?src=stats), with a nationally ranked School of Business (https://www.usnews.com/best-graduate-schools/top-business-schools/mba-rankings?_mode=table), the WSU School of Education is also nationally ranked in the top 10% of schools of education, preparing the highest number of school teachers and leaders in the state. Accredited by the Council for the Accreditation of Educator Preparation, the Council for Accreditation of Counseling and Related Educational Programs and the National Association for the Education of Young Children, it has completed rigorous accreditation expectations. Of those completing our programs and an alumni survey, over 95% are employed in positions for which we prepared them. Since 2003, almost 50 of WSU's alumni have been awarded state and national honors for their leadership, including 25 awards for school leadership (17 principals of the year, 5 superintendents of the year, 2 college presidents and a state superintendent of public instruction). In addition, 18 state or national teacher awards were granted to graduates; 14 teachers of the year, 2 librarians of the year and 2 Milken Awards.

Because WSU prepares the most principals in our state, we have an added responsibility to ensure WSU graduates embody the characteristics of exemplary school leaders, meet or exceed national standards for school leadership, reflect the diversity of our student population and, most importantly, are prepared to be strong leaders of change efforts that reduce educational disparities.

Our social justice focus is embedded in WSU's five-year Strategic Plan, specifically WSU's focus on equity, community engagement, culturally responsive pedagogy and the success of diverse students as well as the School of Education's focus on diversity and inclusiveness which is aligned with our department's mission to encourage democracy and social justice. Although *social justice* is not defined by WSU, our school or our department, we endorse the definition of D. S. Peterson:

> I define social justice as an orientation that includes both a goal and a process (Bell, 2016) in which the dignity of each person's unique identity—including the intersectionality of race/ethnicity, socioeconomic status, home language, national origin, sexual orientation, gender identification, ability, religion, or any other manifestation of diversity that advantages or disadvantages a person by virtue of membership in that group (Gay, 2010)—is respected and enhanced. (D. S. Peterson, personal communication, September 15, 2017)

Educational disparities based on race, ethnicity and socioeconomic status persist in our state, and in this nation, to the detriment of our democracy and the future of public education. Moreover, efforts to achieve an educator workforce that matches the diversity of the children in our schools has not been achieved. In our state, where two thirds of the school districts (63%) have a gap of 40 percentage points or more between the racial/ethnic diversity of students and that of administrators, the administrative workforce is not shifting quickly enough to respond to the increasingly diverse K–12 student body. Although positive influence has been found when leaders who are culturally and linguistically diverse become role models for students from a similar demographic background, we also know leaders of all racial and ethnic backgrounds can effectively lead for social justice (Emdin, 2016; Theoharis, 2018). Moreover, because the majority of current teachers and school leaders in our state are White, it is imperative that White leaders are prepared to—and are committed to—lead for social justice.

Due to persistent educational disparities based on race and ethnicity in our K–12 schools and given WSU's position as the institution that prepares the largest number of school leaders in our state, WSU feels an even greater responsibility to ensure that school change efforts focus on eliminating the correlation of school achievement and the race and ethnicity of the student. Children of color cannot wait for annual standardized test results, for laborious and lengthy state improvement plans or for large-scale improvement efforts to receive corporate, state or federal funding for their learning to commence. Our school leaders must have the tools to begin small-scale change efforts within weeks of noticing a problem of practice in our local schools, particularly when our children of color are at risk of being suspended, expelled, ignored and diminished by policies and practices that exclude them from educational success. As such, WSU's principal preparation program has embraced improvement science as the signature change leadership practice to eliminate educational disparities in our K–12 schools.

This mission of our principal preparation program was developed over time by a team of academic scholars and practitioners who were inaugural members of a prestigious statewide organization focused on leadership for equity and who had significant careers in K–12 education and statewide policy development. Based on groundwork from years of participation in this consortium, input and support from our dean and a recognition that the tenets of improvement science aligned with our team's equity-focused mission, members of our team were invited to explore the use of improvement science as our signature change leadership pedagogy.

Discussion

In 2015, members of our principal preparation team were invited by our dean to explore the use of improvement science as a model for meaningful, sustainable, democratic improvement efforts that include student and teacher voice and enhance the dignity of our students and teachers while positively influencing our schools. Because of our governance structure and faculty contractual rights at WSU, team members were not required to participate; however, the majority of our team members chose to embrace improvement science as our change leadership methodology. This team proposed that as we increase efforts to recruit and prepare school administrators who reflect the demographics of students in our schools, we also explicitly infuse an equity focus and culturally responsive practices into improvement science, and thus, into the leadership practices of our graduates. Two members of our team volunteered to take an improvement science course through Parker School of Medicine and the WSU School of Public Health, to participate in a national improvement science network called a networked improvement community (NIC) that enhanced both the structure of our principal preparation model and the equity and change-based curriculum embedded in it, and meet with a consortium of state teacher union leaders, state department of education leaders and district practitioners exploring the use of improvement science in our state's schools.

Networked Improvement Communities (NICS)

Carnegie Institute: Higher Education Network (HEN)

Most instrumental in our growing understanding of improvement science and the role of this process in school change was our regular attendance in the Higher Education Network (HEN) webinars where novices, expert practitioners and authors of improvement science research shared ideas and offered support. Two faculty members regularly attended these sessions, our program coordinator for the initial administrative license and one professor in the advanced administrative license program. HEN members represented a cross-section of over 30 faculty members across 18 colleges, universities and leadership development programs, including practitioners from across the United States, higher education improvement teams, researchers and staff from the Carnegie Foundation. Several concepts stood out in our critical early learning:

- Do it. Do not talk about it.
- Honor the time devoted to problem-solving.
- Focus on high-leverage, challenging, "wicked," equity-based problems.
- Before you try to improve something, look at the problem from the perspective of those whose work it impacts.
- Honor the voice of the users, including the students.
- Consider IS tools like a screwdriver—useful for turning a screw, if you can avoid stabbing yourself in the leg.
- Recognize that all first ideas are fine—push through the wall.
- Experience improvement science before teaching it.

Though we did not realize it at the time, most of these precepts aligned with the first five of the six improvement science principles (Figure 10.1), and became the basis for subsequent initiatives. The last one, however, "Experience improvement science before teaching it," we put into immediate practice by applying improvement science to a personal project.

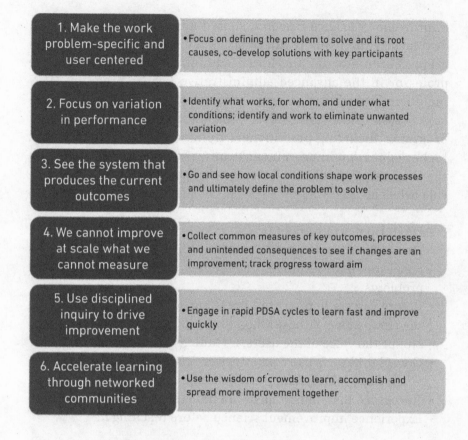

1. Make the work problem-specific and user centered	• Focus on defining the problem to solve and its root causes, co-develop solutions with key participants
2. Focus on variation in performance	• Identify what works, for whom, and under what conditions; identify and work to eliminate unwanted variation
3. See the system that produces the current outcomes	• Go and see how local conditions shape work processes and ultimately define the problem to solve
4. We cannot improve at scale what we cannot measure	• Collect common measures of key outcomes, processes and unintended consequences to see if changes are an improvement; track progress toward aim
5. Use disciplined inquiry to drive improvement	• Engage in rapid PDSA cycles to learn fast and improve quickly
6. Accelerate learning through networked communities	• Use the wisdom of crowds to learn, accomplish and spread more improvement together

Figure 10.1. Carnegie's Six Core Principles of Improvement.
Source: LeMahieu, Grunow, Baker, Nordstrum, & Gomez, 2017 (used with permission of the authors).

This initial experience with a personal improvement project (PIP) in the summer of 2015 synthesized our learning and proved instrumental for the development of our individual understanding of improvement science and formed the basis for long-term curriculum change in our initial administrator licensure curriculum. Under the guidance of Carnegie facilitators, each HEN team member identified a problem of practice and completed a personal improvement project learning using improvement science tools, including a fishbone, driver diagram, aim statement, process map, data run charts and several Plan, Do, Study, Act (PDSA) cycles before sharing the experience online. This project was replicated with our initial administrative students the following academic year. Implementation challenges and successes of the PIP are described in a later section of this chapter.

Essential to our success in these early stages was the regular support of HEN members. In subsequent webinars, the collegial relationships were developed and enriched by face-to-face meetings at the Carnegie Improvement Science summits in 2015, 2016, 2017 and 2018 and the resources/materials made available on the Carnegie Hub. Members of our team also attended improvement science meetings at the twice-annual convenings (in 2016 and 2017) of the Carnegie Project on the Education Doctorate (CPED) or presented in the professional development series on improvement science (spring 2017). These relationships enabled us to explore and share improvement science course and syllabus design, rubrics, student artifacts, game theory, protocol pedagogy, improvement science in the EdD, concept papers and other resources developed and openly made available by members of the NIC.

University Council of Educational Administration (UCEA-PDN)

In fall 2016, our program team participated in the UCEA Program Design Network Improvement Community (PD-NIC) for Candidate Recruitment, Selection, and Evaluation focusing on the domain Increasing the Diversity of Administrative Licensure. Specifically, our problem of practice, "The diversity of the interns in the Woodland State University Initial Administrator Licensure program do not reflect the diversity in state K–12 schools," was supported by an aim statement: Increase the diversity of interns in the 2017–2018 Preliminary Administrator Licensure cohort from 2016–2017 by 5%. Our work with UCEA was absorbed into continued work with the Carnegie Foundation during the launch of the Improvement Leadership Education and Development (iLEAD) initiative in September 2017.

iLEAD

The iLEAD initiative was a rich opportunity for UCEA-PDN members who had been using improvement science in the preparation of educational leaders and had also incorporated IS techniques into an equity-based leadership preparation curriculum to expand the relationship of the institute of higher education (IHE) with a local education district (LEA). The LEA with whom Woodland State University collaborated was a suburban district with 5,100 students, whose makeup included 20% Latinx students, 49% receiving free and reduced lunch and 15% experiencing disabilities, and who identified their three greatest challenges: (a) reducing educational disparities, (b) integrating context-based change leadership through improvement science and (c) meeting the state accountability and school improvement requirements. We were selected based on our potential to use improvement science as a component of our licensure program, ability to collaborate with the LEA on a well-specified, common aim guided by a mutually developed understanding of the problem disciplined by the rigor of improvement science, our capacity to accelerate repaid diffusion into the field in varied educational contests and our goal to build mutually responsive, energizing relationships between the IHE and the LEA focusing on the dual goals of equity and excellence to address educational disparities—a daunting endeavor.

Engagement With the Local Education Agency (LEA) and Woodland State University

Engagement between Woodland State University and the local education agency began in fall 2016 when we introduced our initial administrator licensure interns, who were enrolled in a yearlong cohort model program, to the concepts of improvement science. In the fall of 2016, a four-person team from the LEA, including the district director of teaching and learning, an assistant principal and two teachers (one of whom was in the Preliminary Administrator Licensure cohort and had recently been hired as an assistant principal for the 2017–2018 school year), presented to our 49 interns on how they use improvement science, why they chose improvement science and the influence of improvement science on the work of teachers. These practitioners were clear that teachers in the LEA were reengaged and energized in addressing problems of practice in their schools because an organic process like improvement science that is respectful to teachers and students was in place. In addition, the LEA was one of the participating districts in the February 2016 meeting of local administrators, teachers and the statewide advocacy organization convened by Paul LeMahieu to share promising IS practices and implementation challenges. Our administrator licensure program shared with the LEA a mutual commitment to prepare graduates of our principal preparation program to become strong leaders for equity, leaders who resist the urge to blame teachers, students or families when initiatives fail to create success for all students in our schools.

Guiding our change process were concepts from LeMahieu and Bryk (2017), outlined in Figure 10.2. The first phase, Chartering, is a time when "an initiation team specifies the core problem to be solved and network members are united around it" (p. 13). In this phase, the iLEAD team, under the guidance of Carnegie staff, reviewed the integration of improvement science at WSU to date and identified a problem of practice. A problem encountered by many institutions, including WSU, is providing field-based practicum experiences where leaders directly apply new knowledge to their practice and increase student achievement (Chandler et al., 2013; LeMahieu, Grunow, Baker, Nordstrum, & Gomez, 2017; Peterson, 2017). Consequently, members of our iLEAD were mutually committed to embracing improvement science as a promising school improvement strategy to enrich field-based experience while maintaining focus on our aim statement and key drivers (illustrated in Figure 10.3) to reduce educational disparities.

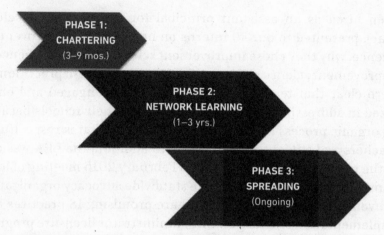

Figure 10.2. The phases in a maturing network improvement community.
Source: LeMahieu & Bryk, 2017 (used with permission of the authors).

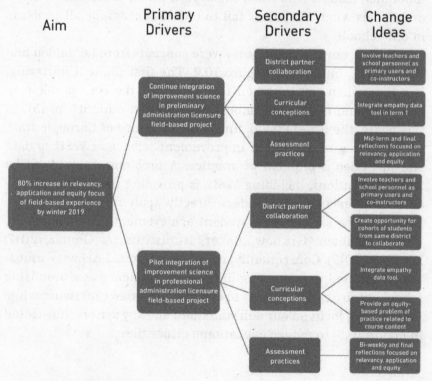

Figure 10.3. Driver diagram.

Our aim, of an "80% increase in relevancy, application and diversity focus of the CAL field-based experience in the academic year 2017–2018," was supported by the following drivers:

- Prepare all our graduates to use improvement science methodologies to interrupt educational disparities.
- Further integrate improvement science into the three-credit educational leadership project of the preliminary administrator licensure program in fall, winter and spring terms of the yearlong Preliminary Administrator Licensure cohort experience to address educational disproportionality.
- Integrate improvement science into the field-based practicum of the professional administrator licensure program to influence equity-based change practices in districts and schools.

A key driver was to recognize and build upon past successes implementing improvement science in the field-based practicum of the Preliminary Administrator Licensure Program. In 2017–18, 49 preliminary and preliminary + MA licensure graduates participated in a yearlong, three-credit IS project that began with individual personal improvement projects in the fall term and culminated in the spring term with school-based team projects such as Latinx family involvement, district counseling programs, culturally responsive instructional practices in classrooms, antibullying efforts at the classroom and school level, attendance and classroom discipline support for beginning teachers.

A second driver was to create a cohort model in the Professional Administrator Licensure Program using improvement science methodology as a signature pedagogy across a sequence of classes by redesigning the field-based experience component of the program. Integrating improvement science to increase relevance and efficacy, including the voices of students, teachers and the community in the change effort, was foundational to our effort. Specifically, currently practicing administrators in our advanced licensure program use improvement science for the 30-hour, field-based project required in each 10-week course.

The first two of the six improvement principles (see Figure 10.1) were particularly useful in this phase as they helped us to further define the problem and include the users, our licensure students, as key participants in program redesign. To make our work problem-specific and user-centered (Principle 1), gain an explicit understanding of the current experience and identify what works and for whom (Principle 2), in fall 2017, we elicited student perspectives using the empathy data tool to analyze experiences of continuing administrator licensure students (LeMahieu, Grunow, Baker, Nordstrum, & Gomez, 2017; Langley et al., 2009).

Our iLEAD team and department chair had several indictors of the need to pilot a redesign of the field-based project in the professional licensure program. An analysis of empathy data, collected in fall 2017 from licensure students representing seven local districts, some of whom had taken as many as five of the nine required classes, indicated a lack of relevancy and application in the field-based project. We also found that though several licensure students from a district were enrolled in the same classes, opportunities for collaboration on their field-based projects were limited. Our goal was to increase collaborative efforts within the same school or district; further, we hoped to encourage cohorts of students from the same district to enroll as a team and use improvement science to address common problems of practice.

In winter and spring of 2017, we integrated improvement science into each of two advanced licensure courses—Course 1: District, School, Staff Supervision and Evaluation, followed by Course 2: District and School Policy, Operation, Facilities and Finance. Advanced licensure students collaborated with a school/district team at their site to identify a problem of practice aligned with standards assigned to the course, and use improvement science tools, including a fishbone, empathy interview, interrelationship diagraph, aim statement, driver diagram and at last three PDSA cycles, to implement and assess their change initiative.

Activities in the Chartering phase deepened our perspective of the problem from the user's perspective. Change ideas included the following:

- Collaborating with district partners, collecting data from PDSA cycles and adjusting over time. The course design for Course 1 in winter 2018 required the iLEAD team to complete several PDSA cycles and to use that information to plan spring courses and the fall Pilot 2. We explained to advanced licensure students that we were using improvement science to teach them improvement science.
- Partnering with districts to increase multiple perspectives and increased voice to contribute to actions that were contextualized, action oriented, collaborative and met emerging district needs.
- Segmenting our work into a small-scale change in Pilot 1, in which a small (10–20) number of advanced licensure students participated, allowed us to measure the impact of the change prior to exploration of other potential solutions, including asking why the intervention works and not just whether it worked. The 42 students in Pilot 2, spring 2017, benefited from our increased knowledge about what worked.
- Another key change idea involved explicit teaching, coaching, practicing and debriefing the empathy interview tool, thus helping students to understand why empathy is an important aspect of improvement efforts and how to use it. The empathy tool increases data concerning users and their tasks, is an iterative process of refinement, helps to identify the whole user experience and develops multidisciplinary skills and perspectives. Empathy interviews are an important companion to data from schools, districts and counties; onsite visits to schools and communities; and analysis of relevant scholarship; they also help us "embrace students' lived realities as part of their schooling" (Delpit, 2018, p. xiii), thus dramatically increasing cultural responsiveness.

New Learning

Coteaching the courses with three administrators from the LEA team had some distinct advantages. One was that the "on-the-ground perspective" from peers about implementation of improvement science at the district, school and classroom levels improved our credibility with practicing administrators in the class. Though instructors from WSU had an academic understanding of improvement science, only one had used the methodology with teachers in schools. Overall, partnering with the LEA provided us opportunity to respond to variability within and among schools and districts, adjusting our structure and content to meet emerging needs.

We used the empathy data tool for the first time in both the Preliminary and Professional Administrator Licensure Programs' field-based project curriculum. Student feedback on bimonthly and end-of-course reflections was uniformly positive. One professional licensure student wrote:

> Using empathy data with key stakeholders is not an ancillary effort for improvement. Rather, interviewing key stakeholders about their perspective and experience is foundational to understanding if a key change is desired. More importantly, empathy interviews serve a dual purpose on engaging those most likely to be impacted while ensuring that their perspective informs the "what" and the "how" of implementing something new.

New learning also applied to our own collaboration. Though our iLEAD team did not experience discord while implementing this pilot program, we recognized that strong working relationships, a dedicated work ethic and mutual trust were central to our success in this endeavor (Goleman, Boyatzis, & McKee, 2013). We learned that when we regularly incorporated social activities into our work with the students during class and within our team during planning time to "create common memories and strengthen bonds" (Wiking, 2017, p. 142), our work was stronger. We were also aware, as Fullan (2013) notes, "Making small progress in meaningful work is the most powerful stimulant to wanting to do more" (p. 21), a core concept in building strong team relationships and implementing improvement science. In this way, change became a social activity. Each of us willingly devoted many uncompensated hours in the planning, delivery and assessment of these pilots.

Implementation Challenges

One challenge was related to our goal of preventing our school leaders, most of whom were White, middle class and native English-speaking, from perpetuating educational inequities by implementing interventions that reflected the biases of the dominant culture. We addressed this issue by providing student teams an equity-based problem of practice related to the course curriculum and requiring that teams disaggregate data based on ethnicity and race. The problem of practice, for example, in one course was identified as "Teacher supervision and evaluation does not consistently lead to improved, equity-based teacher practice and student performance."

Identifying the core problem for the students at the beginning of the term, in lieu of providing teams latitude and the time to create their own, helped to mitigate another challenge: teaching improvement science to novices within a 10-week time frame. Though we did not teach strategies to identify a problem of practice, we used the time for teams to collaborate and apply improvement science tools.

We were also challenged to include the input of adjunct and tenure-line faculty not engaged in this pilot to promote a shared understanding of what we were doing, why we were doing it and what it might mean long term for our professional licensure program. Collaborating with five iLEAD team members and the adjunct professor while preparing six face-to-face class sessions per term and providing feedback to students left inadequate time for appropriate communication with equally busy program members.

The Chartering phase, where early stages of the change are tested at a small scale, and in our case, resulted in our focus on two discreet professional licensure classes, nears completion. Three questions guide our assessment:

1. Was the change implemented as intended?
2. Were the predicted beneficial impacts realized?
3. Did the change cause harm somewhere else in the system?
   (LeMahieu, Grunow, Baker, Nordstrum, & Gomez, 2017)

Initial data indicates that our changes were implemented as intended. Five change ideas—engagement of district partners as resources and coinstructors, teaming of students from the same district, introduction of the empathy tool, equity-based problem of practice and reflection protocols—were designed, tested and refined over winter and spring 2018. Reflections from two professional licensure students suggest progress on the predicted benefits:

> Improvement Science completely changed the way I think about a problem of practice. Starting with identifying the probable causes of the problem is where I see groups linger. Improvement Science allows you to admire the problem for a short while, but then moves you intentionally into selecting the cause to focus on and consider the user.

> Out of all the courses I have taken lately, I have to admit that this has been the only one that has provided me with a tool to implement in my daily professional life. It helps me both create a positive and collaborative tool and also a detailed path to identify and tackle challenging equity issues. Everyone contributes.

We do not know yet if the change caused harm somewhere else in the system. However, key future activities for our community in Phase 2: Network Learning, will include an analysis of which of our changes worked, for whom and under what conditions (LeMahieu, Grunow, Baker, Nordstrum, & Gomez, 2017). In addition, a small-scale test, a 10-week elective improvement science class using the series of six lesson protocols designed and refined in 2018, will be available in winter 2019. Improvement science, using the learning from winter and spring 2018 pilots, has also been embedded in several professional licensure courses in summer and fall 2018.

Though the composition of the original iLEAD team has changed, WSU is committed to strengthening university/district partnerships, advancing improvement science as an equity-based change process, forming networked improvement communities to strengthen our work and focusing on real problems that matter, key considerations for our entry into Phase 3: Spreading, where our improvements have the potential to influence the introduction of improvement science to scale in our licensure program.

An important consideration throughout all three phases is that, as one nationally recognized teacher leader recently reminded us, the *teachers* are counting on us to prepare future leaders to embrace *their* expertise and deep commitment to reducing educational disparities. Improvement science does just that.

Key Concepts

Quality improvement
Networked improvement communities
Educational disparities

Discussion Questions

1. How do improvement science research and networked improvement communities advance social justice and interrupt educational disparities?
2. What was the role of the networked improvement community in the program changes within Woodland State University? For the local educational agency? For students in the Preliminary and Professional Administrator Licensure Programs?
3. How can faculty in institutions of higher learning, who often bring an academic understanding of improvement science work, prepare themselves to work with practitioners to identify and solve problems of practice?

References

Bell, L. A. (2016). Theoretical foundations for social justice education. In M. Adams & L. A. Bell (Eds.), *Teaching for diversity and social justice* (pp. 3–26). NY: Routledge.

Bryk, A., Gomez, L., Grunow, A., & LeMahieu, P. (2015). *Learning to improve: How America's schools can get better at getting better.* Cambridge, MA: Harvard Education Press.

Chandler, C., Chan, T., & Jiang, B. (2013). The effectiveness of an embedded approach to practicum experiences in educational leadership: Program candidates' perspectives. *International Journal of Teaching and Learning in Higher Education, 25*(1), 79-91.

Delpit, L. (2018). Foreword. In M. Khalifa, *Culturally responsive school leadership* (p. xii). Cambridge, MA: Harvard Education Press.

Emdin, C. (2016). *For white folks who teach in the hood . . . and the rest of y'all too.* Boston, MA: Beacon Press.

Fullan, M. (2013). *Stratosphere: Integrating technology, pedagogy, and change knowledge.* Toronto, ON: Pearson Canada.

Gay, G. (2010). *Culturally responsive teaching: Theory, research, and practice.* New York, NY: Teachers College Press.

Goleman, D., Boyatzis, R., and McKee, A. (2013) *Primal leadership: Unleashing the power of emotional intelligence.* Boston, MA: Harvard Business Review.

Langley, G., Moen, R. Nolan, K., Nolan, T., Norman, C., & Provost, L. (2009). *The improvement guide: A practical approach to enhancing organizational performance.* San Francisco, CA: Jossey-Bass Publishers

LeMahieu, P., Grunow, A., Baker, L., Nordstrum, L., & Gomez, L. (2017). Networked improvement communities: The discipline of improvement science meets the power of network. *Quality Assurance in Education, 25*(1), 5-25.

Peterson, A. (2016). Getting "what works" working: Building blocks for the integration of experimental and improvement science. *International Journal of Research & Method in Education, 39*(3), 299-313.

Theoharis, J. (2018). *A more beautiful and terrible history: The uses and misuses of civil rights history.* Boston, MA, Beacon Press.

Wiking, M. (2017). *The little book of hygge: Danish secrets to happy living.* New York, NY: Harper Collins Press.

CHAPTER ELEVEN

Unraveling Gateway Course Complexity

Graphic Visualizers to Map Improvement

BRANDON SMITH

Brevard College

Abstract

Blue Mountain College (BMC) is in the midst of a multiyear retention improvement initiative that has proven extremely complex, despite the college's small size. In general, as insider research progresses, the resulting data which are accumulated can become difficult to organize. Complexity builds quickly in organizations, and rather than finding new ways of communicating in new data-rich environments, stakeholders often rely on habitual, or outdated formats for organizing information (Bolman & Deal, 2013, pp. 28-40). This improvement project did not begin with knowledge of improvement science (IS) tools; however, the adoption of IS frameworks and graphic visualizers has allowed BMC to better organize, communicate and operationalize complex data resulting from insider research. Thanks to early successes, the college is revising committee reporting practices and increasing usage of graphic visualizers as a means of reimagining data presentation to create a more nimble and trackable improvement effort.

Keywords

gateway course, retention, course redesign, persistence, completion, insider research, action research, student success, graphic visualizer

Background

Blue Mountain College (BMC) was established in the mid-1800s as a private, religious two-year college. Nestled in a small valley in the Appalachian Mountains, the college is surrounded by a low stone wall and sits on a hillside in the center of a charming Appalachian town. The school has a long history of providing educational experiences which capitalize on small class sizes, outdoor adventures and the liberal arts. Total student enrollments have never exceeded 750 students. At one point during the 20th century, the college served as a premier two-year school sending students off to complete degrees at some of the most well-regarded universities in the country. The college has a proud history informed by its motto, the Latin phrase *Ad discendum vita servitium*, which roughly translates to "Learn for a life of service."

Just before the turn of the last century, BMC made a major cultural shift and became a four-year college, offering bachelor's degrees for the first time in its more than 100-year history. Not long after this move, the college began a slow creep toward financial insolvency. The economic downturn in the early 21st century hit the school extremely hard, and the endowment has remained small despite concerted efforts in the development office. For some time, most of the money raised by development each year has gone directly to pay bills rather than add to the endowment.

To combat the financial strain during those early years as a four-year school, the president at that time greatly expanded the athletics program. This action led to an immediate bump in enrollment from new student-athletes, but the very next year enrollment dropped back down to previous levels. One longtime professor described the decline in enrollment as a collegial identity crisis, noting that the established student base was leaving the college as the campus culture made a dramatic switch toward prioritizing athletics. Ten years later, the college continues to have flat enrollments and now has the added costs of maintaining, staffing and transporting numerous sports teams. The irony is that these teams, which many view as a drain on campus resources, have also kept enrollments from plummeting. More than half of all students at BMC are athletes.

Some faculty who have been at the college for more than 40 years will say that there has always been financial hardship at BMC. When looking over the last 10 years, retention numbers at the college have been low but stable, leaving the school in a state of economic hardship that makes growth and improvement a challenge.

Isolating the Issue: Retention

Amazingly, the college recruits and enrolls far more students each year than it can sustain. If the college maintained student retention at the national average, it would likely run out of housing, classrooms and professors within a year or two. The freshman classes at BMC often make up nearly half of total enrollment on the campus, but in 2015–2016, 51% of incoming freshmen chose not to return the next fall. Half of the freshman class leaving the campus set off alarms in the administration offices and signaled to many that the college was supporting neither its mission nor student needs. Worse still, this loss of students equated to about one-quarter of the total tuition revenue, a staggering sum. Upon further investigation, it was realized that the college had been losing about half of the freshman class for some time. To further complicate the situation, the college typically sees further attrition between 20 and 30% during the sophomore year. Four-year graduation rates hover in the 20% range, whereas the national rates for private colleges is close to 70% (NCES, 2016). As one begins to look at the retention numbers, one realizes how a college can fail to thrive despite bringing in record-setting freshman classes year after year.

The question the college was faced with was simple: why would so many students leave after just one year of college? For some, this line of inquiry was the beginning of the complexity issue and also the point at which the conversation spiraled into a whirlwind of suppositions and tangents that made taking targeted action challenging.

In a broad sense, the reason that students were leaving the campus could be simplified in a single word—*value*. A person who perceives that the quality of an endeavor is not in line with the total costs will stop investing time and resources in that endeavor (Langley et al., 2009, p. 218). The perception of value can drive behavior, and ultimately this complex concept is perceived by organizations in terms of systems, relationships, supportive infrastructure, overall integration of services and price (Sakyi-Gyinae & Holmlund, 2018). The current solution for overcoming BMC's low value to freshmen is to bring in ever-increasing freshman classes to maintain the enrollment status quo. This solution is only a stopgap, a way of buying time, and as the campus ages and faculty salaries stagnate, pressure to improve retention numbers has mounted.

The human impact of these low retention numbers has had an erosive and debilitating creep across the campus over the years. Faculty and staff salaries are some of the lowest in the state, with many veteran employees seeing salary compression, which often means they are paid less than new hires in their field of study. Deferred maintenance slowly eats away at building infrastructure and spaces across campus, and the financial strains of the institution often leave stakeholders with scarce resources when it's time to find innovative ways to offer value and quality educational experiences to students.

The school, like many colleges, is heavily dependent on enrollment revenue. Low retention makes it difficult to build financial momentum, and despite the concerted effort of the leadership team the college has been in a position of financial instability for nearly a decade. Hope and direction have come from the recent appointment of a president who secured significant capital funds, balanced the budget and built positive relationships on the campus and in the community. However, for the college to be positioned to develop long-term solutions it must create a new model for serving and retaining students. Without a more effective retention model it will continue to be difficult for the organization to invest in faculty, staff, students and infrastructure.

Retention: The Multiheaded Hydra

Raising retention rates, especially in the first two years at BMC, has been a confounding challenge. From both a financial and philosophical position, having more successful freshman and sophomore students is an easy sell for most stakeholders on campus. To better understand the persistence problem, Blue Mountain College began a partnership with one of the nation's leading consultancies on student persistence, the Farmer Institute for Academic Advancement (FIAA). The FIAA is composed of academic leaders from across the country, all of whom have firsthand experience guiding higher education improvement projects driven by large-scale data collection.

Complexity Cannot Be Avoided

To begin, the Farmer Institute asked the college to assign a committee charged with compiling information on student demographics and final grades in courses. What the college found was troubling. Early data showed that when freshmen earned two or more grades of D or F or withdrew from just two classes, they were 81% more likely to leave the school (Frick-Rupert, 2014). Courses with high enrollments, coupled with large numbers of final grades in the D, F, Withdrawal, or Incomplete range (DFWI) have been classified as gateway courses—so called because these classes either launch students into upper level studies or bar access to the coursework required for degree completion (Koch, 2017).

A faculty written report on the study from 2014–2015 was keen to mention that low course grades was not the only factor impacting retention at Blue Mountain College; more students were leaving the school than were earning low grades. The early report made recommendations that leadership consider some of the following improvements: refine how students were placed in early courses, refine the academic warning system and refine advising methodology. These recommendations recognized that gateway courses were part of the problem, but the initial recommendations focused on external systems rather than considering course redesign. Some changes were made to these systems, but tracking of formative measures in the improvement efforts proved difficult, and the summative assessments yielded sparse change in academic outcomes. If improvements were made through the early efforts, there is little to no documentation tracking how the methods used influenced outcomes. Perhaps in part because of this limited documentation, the retention efforts stalled, and what was learned was never operationalized. In the initial efforts, it seems that as the data increased and curricular and cocurricular causes began to be identified, the sheer volume of information being collected slowed the project. Whatever the reason, the work with the FIAA on campus was put on hold.

However, in 2015–2016, the college had the aforementioned 51% of the freshman class choose not to reenroll at BMC, many of them leaving after just one semester (NCES, 2016). This mass exodus catalyzed a renewed commitment to increasing persistence and degree completion. In one meeting to address the issue, a campus administrator referred to retention as a multiheaded hydra. "You try to deal with one issue," he said, "and two more pop up in its place!" It was clear that many of the stakeholders in the room were frustrated by the complexity of the persistence puzzle. The FIAA and leadership had a frank discussion about next steps and opted to focus the majority of the college's efforts on improving curricular outcomes, rather than splintering efforts across multiple fronts. Although there are many factors at play when working to unpack the complexities of retention, the college realized that if it tried to make every aspect of retention important, it would continue to be hampered by the volume of possibilities. Gateway courses were clearly a problem at the school, and by focusing on academic outcomes in these foundational classes, BMC hoped to better serve freshman and sophomore students.

Improving Academic Outcomes in Foundational Courses

The Farmer Institute for Academic Advancement had been encouraging the college to participate in their proprietary Gateway Improvement Project (GIP) for some time as a means to help improve academic outcomes, and thus retention rates. There is a growing body of literature indicating that curricular redesign can improve academic outcomes (Daiek, Dixon, & Talbert, 2012; Eliason & Holmes, 2012; Merseth, 2011; Schmidt et al., 2010; Twigg, 2003; Van Campen, Sowers, & Strother, 2013; Yamada & Bryk, 2016) However, the gateway courses that most significantly impact freshmen and sophomores, the group most likely not to persist, are often marginalized by faculty and students and, instead, a premium is placed on upper level coursework (Mathews & Newman, 2017).

In the spring of 2017, the college opted to pilot the GIP process and started with two classes: Math 101 (MAT 101) and English 101 (ENG 101). These two gateway courses were chosen because they have some of the highest enrollments on campus and therefore the potential to positively (or negatively) impact the educational experiences of almost every first-year student on campus. The GIP that the Farmer Institute has developed offers schools an online portal to guide an insider research process that depends on mixed methods data collection. The tool is exceptionally comprehensive, and usually invites schools to spend a full year gathering and collating data linked to gateway courses and academic systems. An FIAA scholar is assigned to each participating institution to help collect, organize and synthesize data into reports meant to guide the improvement efforts. The data-collection process is systematic and well informed, but the timeline proved exhausting for some participants at BMC. The full GIP improvement cycle normally takes a minimum of three years, and participants often spend long hours recording and organizing the data.

Committing to the Program

The GIP starts by asking participating schools to commit to seven goals: improved teaching and learning, increased student success as measured by grades, increased student success as measured by retention, increased graduation rates, promotion of a culture of continuous improvement, reflection and additions to the academic conversation on retention and student success and to provide feedback to the FIAA. BMC had no problem agreeing to this partnership and program, as these goals linked directly to the needs of the institution.

Data Collection and Synthesis

The GIP data collection process began during the spring semester of 2017 and was progressing on schedule for the first few weeks. However, because of financial pressure, leadership asked the participating GIP faculty to consider expediting the process. Though the FIAA process usually would have allowed a year for data collection and planning, the college felt they could not afford to wait a full year to test improvements in gateway courses. This decision was fueled by increasing DFWI rates and a larger than expected midsemester exodus of students. The FIAA agreed that even though the data collection for the improvement project was not tapped for completion until January of 2018, a partial redesign was needed for the start of school in August 2017. The task force was wary of redesigning without completing the FIAA process and worried that without fulling delving into the problem, the work might fall victim to the short-term rewards cycle described by Bolman and Deal (2013) in Figure 11.1.

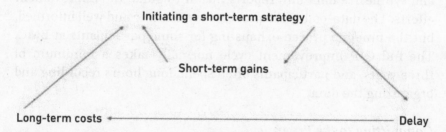

Figure 11.1. Bolman and Deal's systems model with delay illustrates the effects of short-term solutions over time.

In the book *Reframing Organizations: Artistry, Choice, and Leadership*, Bolman and Deal (2013, p. 34) use a systems model with delay to describe what often results when short-term strategies are adopted without considering unintended consequences.

Essentially, short-term strategies that fail to consider complexity often yield short-term gains but, after a delay, may incur long-term costs. This cycle, if unchecked, can repeat itself until resources become so scarce that an organization ceases to function.

To combat this, the team and FIAA looked carefully at the available data as well as at promising practices for improved academic outcomes in gateway courses and formulated a plan that would allow for collection of leading measures and which considered balancing measures to minimize unintended outcomes.

Reimagining Academic Systems

There is mounting evidence of a link between learner-centered teaching and success in gateway courses (Eliason & Holmes, 2012; Merseth, 2011; Twigg, 2015; Yamada & Bryk, 2016). To that end, the FIAA provided a library of webinars and scholarly articles to guide the first course redesign pilot at BMC.

One of the challenges faculty recognized across all courses related to communicating the academic progress and needs of students to a variety of stakeholders. The current model for communicating the academic progress of a student was clunky, time-consuming and lacked uniformity. The process required faculty to fill out a form online that was then relayed through a third party to the student. The student then met with academic support services, but the meetings were rarely documented, and the nature and quality of academic support were not always apparent. In many cases, the missed learning outcomes that were the source of the alert were never clearly communicated, nor was an opportunity to remediate offered. Timing and communication of academic outcomes were challenges that all the faculty agreed was important to address as part of course refinement.

As a first step in the course redesign process, the participating faculty opted to map engagement points in each class where significant learning outcomes were assessed. These engagements points were soon dubbed "Milestones" and were formative assessment points which faculty could use as leading measures of curricular change.

At each Milestone, students who were mastering the outlined learn-ing targets were given green marks on an online spreadsheet system; borderline students were marked with yellow, and students at high risk of failure were marked as red. The faculty also included support assignments for each Milestone. Support assignments were designed with learning outcomes in mind and offered students supplemental opportunities to improve their knowledge of learning outcomes and, in many cases, improve their grades. This system helped to quickly alert faculty, support staff and students to student understanding and application of knowledge at key intervals. These Milestones were also meant to function as balancing measures and serve as a time when faculty were invited to reflect on the process, offer feedback to the entire group and consider whether or not to continue the pilot.

Faculty had designed a system that would allow curricular and pedagogical adjustments to be measured and visualized quickly. This would then allow them to isolate learning outcomes which required further attention, as well as identify pedagogical innova-tions. During the fall pilot, the overall reaction to the work was that it was beneficial for students, but the spreadsheets and monitoring of the Milestones were cumbersome to navigate. It was apparent that a more streamlined model for communicating and visualizing the data would be necessary for the work to continue.

Implementation and Data Collection: Semester One

In the fall of 2017, the GIP faculty were simultaneously piloting Milestones and uploading vast amounts of qualitative and quanti-tative data to the FIAA servers for processing. Bimonthly meetings continued to yield innovation and clearer understanding of prob-lems of practice in gateway courses, but faculty were beginning to fatigue. The team fluctuated between excitement, when new dis-coveries were made in the classroom, and exhaustion, as the data collection and sense-making process took up more and more time.

At the end of a semester the committee had finished the online GIP data upload and began writing a report to synthesize the information housed on the FIAA servers. The resulting report was more than 20 pages in length and included over 60 pages of appendices. Faculty, even those who were vested in the improvement effort, found it difficult to operationalize and track the vast amount of information housed in the report. As the document was being finalized, grades were pulled for the courses participating in the Milestone pilot and the results were heartening. It was found that both math and English grades were the highest they had been in five years. Math was up by 13.2%, whereas English was up 5.8%. Much of the English gains came from non-GIP sections of the course, but the results still bolstered spirits. Most faculty were excited to see academic improvement as a result of their labor; however, others were clearly weary of the effort and cited the bureaucracy and time required to manage the data as limiting factors if the improvement project was to continue.

Improvement Science Tools as Frameworks to Organize Complexity

Committee leadership realized that the current methods of data management and sense-making were cumbersome. The report had useful data, but the sheer volume of information made it challenging for some stakeholders to make use of it. One member of the committee had recently learned of improvement science tools through his graduate program, and he shared processes from four texts with the team which proved foundational in refining the GIP effort at BMC: *Learning to Improve* (Bryk, Gomez, Grunow, & LeMahieu, 2015); *Reframing Organizations: Artistry, Choice, and Leadership* (Bolman & Deal, 2013); Carnegie *90-Day Cycle Handbook* (Park & Takahashi, 2013); and *The Improvement Guide* (Langley et al., 2009). In all of these books, the authors stress the importance of unraveling complexity with graphic visualizers and mental maps. In doing so, large amounts of data can be organized and more easily leveraged for innovation and systems redesign. The tools proved transformational in the GIP team's approach to managing information and reimagining their internal improvement cycles on campus.

Believing Is Seeing: Reimagining Data Organization and Reporting

When considering how to approach sense-making in complex organizational structures, Bolman and Deal advocate that "believing is seeing" (p. 36). The first way the college opted to utilize improvement science tools was in trying to reframe causal data in the annual report.

The Farmer Institute process invited the faculty to collect causal data in two main categories: Principles and Performance Indicators. As mentioned earlier, these data were originally compiled in an online database and then synthesized into a narrative report. The original process, although useful, took the committee months to complete. These data were crucial in understanding the problems surrounding the course redesign process, but because of the online interface it was difficult to visualize the narrative as an interconnected system; despite the use of bullet points and summaries, readers were still losing track of how the systems interacted to yield undesirable results.

A causal systems map, or fishbone diagram, is a mental map for organizing causal factors and underlying problems in a system (Bryk et al., 2015; Langley et al., 2009; Park & Takahashi, 2013). This graphic visualizer served as a useful tool for arranging the causes of low pass rates in gateway courses at BMC. Each larger category, or "big bone," represents a principle from the GIP process (see Figure 11.2).

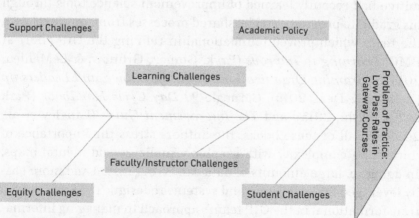

Figure 11.2. Basic fishbone diagram.

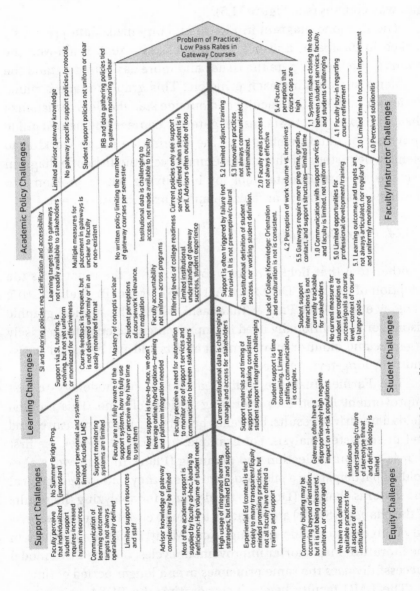

Figure 11.3. Detailed fishbone diagram.

Each larger category is unpacked in subcategories via "small bones," which further reveal how challenges within the systems of each principle are linked to the larger issue of low pass rates in gateway courses (see Figure 11.3).

The fishbone diagram in Figure 11.3 organizes data previously locked in databases and long narratives. As a tool, it allowed the team to quickly navigate the issues and more easily understand the problems surrounding each principle. This graphic made it much easier for both the GIP faculty and outside stakeholders to visualize the complexity tied to success in gateway courses and helped guide conversations and meetings. As the committee began working to identify next steps in the improvement cycle the fishbone diagram became an instrumental tool for identifying which problems to tackle next and how to organize plans to drive improvement.

PDSA: Plan, Do, Study, Act

Another tool that helped reduce complexity in the report was the adoption of the Plan, Do, Study, Act (PDSA) cycle (Bryk et al., 2015; Langley et al., 2009; Park & Takahashi, 2013). This cyclical graphic visualizer is traditionally used in improvement science to concisely organize and monitor improvement efforts and can be scaled across short- or long-term projects.

The Farmer Institute utilizes a similar methodology to test improvement hypotheses over long periods of time. This method yields data-driven results, but relies heavily on lagging measures and end-of-semester analysis. For example, in the FIAA model, the first year is for data collection and planning (Plan). In year two, stake-holders participate in a pilot program where they initiate pedagogical and systems changes (Do). The third year is for analyzing the results of the changes (Study) and creating a plan to either scale up success-ful change or continue revising (Act). Many PDSA applications in the literature map shorter improvement cycles, but the FIAA model successfully uses the same principles over a longer period of time.

The BMC faculty began incorporating the PDSA as a means of visualizing the end-of-semester results from the Gateway

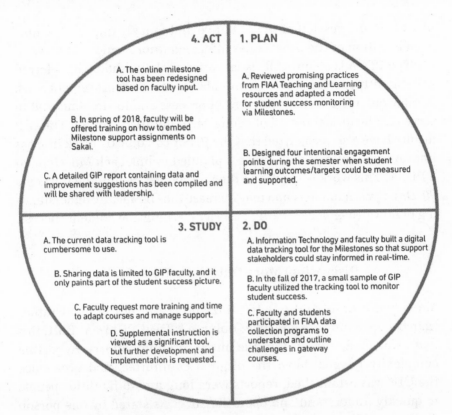

4. ACT

A. The online milestone tool has been redesigned based on faculty input.

B. In spring of 2018, faculty will be offered training on how to embed Milestone support assignments on Sakai.

C. A detailed GIP report containing data and improvement suggestions has been compiled and will be shared with leadership.

1. PLAN

A. Reviewed promising practices from FIAA Teaching and Learning resources and adapted a model for student success monitoring via Milestones.

B. Designed four intentional engagement points during the semester when student learning outcomes/targets could be measured and supported.

3. STUDY

A. The current data tracking tool is cumbersome to use.

B. Sharing data is limited to GIP faculty, and it only paints part of the student success picture.

C. Faculty request more training and time to adapt courses and manage support.

D. Supplemental instruction is viewed as a significant tool, but further development and implementation is requested.

2. DO

A. Information Technology and faculty built a digital data tracking tool for the Milestones so that support stakeholders could stay informed in real-time.

B. In the fall of 2017, a small sample of GIP faculty utilized the tracking tool to monitor student success.

C. Faculty and students participated in FIAA data collection programs to understand and outline challenges in gateway courses.

Figure 11.4. A PDSA of the first semester of the GIP improvement process can be seen in this diagram, which captures the first semester of improvement efforts and offers insight on future improvement.

Improvement Project (Figure 11.4). As a planning and reporting tool, the PDSA made it much easier for outsiders to process the work being undertaken by the GIP faculty by clarifying the linear progression of the improvement process.

The PDSA has been such an effective organizational tool that the committee chairs have since chosen to simplify the biannual reporting model for the committee. Instead of adding lengthy narratives to the report each semester, the committee now updates the ongoing GIP report with an executive summary and a fresh PDSA for each semester. This should make it easier for readers to see the historical progression of the initiative and quickly understand how each iteration of the process has informed improvement efforts.

The PDSA is a powerful visualization tool and should be referred to frequently to remind participants about current improvement aims, to offer outsiders a clear overview of process and future aims and to serve as a historical record of a long-term iterative process. The GIP faculty have also recognized that the PDSA can quickly track in-class improvement efforts and a pilot is planned to link each Milestone to a PDSA. This work is similar to the method detailed in the Carnegie *90-Day Cycle* handbook and may increase the GIP faculty understanding of how pedagogical changes impact learning and student success.

Discussion: More Data, Less Complexity

Many institutions continue to utilize processes out of habit rather than because they are effective (Bolman & Deal, 2013). At BMC this truth was made manifest in the initial retention efforts. Reporting complexity bogged down the original committee, and even once the GIP was established, reports were long and difficult for people to quickly understand and operationalize. As stated by one person involved in the GIP project at BMC, "In an ideal world, we would have known how to utilize improvement science tools sooner in this process. It's a very effective way to organize the data."

As stated before, the college plans to pilot further use of formative PDSAs in every GIP class moving forward. The pilot will increase the frequency of the cycles in a modification of the Carnegie *90-Day Cycle* (Park and Takahashi, 2013). Instructors will monitor the learning outcomes for Milestone assignments at 15- to 30-day intervals over the course of the semester and share innovations with faculty. This should allow for a more nimble and uniform improvement effort and may permit discontinuing time-consuming spreadsheet tracking, which proved onerous to many of the faculty in the initial project pilot. These course-level PDSA cycles should quickly and succinctly provide much of the data needed for the larger Gateway Improvement Project reports.

These minor modifications to the Farmer Institute process have not gone unnoticed at FIAA, and they have plans to work with BMC faculty to discuss the inclusion of graphic visualizers as revisions to their overall processes. It is clear to the FIAA team that improvement science tools have the potential to increase efficiency, facilitate visualized data and operationalize improvement effectively.

Improvement is iterative; you can't apply skills you haven't learned, and you can't abandon a project just because it seems too complex to tackle. The use of improvement science tools at Blue Mountain College was not part of their original design, but the integration of these tools proved useful and informed how the college approached future improvement efforts. The Gateway Improvement Project at BMC is in the early stages, but the improvements to end-of-course grades in the math and English pilots, combined with the positive feedback from many of the participating faculty, are propelling further improvement efforts. The project is building momentum on campus and will be expanding to five additional courses in fall of 2018. This expansion means added complexity for researchers, but the GIP leadership has said that it feels better positioned to manage complex systems and data through the use of improvement science.

Key Concepts

Using graphic visualizers to map complexity
Plan, Do, Study, Act (PDSA)
Causal systems map/fishbone diagram

Vocabulary

Action research: A form of practitioner research that often takes place in educational settings and which is conducted by individuals who will then execute internal organizational change based on the outcome

Gateway course: Classification assigned to courses with high enrollments coupled with large numbers of final grades in the D, F, Withdrawal or Incomplete range (DFWI)—so called because these classes either launch students into upper level studies or bar access to the coursework required for degree completion

Graphic visualizer: A visual representation of a system, structure, plan or other complex organizational framework

Lagging measure: A summative assessment that happens late in an improvement project; knowledge learned from a lagging measure is often difficult to leverage for the benefit of the population from which it was measured

Leading measure: A formative assessment that can be used early in an improvement project as a measure of change efficacy and which can often lead to immediate beneficial change

Discussion Questions

1. What graphic visualizers and mental maps do you see being used most often within your organization? How do they impact workflow and improvement efforts?
2. Where do you see complexity overwhelming improvement efforts in your own organizational context? Can you imagine utilizing graphic visualizers like the PDSA and fishbone to unpack that complexity? What challenges or benefits do you predict might result?
3. If you were part of the GIP team at BMC, what other improvement science tools would you try to incorporate in the effort? What would make incorporation challenging, and how do you imagine these tools would benefit the project?

Class Activities

1. Break into small groups. Find a common organizational challenge (professional development, purchasing, faculty assessment). As a group, work to develop a fishbone diagram that maps the complexity and causes of your shared problem.
2. The fishbone in this study illustrates considerable operational complexity. Choose one bone from the study and work in groups to design a PDSA that might drive improvement.
3. A driver diagram is another tool for improvement that takes the problem established in the fishbone and reframes it as an improvement aim; the causes from the fishbone become change actions that can be tested for improved results. Break into groups and choose one "big bone" from the fishbone in this study and design a driver diagram that might inform future efforts for the GIP.

References

Bolman, L. G., & Deal, T. E. (2013). *Reframing organizations: Artistry, choice, and leadership*. San Francisco, CA: Jossey-Bass.

Bryk, A., Gomez, L., Grunow, A., & LeMahieu, (2015). *Learning to improve*. Cambridge, MA: Harvard Education Press.

Daiek, D., Dixon, S., and Talbert, L. (2012). At issue: Developmental education and the success of our community college students. *The Community College Enterprise*, 18(1), 37–40.

Eliason, S., & Holmes, C. L. (2012). A course redesign project to change faculty orientation toward teaching. *Journal of the Scholarship of Teaching and Learning*, 12(1), 36–48.

Frick-Rupert, J. (2014). *Gateways team report to high impact practices action team*. Unpublished internal report, Brevard College, Brevard, NC.

Koch, A. K. (2017). It's about the gateway courses: Defining and contextualizing the issue. *New Directions for Higher Education*, 2017(180), 11–17.

Langley, G. J., Moen, R. D., Nolan, K. M., Nolan, T. W., Norman, C. L, & Provost, L. P. (2009). *The improvement guide* (2nd ed.). San Francisco, CA: Jossey-Bass.

Matthews, R. S., & Newman, S. (2017). Chief academic officers and gateway courses: Keys to institutional retention and persistence agendas. *New Directions for Higher Education, 2017*(180), 63–73.

Merseth, K. K. (2011). Update: Report on innovations in developmental mathematics—Moving mathematical graveyards. *Journal of Developmental Education, 34*(3), 32–39.

National Center for Education Statistics. (2016). *Integrated postsecondary education data system.* Available from https://nces.ed.gov/collegenavigator/?s=all&zc=28712&zd=0&of=3&id=198066

Park, S., & Takahashi, S. (2013). *90-Day Cycle Handbook.* Stanford, CA: Carnegie Foundation for the Advancement of Teaching.

Sakyi-Gyinae, K., & Holmlund, M. (2018). What do business customers value? An empirical study of value propositions in a servitization context. *Technology Innovation Management Review, 8*(5), 36–43.

Schmidt, H. G., Cohen-Schotanus, J., Van der Molen, H. T., Splinter, T. W., Bulte, J., Holdrinet, R., & van Rossum, H. M. (2010). Learning more by being taught less: A "time-for-self-study" theory explaining curricular effects on graduation rate and study duration. *Higher Education: The International Journal of Higher Education and Educational Planning, 60*(3), 287–300.

Twigg, C. A. (2003). Improving quality and reducing cost: Designs for effective learning. *Change, 35*(4), 22–29.

Twigg, C. A. (2015). Improving learning and reducing costs: Fifteen years of course description. *Change, 47*(6), 6–13.

Van Campen, J., Sowers, N., & Strother, S. (2013). *Community college pathways: 2012-2013 descriptive report.* Stanford, CA: Carnegie Foundation for the Advancement of Teaching.

Yamada, H., & Bryk, A. S. (2016). Assessing the first two years' effectiveness of Statway: A multilevel model with propensity score matching. *Community College Review, 44*(3), 179–204.

CHAPTER TWELVE

Learning to Improve While Improving Assessment of Family Medicine Residents on an OB/GYN Rotation

BROOK A. HUBNER, CECIL ROBINSON,
AND MICHAEL A. LAWSON
University of Alabama

Abstract

This chapter describes a project to improve obstetrics and gynecology (OB/GYN) department evaluations of family medicine (FM) residents. Our work began after recognizing that FM residents on the OB/GYN rotation do not have access to timely data to identify clinical deficits. We summarize initial steps to improve and describe how adding improvement science methods impacted our improvement approach.

We used causal system analysis to establish an understanding of the system and develop predications for improvement (Bryk, Gomez, Grunow, & LeMahieu, 2015). Our working theory hypothesized that improving assessment practices would impact the aim of residents receiving feedback at the two-week point of a 30-day rotation. Our first Plan, Do, Study, Act (PDSA) cycle (Langley et al., 2009) was based on the prediction that if we codified assessment language onto a feedback card, then residents would receive feedback during the rotation. Results from our first PDSA cycle indicated that for faculty to complete timely evaluations, we needed a tool that more directly responded to faculty time constraints and the physical context of the patient care setting.

We discuss lessons learned about the common challenges of an improvement project. We conclude by discussing some unexpected outcomes that have implications for other educators embarking on improvement projects.

Keywords

improvement science, evaluation, family medicine resident

Setting and Background

This chapter presents an ongoing educational improvement project within an obstetrics and gynecology (OB/GYN) rotation of a family medicine (FM) residency program. The improvement project was initially developed at the request of the OB/GYN department chair. She was concerned about the residency program's evaluation process and its utility in helping residents develop, reflect on and learn about their own practice. The improvement project was further facilitated by the primary authors' participation in a university-wide seminar on improvement science. These twin developments structure the primary aims of the chapter: (a) to document our initial lessons learned about improving the evaluation of FM residents during an OB/GYN rotation and (b) to document our learnings about the emergent methodology of improvement science in this setting. Accordingly, the chapter begins with a brief introduction into the assessment structure and rationale for this residency program.

Assessment in Residency Programs

Nationally, FM residents are assessed using milestones—competency-based developmental outcomes of knowledge, skill, attitude and performance—that can be progressively demonstrated throughout residency. For example, to satisfy one competency the practitioner "performs specialty-appropriate procedures to meet the health care needs of individual patients" (Accreditation Council & the American Board of Family Medicine, 2015). Consistently demonstrating this competency is essential to the daily practice of medicine. However, this competency is difficult to assess. It requires assessment of general procedural competence, not the specific *activities* where observation of the resident occurred.

To address this difficulty, medical educators have started to develop assessments that are focused on the activities that comprise these competencies (Shaughnessy et al., 2013). The idea is that faculty assess resident competence within a specific activity. When residents consistently demonstrate performance in an activity over time, in multiple settings or on multiple cases, faculty can make decisions about that resident's competence. In other words, by observing resident performance of an activity, faculty can determine whether the resident can be *entrusted* to perform the activity independently (ten Cate & Scheele, 2007). This type of assessment model has been termed entrustable professional activities (EPAs).

For example, within the OB/GYN rotation, the patient care competency to "perform specialty-appropriate procedures" could be assessed with an activity-specific EPA—"manage an uncomplicated labor and delivery." The emerging practice of codifying and utilizing EPAs to transform broad competencies into "practical, manageable, measurable activities" (Schultz, Griffiths, & Lacasse, 2015, p. 888) permit faculty to provide residents with meaningful formative feedback.

Need for Improvement

This improvement project began after a few FM residents were not successful on their OB/GYN rotations. It is rare that residents do not meet the rotation requirements, but those infrequent failures impact residents and faculty. A repeating resident requires additional faculty oversight, compressing the physicians' time available for teaching, administrative responsibilities and, ultimately, patient care. Residents who repeat rotations delay program completion and are also at risk of not progressing academically.

Residents receive milestone competency-based summative evaluations after completing the OB/GYN rotation. However, the department chair was concerned that these general evaluations did not provide specific guidance for future learning. Although faculty provide formative verbal feedback to residents, the comments are not captured for later reference. Given the cognitive demands and high stress of patient care, the department chair was concerned that residents may struggle to assimilate verbal feedback. These concerns led the department chair to request help in improving the evaluation process for FM residents on the OB/GYN rotation.

Our improvement journey began before fully understanding improvement science language. Initial steps began when one of the coauthors, a curriculum design expert, worked with a medical practitioner to develop the language of EPAs for use in OB/GYN department evaluation of FM residents. This initial stab at the problem was facilitated by disciplinary knowledge about medical education and evaluation and by engineering backgrounds which included training in design thinking and analysis. Using a backwards-curriculum design approach, they generated the goals of the rotation, reached consensus with department faculty and developed EPA language. They created a prototype evaluation tool but did no systems analysis. Their approach was intentional, but they did not thoroughly analyze the system or work to develop a theory of the problem. About the time they were completing the prototype tool, this initial design work was augmented by engagement with an improvement science doctoral seminar. This exposure facilitated a deeper dive into the systems-level processes which could facilitate or impede the development of an enhanced evaluation system.

Accordingly, the first step in our improvement journey was to assess our organizational capacity and readiness to engage in improvement-oriented work (e.g., Bryk et al., 2015; Langley et al., 2009, Lewis, 2015). Three questions were especially salient to our self-evaluation:

- Do we have the disciplinary and practical know-how to pursue this important work?

- Do we have the organizational and human capability to make changes across the organization?
- How can we best engage the targeted recipients and/or users of our change ideas?

Our team included discipline and practitioner experts and novices in improvement science. Although the department chair was the initiator of the project, we were not confident that there was readiness for change across the organization. In keeping with design thinking, we decided to test our initial change ideas using the department chair. This strategy enabled us to fail and learn quickly, thereby avoiding the challenges associated with trying to scale up too quickly (Langley et al., 2009).

To tackle the issue of improving the existing evaluation process, we followed principles of improvement science methodology. We began by analyzing the system producing the negative outcomes, developing a working theory of the problem, identifying high-yield targets, then testing our theory.

Testing the Change

To understand the system and sources of the undesirable outcomes, we needed to understand the daily, routine activities of the physicians. Bryk and colleagues (2015) describe using causal system analysis to make visible the daily process and standard work that comprise the overall "system of work." To improve, we needed to expose system structures and identify the root causes that we hypothesized create the problem for timely written feedback (Langley et al., 2009).

Our work began by meeting with the department chair. During these meetings, we asked a series of probing questions developed to help us understand the system from the perspective of administration (Bryk et al., 2015). The meetings helped us understand the range of teaching, administrative and clinical responsibilities required by residency faculty. We also began to understand the nuances of the busy patient care environment and the competing priorities for faculty time. The discussion illuminated the layers that created a complex system for analysis and helped us begin to visualize the overall structure that hinders resident evaluation.

Bryk and colleagues (2015) explain that a cause and effect diagram can assist with understanding some of the workflow dynamics that accompany the development of resident- and patient-responsive residency programs. Our problem analysis, represented in Figure 12.1, adopted the following improvement-oriented research question: "Why do residents not have timely access to data that can help them identify their clinical deficits while they are engaged in their OB/GYN rotation?"

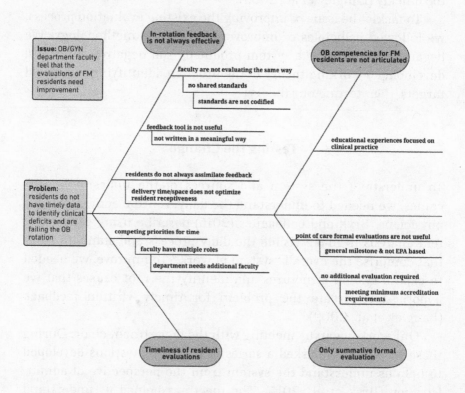

Figure 12.1. Fishbone diagram representing key factors contributing to lack of timely data on residents' clinical deficits.

Our causal systems analysis enabled us to identify four key factors related to this important question. Two of the four are described here. For instance, we learned that although residents are evaluated by faculty, the evaluations are often not delivered in a timely manner. We also learned that a key reason for this difficulty can be traced to the fact that faculty have multiple academic and clinical roles and that the department is not fully staffed. In short, faculty appeared to be bogged down in competing priorities.

Our question about these underlying dynamics also revealed that when faculty provide residents with "in-rotation" feedback, it is not always delivered in an effective or responsive manner. For example, faculty did not have codified or shared standards for resident evaluation, and they also lacked an evaluation tool that enabled them to identify specific skills deficits.

Finally, causal systems analysis helped us learn that residents were receiving feedback from the faculty verbally, and this practice often made it difficult for them to reflect on and learn from their own clinical experiences. For this reason, we began to theorize that an improved evaluation system would need to lessen the cognitive load experienced by residents while they were "on the floor" so that they could assimilate feedback more effectively.

After iterative questioning, we started to develop confidence that we were "seeing the system" (Bryk et al., 2015, p. 58) that gives rise to the current set of evaluation practices and outcomes. For this reason, we decided to test our knowledge of the system by developing a driver diagram. This driver diagram (Figure 12.2) depicts our "theory of change" for how we might improve the system in service of our primary aim. In this case, our aim was to complete two-week rotation evaluations for 50% of residents by the midpoint of the rotation.

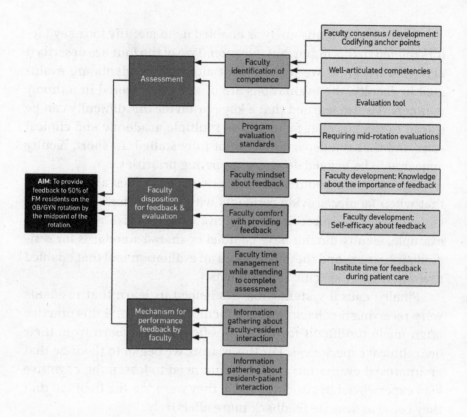

Figure 12.2. Driver diagram of theory of change.

In this initial driver diagram, we hypothesized that our primary opportunities for impacting the timeliness of resident evaluations were driven by three primary drivers: (a) regular and consistent assessment, (b) faculty disposition for feedback and evaluation and (c) the mechanisms for performance feedback by faculty. We further hypothesized that our ability to move those primary drivers depended on our ability to impact several systemic processes. These system processes are represented in our driver diagram as secondary drivers. For example, our casual systems analysis led to believe that regular and consistent assessment is a primary driver impacting the timeliness of resident evaluation. However, for assessment to be effective, faculty need to have access to shared measures, and they also need to have shared definitions for how they are defining resident competence.

Once our driver diagram was developed, the next step in our improvement journey was to identify the most optimal "point of entry" into the system. Put differently, given the complexity of the resident education and evaluation system, we needed to develop some sort of systematic process that could help us understand the best place to start.

To assist in this effort, we developed an interrelationship diagram, graphically presented as Figure 12.3. The interrelationship diagram is a tool that can help improvers identify those systems processes that, if properly manipulated, can have the most broad-reaching impact. In our case, we decided to use the interrelationship diagram to help us identify the most potent/high-leverage primary driver.

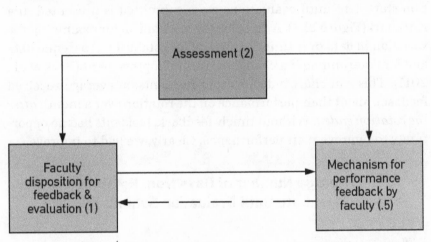

Figure 12.3. Interrelationship diagram showing cause and effect relationship between drivers.

Our interrelationship diagram indicated that assessment represented the highest leverage primary driver. The arrows pointing toward the other two drivers indicate that we think changes in assessment can and will positively impact faculty disposition for giving feedback and the mechanism by which faculty gather evaluation data. Accordingly, we began to formulate initial change ideas that might impact key aspects of the overall assessment system. We directed our initial change ideas toward improving the accompanying secondary drivers depicted in Figure 12.2—namely, program evaluation standards and faculty recognition of resident competence. More concretely, we theorized that changes to the assessment tool would enable us to achieve our aim of evaluating 50% of the residents on the OB/GYN rotation by the midpoint of the 30-day rotation.

Developing Our Initial Change Idea

Before we tested our change idea, we needed to collect baseline data to understand the extent to which our change ideas resulted in an improvement. Our data of the average number of days from the rotation start date until evaluations were submitted is presented in a run chart (Figure 12.4). A run chart is mechanism for examining the variation in data over time. It is useful for establishing baseline data and for determining if a change results in improvement (Bryk et al., 2015). This run chart indicates that residents on average received feedback about their performance on the rotation over a month *after the rotation ended*. Without timely feedback, residents had no opportunity to improve their performance. Clearly, we had to improve.

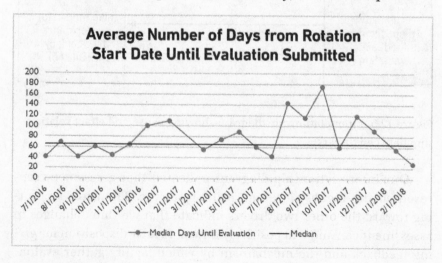

Figure 12.4. Run chart indicating length of time between rotation start date and evaluation submission.

Plan, Do, Study, Act Cycle

With these data in hand and a theory of change elucidated, we began our first PDSA cycle (Langley et al., 2009). This cycle tested the process of residents receiving specific feedback by the end of the rotation. We theorized that a simple feedback card with agreed-upon assessment language would facilitate timely feedback. We hypothesized that the department chair would ask residents for the evaluation card and find it a quick task to complete. Cards were placed at high-traffic nurses' stations.

During the first PDSA cycle, the department chair used one evaluation card, obtained from her secretary. The resident was evaluated on an activity that he had performed on the OB/GYN rotation two months prior. Neither resident on the current rotation received a written feedback card.

To understand why the first test yielded suboptimal results, we conducted empathy interviews (Langley et al., 2009) with the department chair and with the residents on the rotation. These interviews enabled us to develop a user-centered view of the evaluation process from the perspective of both residents and faculty. The department chair commented on the availability of the tool and the evaluation wording. She explained that the complexity of the patient care environment was not conducive to searching for an evaluation of care. She remarked that often she had time to reflect on residents' work during protected administrative time and valued having an evaluation tool at her fingertips. She felt the anchor points were helpful for the card that she completed.

The resident interviews were illuminating. Residents could not carry the card with them because it did not fit in their scrub pocket. They described the busyness of the wards and did not think that a card at the nurses' station would be utilized. They suggested a mobile tool as they always have their phone, which fits in their scrub pocket.

This cycle led us to revisit our driver diagram. The provisional nature of the theory (Bryk et al., 2015) makes driver diagrams living documents (Langley et al., 2009). We developed a new theory of change by reexamining the driver diagram (Figure 12.5).

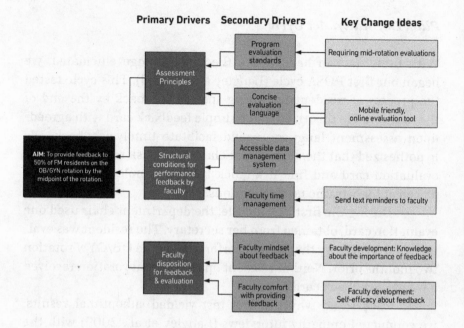

Figure 12.5. New theory of change after PDSA Cycle 1.

In this new driver diagram, our theory of change remains focused on assessment. We modified the change idea based on what we learned in the first PDSA cycle—ease of access to the assessment tool impacts its timely use. Because the tool was not used in a timely manner, we added a change idea of text reminders for future PDSA cycles.

PDSA Cycle 2

Our second PDSA cycle was determined by the Study and Act phases of our first PDSA cycle, which highlighted problems with our initial assessment tool. For this second cycle, we predicted that developing an online, mobile friendly tool had the potential to impact the timeliness and ease of feedback as well as the faculty's disposition for giving feedback. We developed an assessment tool, and PDSA Cycle 2 was underway at the time this chapter was written.

Discussion

Design thinking (Brown, 2008) is both problem- and user-centered, and is a philosophy that guided our approach. Our efforts focused on visualizing the standard work processes (Bryk et al., 2015) that impacted faculty's ability to complete evaluations in a timely manner. We learned that focusing on the users and understanding the context of the problem is much harder than originally anticipated.

We visualized the daily work practices and developed an understanding of the complexities of the system using a fishbone diagram. The fishbone diagram nicely explained the system, but it was hard to not become overwhelmed by the complexity. It was tempting to focus on multiple processes instead of beginning with one small change.

We followed the philosophy of being minimally intrusive and learning quickly (Bryk, 2015). By starting small we could quickly learn if our provisional theory was on track. We decided on an aim of providing an evaluation to 50% of the residents by the midpoint of the 30-day rotation.

Byrk and colleagues (2015) suggest that measurable improvement can be scaled provided that mechanisms are in place for systematic and meaningful organizational learning. To this point, while our aim statement was clear and measurable, we also needed to develop a well-articulated theory of action that would enable others to understand the "logic" of our work, as well as the lessons we learned along the way.

What We Learned

Byrk and colleagues (2015) describe *solutionitis* as "jump[ing] quickly on a solution before fully understanding the exact problem to be solved" (p. 24). Solutionitis impacted this project. Our initial user-centered approached focused on solving the problem for the faculty. We theorized that uniform assessment language on a card would facilitate faculty evaluation of residents. Although we tried to approach our theory of the problem with a blank slate using the tools of improvement science, the idea of an EPA card had been developed before the engagement with the improvement science seminar.

This solution influenced our thinking and highlights a challenge with improvement work. Those involved in the system will have ideas about how the issue can be fixed. It is difficult to not let preconceived notions filter into the improvement thought process. Purposefully examining the system and developing a data-driven theory of change was challenging, as it was often far too easy to allow prior assumptions and ideas about how to best "fix" things guide our process.

The suboptimal outcomes of the first PDSA cycle also highlighted that we ignored a key part of the system. Digging deeply to identify all elements of the system would have helped us visualize the standard work of faculty *and* residents. We focused on the faculty piece of the equation first, thinking that we were being user-centered. But in focusing on faculty and not the learners, we failed to fully appreciate the context of implementing this change idea in relation to the impact on the residents. We should have included the residents in the development of our initial theory of the problem. This led us to ignore Bryk's (2015) advice about being careful to not impose change on others.

The fact that one card was completed led us to believe that there was motivation to use the evaluation tool. It also demonstrated that the EPA language and anchor points on the tool were helpful. We also learned that faculty may prefer to evaluate a resident when it is convenient for their daily schedule rather than in the hectic patient care environment.

Our study of the first change idea reflects the importance of examining the kernels of behavior in the process. Embry and Biglan (2008) discuss evidence-based kernels as a way to drill down to essential units of behavior. By finding these "fundamental units of behavior" (p. 75), we can test these kernels to understand if the intervention is efficacious. The activities described by faculty and residents indicate that their behavior in the patient care environment is not conducive to finding an evaluation card and completing it by hand. Focusing on the unit of behavior that prompts evaluation, we determined that the tool should be at the residents' or faculty's fingertips.

From this first PDSA cycle and subsequent empathy interviews, we learned how important seeing the entire system is to improve outcomes. Our empathy interviews indicated that residents were an integral part of the system. We learned that we could not understand the exact problem to be solved without understanding the perspective of this core part of the system.

We also learned the importance of intervening by impacting the conditions that affect improvement. Our first PDSA cycle hypothesized that an improved assessment tool would result in in-rotation feedback to residents. The outcome and attempts to develop a second PDSA cycle with a modified tool highlight the larger ecology of the system. In an organization, multiple systems are at work, and these systems impact each other. We discussed how faculty have multiple responsibilities, and this is also true for the coauthors.

Our attempt to implement a second PDSA cycle was hampered by competing responsibilities. In this case, improvement work was not the standard work of the coauthors. The improvement project was an add-on to regular responsibilities and this comes at a cost. With multiple competing interests, something must give. Typically, the standard work needs to be done; add-ons are attended to when there is more time. Pulling back to a high-level view of the problem, could it be that time should feature more prominently in our change theory? The results of our second PDSA cycle will be instructive in this regard.

This improvement journey is situated in the context of medical education. Although medical education may have nuances that differentiate it from other levels of education, at the core it is a system in which instruction and learning occur. Medical practitioners are still educators who benefit from learning more about their teaching practice. In this case, the faculty involved learned more about the importance of assessment.

The concept of faculty learning about their own teaching can be shifted from the hospital setting to school districts. If schools are to work better, it is important to measure if learning is happening. An improvement project focused on impacting student learning can also help faculty make their own learning objectives more explicit. In this case, our aim was not met in the first PDSA cycle. However, the PDSA cycle had an unintended consequence of impacting our own metacognition. Learning occurred unexpectedly as faculty recognized the importance of assessment. The affordances for impacting professional development make this case less about improving resident evaluation and more about how an improvement project can have implications for enhancing the ability of faculty to understand and improve their own practices.

Key Concepts

Causal system analysis
Driver diagram
Fishbone diagram
Interrelationship diagram
Plan, Do, Study, Act cycle
Run chart
Solutionitis
Theory of change

Discussion Questions

1. What are some strategies to keep solutionitis out of design-based thinking if our natural inclination is often to think about a solution when faced with a problem?
2. How might you tell when you've done enough questioning to "see the system" and begin developing a theory of change?
3. What does the run chart tell us about stable or unstable processes in the system?

Class Activities

1. Work through a hypothetical, second PDSA cycle using our hypothesis that an online feedback tool will impact the timeliness of feedback, the ease of providing feedback and the faculty's disposition for giving feedback.
2. Examine the run chart for runs, shifts and trends and describe what was found.
3. You have started working on an improvement project when you learn about improvement science. Describe how you will keep solutionitis out of your design thinking, given that you have already started working on a solution.

References

Accreditation Council for Graduate Medical Education and the American Board of Family Medicine. (2015). *The Family Medicine Milestone Project.* Available from http://www.acgme.org/Portals/0/PDFs/Milestones/FamilyMedicineMilestones.pdf?ver=2017-01-20-103353-463

Brown, T. (2008). Design thinking. *Harvard Business Review, 86*(6), 85–92.

Bryk, A. S. (2015). 2014 AERA distinguished lecture: Accelerating how we learn to improve. *Educational Researcher, 44*(9), 467–477.

Bryk, A. S., Gomez, L. M., Grunow, A., & LeMahieu, P. G. (2015). *Learning to improve: How America's schools can get better at getting better.* Cambridge, MA: Harvard Education Press.

Embry, D. D., & Biglan, A. (2008). Evidence-based kernels: Fundamental units of behavioral influence. *Clinical Child and Family Psychology Review, 11*(3), 75–113.

Langley, G. J., Moen, R. D., Nolan, K. M., Nolan, T. W., Norman, C. L., & Provost, L. P. (2009). *The improvement guide: A practical approach to enhancing organizational performance.* Charlottesville, VA: Wiley.

Lewis, C. (2015). What is improvement science? Do we need it in education? *Educational Researcher, 44*(1), 54–61.

Schultz, K., Griffiths, J., & Lacasse, M. (2015). The application of entrustable professional activities to inform competency decisions in a family medicine residency program. *Academic Medicine, 90*(7), 888–897.

Shaughnessy, A. F., Sparks, J., Cohen-Osher, M., Goodell, K. H., Sawin, G. L., & Gravel, J. Jr. (2013). Entrustable professional activities in family medicine. *Journal of Graduate Medical Education, 5*(1), 112–118.

ten Cate, O., & Scheele, F. (2007). Competency-based postgraduate training: Can we bridge the gap between theory and clinical practice? *Academic Medicine, 82*(6), 542–547.

Contextualizing Improvement Science in K–12 Education

CHAPTER THIRTEEN

Growth and Grading
Overcoming "Grades Don't Matter" in Middle School

CASSANDRA THONSTAD

Newberg Public Schools and Portland State University

Abstract

In this chapter, the author will focus on the process of implementing improvement science as a new administrator in a struggling building. Students at Mystery Middle School, a high-poverty grade 6–8 school that houses just over 500 students, have traditionally underperformed compared to their partnered middle school within the district on grades, normed formative assessments and state tests including the Smarter Balanced. (The Smarter Balanced Consortium is a national standardized test for mathematics and English language arts based on the Common Core State Standards English Language Arts and Math exams.) The problem of practice being explored in this case study is common to many educational institutions: Over 20% of our students were failing nearly half of their classes only two months into the school year and the failure rates were disproportionately representing males and students of color.

Through the use of improvement science principles, beginning with empathy interviews, seeking to see the system at large and brainstorming many potential change actions, staff at Mystery

Middle School were able to implement one change idea at a small scale that is now creating big changes across the system.

From once a week meetings between the assistant principal and 14 individual students to building-wide grade checks and the implementation of a homeroom system, course failures have dropped dramatically and growth on normed formative assessments and state tests has increased as well. The process for the empathy interviews, questions asked and sample response, fishbone and driver diagrams, results and change implementation throughout PDSA cycles, and next steps will all be shared as a way to model how small changes that stem from a solid understanding of the overall system creating the problem at hand really can lead to large-scale changes that impact student learning and success.

Although most applicable at the PK–12 system level, the process used in this case could be replicated across buildings in community colleges and in higher education institutions. The goal of this chapter is to share a case study where improvement science principles have been utilized to take steps toward solving a common problem of practice experienced across the nation in PK–12 schools.

Keywords

empathy interviews, intervention, variability, middle school, failing grades

The Setting/Background

Mystery School District (MSD) is a smaller district serving approximately 5,000 K–12 students across 10 schools: 6 elementary schools, 2 middle schools, 1 high school, and 1 alternative high school. MSD is situated in a rural community of 22,500 people with strong industries of wine production and agriculture and is well known for recreational opportunities in and around the area, making tourism a large contributor to the local economy. Two of the elementary schools qualify as Title I schools and both of these feed into Mystery Middle School.

Mystery Middle School is a grade 6–8 school and has approximately 500 students with self-selected racial identifications of 1% Asian, 1.8% Black/African American, 25.3% Hispanic, 4.8% multiracial, and 66.5% White. Approximately 15% of the students receive special education services and 49% applied and qualified as economically disadvantaged. There are 11 languages spoken by the students and 21% qualify as English Language Learners.

In comparison, the district's other middle school, Close Middle School, is also a grade 6–8 school that has approximately 600 students with self-selected racial identifications of 2% Asian, >0.01% Black/African American, 16.5% Hispanic, 4.3% multiracial, and 76.2% White. Approximately 15% of the students receive special education services and 39% applied and qualified as economically disadvantaged. There are 6 languages spoken by the students and 15% qualify as English Language Learners.

Between the two middle schools, Mystery Middle School is known for being more racially diverse when looking at student demographics, with a higher population of students receiving special education (SPED) services, English Language Learner (ELL) services and qualifying for free and reduced lunch. Mystery Middle School also has a reputation for a more challenging environment, with student discipline issues and a perceived lack of both family and community support.

Need for Improvement

In the spring of 2017, one administrator left the district, leaving a vacancy and opening up the opportunity for administrative shifts throughout the system. The superintendent opted to meet with each administrator across the district and discuss skillsets, needs for growth, aspirations and building needs. In the end, 8 out of 10 buildings were impacted by administrative shifts announced in early May for the following school year.

In these shifts, both the principal and assistant principal at Mystery Middle School were shifted to other buildings and Olivia, a veteran principal with nearly a decade of experience in administration and over 35 years of experience in education overall, was moved into the principal role. Diana, an instructional coach with 4 years in educational leadership roles and 12 years in education, was just completing her administrative license and was appointed to the assistant principal role. With leadership changes across the district, it was well known that Mystery Middle School was being assigned these two new leaders because the school was not meeting performance expectations and significant changes needed to be made. This was the environment that Olivia and Diana were stepping into in August of 2018.

Knowing failing grades had been a significant issue the last several years at both middle schools, but at Mystery Middle School in particular, Diana used the student grading system to pull grades in October. It was astounding to see that 14% of the students were already failing three or more classes only seven weeks into school. Only two weeks later, that number had raised to 21.3%, meaning roughly one in every five students was failing nearly half their classes or more. Looking deeper into that 21.3%, the data showed an even more disparaging picture (Table 13.1).

Table 13.1. School Demographics and Demographics of Students Failing Three or More Classes

	Female	Male	Hispanic	White
School demographics	50.0%	50.0%	25.3%	66.5%
Demographics of students failing three or more classes (percentage)	37.5%	62.5%	39.3%	53.6%

The school was disproportionately failing males and Hispanic students at an alarming rate, continuing to increase the achievement gap for students that moved through the system within the district. Something had to be done.

Testing the Change

Study and Act: Using Empathy Interviews to See the System

Having learned, studied and used improvement science for three years, Diana sought to use this structure to better understand the system as it currently existed and to have an impact on student learning. The first step was seeing the system through the eyes of those closest to these failing grades through empathy interviews with students, families and teachers. Students were chosen randomly through hallway encounters, disciplinary conversations and lunchtime interactions. Families of some of those students were contacted through phone calls or at parent-teacher conferences. Teachers were selected based on those that currently assigned the most failing grades and the least failing grades. Results from these conversations were used to create the fishbone diagram in Figure 13.1.

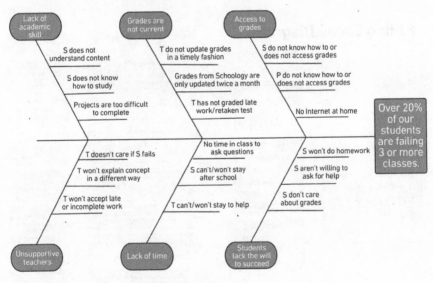

Figure 13.1. Failing grade fishbone diagram.

Based on conversations with all of these users, themes that contributed to current failing course grades were student lack of academic skill, unsupportive teachers, out-of-date grades, lack of time for students to receive support, students' attitude towards grades and willingness to succeed and inadequate access to see student grades. Armed with a better understanding of the system as it currently existed, Diana sought to determine possible drivers and action items.

Plan: Seeking to Determine Action Steps

Working through the improvement science driver diagram process, Diana collaborated with colleagues to identify several possibilities for action items that might impact student learning and, over time, allow for greater student success as measured by course grades. Some of the options could be implemented immediately whereas others required systemic change that would prove difficult for both a new leader in the building and a new-to-the-profession administrator. The driver diagram in Figure 13.2 was created.

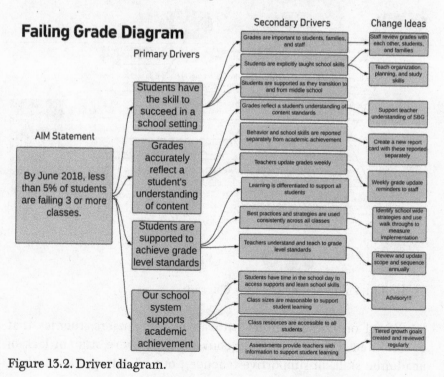

Figure 13.2. Driver diagram.

Based on the improvement science concept of starting small with a bias toward action, Diana chose 14 students who had a high frequency of office visits because of disciplinary concerns and were also on the list at the beginning of November for three or more failing grades. These students would be called into the assistant principal's office once each week to check grades and create an action plan for improving academic performance.

Do: Trying Out a Small Change

Once a week, Diana sent call slips to see students out of the classroom. There was not a strict discipline about when this happened, rather a strict discipline within the conversation around grades, using the following structure:

1. Check-in/Relationship-Building
   a. Diana asked general, nonacademic questions:
      i. How are you?
      ii. How was your weekend?
      iii. Is that a new shirt?
2. Academic Check-In Predictions
   a. Diana asked specific academic questions:
      i. What are you proud of from this week?
      ii. What will we see when we look at your grades?
      iii. How do you think your grades have changed and why?
3. Grade Check
   a. Diana accessed grades online
   b. Student wrote grades as percentages, noting growth with stars
   c. Diana asked student about changes:
      i. Why do you think that grade changed?
4. Planning
   a. Diana asked specific, directive questions for planning:
      i. What grade or grades would you like to focus on this week?
      ii. Why are you choosing that class?

               iii. What are your next steps?
       b. Diana asked specific questions for support:
            i. What do you need help with?
           ii. Do you know how to access that help?
5. Conclusion
       a. Diana reviewed the plan with the student as the student wrote the plan on the grade check form
       b. Students repeated back the plan as Diana wrote the plan on a Post-it Note
       c. Diana kept the grade check form, Student kept the Post-it Note and placed it in the agreed-upon place for reference
           i. Post-it might have gone on a planner page, the front of the student's binder or other location

Study: Taking a Closer Look at the Changes

Over the first two weeks, 3 of 14 students improved one or more grades by a full letter grade, 1 increased by a single failing grade, and 8 of the 10 remaining students had improved grades based on percentages in more than half of their classes. Students reported being less overwhelmed by failing grades after making plans each week to focus on one or two specific classes and were amazed at the grade changes they were seeing so quickly. (Note: One of the strategies used in the structured conversations was to teach students how to identify and prioritize which assignments would have the biggest impact on their grades.)

Act: Adapting the Change

After talking with students and seeing the results after only two weeks, Diana went to her principal to discuss what she was seeing. As a team, Diana and Olivia determined the next step would be to adapt the process by scaling it to a few more staff members, specifically the administrative and counseling team.

Plan: Setting Up the Next Cycle

Olivia agreed to take on 10 students from the list and asked counselors if they would do the same. Each of these three staff chose students based on already knowing them and having some relationship with them, determining they could have an impact on these students through that connection. They would also go through the process of grade checks with their students each week and, as a team, they would continue to measure academic progress.

Do: Adapting the Adaptation

Within a couple of days, word got out about what the administrative and counseling team was doing as students were pulled out of class, returning 10 minutes later and sharing why they had been called to the principal's or counseling office. Between the four on the team, 45 students (approximately 9% of the student population) were being pulled out in those initial days.

This created a buzz around the school and 10 other staff members, including secretaries, teachers and educational assistants, reached out to choose students they had relationships with from the list as well. By the end of the fourth day, there were 86 students with a mentoring adult. Staff met with their students using a similar protocol for the next three weeks. Although staff were asked to stay as close to the procedure as possible, variability within these conversations and with the frequency of the conversations themselves was inevitable.

Study: Reviewing the Scaled Changed

After three weeks, the administrative and counseling team reviewed the data comparing the 86 students who were receiving support to the 26 students who were not based on the original list of failing students generated in November. The results are shown in Table 13.2.

Table 13.2. Comparison of Changes of Grades for Students Receiving Support or Not Receiving Support

.	November to December	
	With Support	**Without Support**
N	86	26
Less D/F (percentage)	24.42%	23.08%
More D/F (percentage)	12.79%	19.23%
Students with all passing grades (percentage)	3.49%	0.00%
Average number of D/F difference	-0.22	-0.08

Most notably, three students receiving support no longer had any failing grades and although the percentages of students with fewer D's and F's were similar, the percentage of students without support now failing more classes was astounding.

Act: Adopting the Plan to Seek Additional Evidence

The team felt like they were providing a stopgap to the worsening grades at least and wanted to continue the work. All 14 staff agreed to continue supporting their students until the end of the semester, which was six weeks away, with a midpoint check-in scheduled in three weeks to review results.

In December, the administrative team created student profiles and invited all staff to select one, share with others and reflect on the current reality for many of their students at the monthly professional staff development. These profiles included racial, gender and grade demographics; current academic standing; and a short narrative about each student. The goal of this activity was to help build empathy for what students were going through and to help staff see potential barriers for academic success.

At the staff professional development in January, the administrative team walked the staff through a crosswalk of the district equity and grading policies, asking partnered staff members to each read one policy and share out connections, wonderings and epiphanies during their conversation. By reviewing board policy, staff better understood the K–12 perspective on the purpose of grades and the stance on equitable outcomes for all students.

In January, the team also decided to share the November to December and December to January data with the whole staff. At that time, 4 staff members not included in the initial 14 volunteers saw the results and chose to start implementing grade checks each week with all of their students through the end of the first semester. This resulted in some students connecting with two or three adults about their grades each week and nearly 200 additional students engaging in grade checks from January to February weekly with staff, meaning approximately half the staff and students were now participating in weekly grade checks. The data the team reviewed at each point are presented in Table 13.3.

Table 13.3. Month to Month Comparison of Failing Grades for Students With a Support Person Versus Students Without a Support Person

	November to December		December to January		January to February	
	Students With Support Person	Students Without Support Person	Students With Support Person	Students Without Support Person	Students With Support Person	Students Without Support Person
N	86	26	86	23	83	21
Fewer D/F (percentage)	24.42%	23.08%	15.20%	15.40%	44.58%	76.19%
More D/F (percentage)	12.79%	19.23%	10.50%	23.10%	15.66%	0.00%
Students with all passing grades (percentage)	3.49%	0.00%	7.10%	0.00%	13.25%	9.52%
Average number of D/F difference	Down 0.22	Down 0.08	Down 0.38	Down 0.06	Down 0.13	Up 0.02

In addition, there were significant changes in work toward closing the achievement gap, with a higher percentage of students identifying as male or as Hispanic improving their grades by the end of the semester (see Table 13.4).

Table 13.4. Comparison of Demographics Of Students in the School and Demographics of Students With Improved Grades From November to February

	Female	Male	Hispanic	White
School demographics	50.0%	50.0%	25.3%	66.5%
Failing students with improved grades from November to February (percentage)	42.6%	57.4%	39.7%	48.5%

Another significant data point was the number of students with three or more D's and F's dropped from 23.5% in November to 13.5% in February. Although there was still a lot of work to be done, the team felt grade checks were helping to support student academic success.

Implementation

What was most notable from January to February was the significant change for students without a documented support person in ways that were showing academic success. When the team met to discuss these results, they recognized the substantial increase in the number of students participating in grade checks each week for the last few weeks and wondered what might be the next step. The staff of Mystery Middle School asked if they could trade the weekly planner checks for weekly grade checks instead. As a staff, the agreement was made to have all students do weekly grade checks in their Humanities classrooms. Because of this, some of the original 14 staff stopped doing weekly grade checks, knowing these were happening in a different classroom environment. Olivia and Diana continued meeting with their students for weekly grade check-ins, as did some of the other staff volunteers, but the regularity of these interactions was lessened. After a full semester of weekly grade checks across the entire system, the team reviewed extensive data at the end of the year, including course grades (see Table 13.5), a nationally normed local formative assessment (see Table 13.6), and Smarter Balanced Test results (see Table 13.7).

Table 13.5. Overall Comparison of Grades for Students Receiving Support and Students Who Did Not Receive a Support Person

	February to June	
	Students Receiving Support	Students Who Did Not Receive a Support Person
Fewer D's and F's	34.94%	36.36%
More D's and F's	33.73%	45.45%
Improved two or more grades to passing	8.43%	4.55%
No longer have failing grades	14.46%	9.09%
Average number of D's and F's	Down 0.11	Up 0.54

Table 13.6. Comparison of Local Normative Assessment Data Between the Two District Middle Schools-One With and One Without Grade Check Interventions in Place

	Winter ELA Local Exam	Spring ELA Local Exam	Change	Winter Math Local Exam	Spring Math Local Exam	Change
CMS	65.5%	66.2%	0.7%	55.3%	51.9%	-3.4%
MMS	65.2%	73.4%	8.2%	53.0%	52.7%	-0.3%

Table 13.7. Comparison of Nationally Normed Assessment Data Between the Two District Middle Schools-One With and One Without Grade Check Interventions in Place

	2017 ELA SBAC	2018 ELA SBAC	Growth	2017 Math SBAC	2018 Math SBAC	Growth
CMS	53.9%	48.0%	-5.9%	40.6%	35.4%	-5.2%
MMS	49.4%	56.7%	7.3%	32.1%	38.9%	6.8%

In implementing grade checks across the building, the team determined two main ideas they wanted to focus on based on observations during the second semester.

1. Students seemed to benefit from having grade checks on a weekly basis. Specifically, having weekly grade checks was helping close the achievement and learning gaps seen at MMS.
2. Students benefited from these conversations more when the conversation was with a staff member whom they had a relationship with, regardless of whether they were in an academic class with that staff member.

With these two main ideas at the center of their work, Mystery Middle School decided to institute a homeroom class for the 2018–2019 school year, where smaller numbers of students would be assigned a specific staff member, including teachers, educational assistants, secretaries and administrators who would meet with that small group of approximately 15 students to review grades, support through study hall and focus on community-building. These groups will be mixed grade levels and mixed gender, meeting four times a week for 25 minutes each day, with a focus on supporting students both academically and socially.

One of the greatest challenges with this radical scale-up and class creation is the variability the staff acknowledges will exist in a building-wide implementation. Questions have already been asked, such as, "How do we know grade checks will be implemented uniformly across the building?" or "How do we know the grade checks are what is making the difference?"

With data stored for nearly a decade, Mystery Middle School will be able to look at overall trends for grade changes at the end of each semester to see what changes might be observed, including the following:

- Number of failing grades
- Number of students failing three or more classes
- Failure comparisons by gender, race and grade

- Homerooms with the least and most academic growth
- Empathy interviews with students, families and staff

In the shorter term, the administrative and counseling team will partner to look at grades on a monthly basis, reporting out students they are concerned about and noting general trends across the building. One greatly anticipated difference the team is looking forward to is that any student identified as being at risk with failing grades will already have a person assigned through the homeroom system to provide support and guidance.

It is the hope of the team, that by looking at data each month, additional adjustments and changes can be made throughout the year to the new homeroom class to encourage academic success that will result in passing grades at the end of each semester and higher overall achievement.

Discussion

Really Understand YOUR System

Ask questions and emphasize both local data and the voices of users. In understanding a problem deeply, it is important to recognize that your system is set up to get exactly the results it is getting. If students are failing, your system is set up for that to happen. If staff are excited and collaborating together regularly, your system is set up for that, too. It is essential to deeply understand your system from the eyes of the users. Also, do not be afraid to use empathy interviews as data. Some of the best learning the staff at Mystery Middle School accomplished was through empathy interviews.

Start With the Coalition of the Willing

Allow early adopters to share the work. Many different works now discuss what Malcolm Gladwell (2002) calls "the tipping point," acknowledging that there is an initial group of early adopters who will be excited about the latest and greatest ideas, whereas others will hold out until the bitter end. By starting small and sharing data and discoveries, asking questions throughout the process, early adopters at Mystery Middle School signed on and shared their excitement. Other staff followed, taking initiative from staff leaders' suggestions and experiences, keeping the work user-centered and having a great impact on the classroom.

Be Prepared to Be Flexible

Don't wait to change what you are doing for one student if it will help. In starting small, it was easy to adjust grade checks for each student. As the scale got larger and more students were involved, it was more difficult because variability meant there was more to track and focus on for staff members. Most staff wanted to have a set routine and procedure they would follow each time to ensure consistency and authenticity in the grade checks happening across the building. The continual challenge is to balance consistency with quality support. Do not be afraid to change a routine if it means a student will benefit. We are, after all, here to support students first and foremost.

Share Data Often

Keep the conversation alive and data driven. Each time data was shared, whether it was in a small team meeting or an all staff professional development, the conversation was open to questions and reflections. This opportunity to think deeply about the work requires great trust, but it allowed all staff members the opportunity to engage and to support forward progress. As data was shared, staff were able to make suggestions that better supported students and to step up as leaders of the work.

Key Concepts

PDSA cycle
Empathy

Discussion Questions

1. How might you use empathy interviews to better understand your system from the users' perspective and to gather actionable information?
2. What is the value in sharing data and what is the most effective way to share that data based on desirable outcomes?
3. How can you engage colleagues and staff in asking more questions to see the system that currently exists?

References

Gladwell, M. (2002). *The tipping point: How little things can make a big difference.* Boston, MA: Back Bay Books.

CHAPTER FOURTEEN

Using Improvement Science in Professional Learning Communities

From Theory to Practice

RYAN CARPENTER
Estacada School District

DEBORAH S. PETERSON
Portland State University

Abstract

Improving student outcomes in schools has proven elusive in too many schools and districts in our nation, persistently leaving behind the most vulnerable students and families in our communities. Although many districts are using professional learning communities (PLCs) to bring teachers together to improve teaching practices through collaboration, additional strategies may improve the efficacy of PLCs. Over time, the purpose and effectiveness of PLCs may have diminished, requiring a fresh look at the tools, instruments and theories that will help schools improve. This chapter provides a case study of how one district combines the tools and theories of improvement science within the structure of the DuFour PLC model, and how the district will evaluate the impact of this strategy on student achievement, particularly the success of students of color, students with disabilities and students experiencing poverty.

Keywords

improvement science, PLCs, school improvement, school change, teacher leadership, equity

Background for Improvement Science

Improvement science has garnered successful outcomes in other fields such as healthcare, and although the research on the impact of using improvement science in schools is developing, evidence from schools in our state piloting improvement science indicates it has promise as we work to reduce educational disparities in our state and nation. As Peterson and Carlile share in chapter 8 of this book, these disparities are pervasive and have created an educational system in which the race and ethnicity of our nation's students predict the student's educational attainment. This injustice cannot continue in public schools in our country. Thus, the Cascade Falls School District (CFSD), where Superintendent Rao is now in his second year, has used professional learning communities (PLCs) for the past year and is now using PLCs as a strategy for implementing IS. Although the name of the district and superintendent are fictional, the chapter draws on teacher, superintendent and coauthor experiences in their work with IS in several districts.

The improvement science model (Bryk, Gomez, Grunow, & LeMahieu, 2015) employed by Superintendent Rao in this case study includes Plan, Do, Study, Act (PDSA) cycles to examine an organization's or team's work and processes. PDSA cycles require the team to examine how the context (Lewis, 2015) creates variability that results in inconsistent outcomes. IS asks the following questions:

1. What specifically are we trying to accomplish?
2. What change might we introduce and why?
3. How will we know that a change is actually an improvement?

Given that PLCs and IS complement one another, Superintendent Rao is using PLCs to implement IS.

Background

This case study describes work in the Cascade Falls School District, made up of public schools in a rural district in the northwest United States. Cascade Falls School District (CFSD) serves students in grades K–12 with two K–5 elementary schools, one 6–8 middle school and one 9–12 high school. The student population consists of more than 1,500 students and is 80% White, 17% Hispanic/Latino, 1% African American, 1% Asian and 1% American Indian. Fifty percent of students qualify for free and reduced lunch, 10% were classified as English Language Learners and 16% receive special education services.

The district's 300 staff members consist of 8 administrators, 100 teachers and almost 200 support staff. Superintendent Rao is a new leader in the district, and in his first year of leadership, CFSD embarked on a transformational leadership effort focused on a system-wide implementation of DuFour model professional learning communities (PLC) for all grade- and content-level teaching teams in the district. The collaborative culture being installed in the CFSD is a new practice. Teachers in the past have primarily worked in isolation and have seldom shared student outcomes and teaching strategies with their peers.

Several school structures exist to encourage and support teachers in their development of curriculum and project design, including eight days of professional development training and two hours every Wednesday to practice the DuFour PLC framework. One third of the teaching staff attended a national PLC summit sponsored by Solution Tree. In addition, a nationally recognized speaker visited the CFSD to work with individual teacher teams. The majority of the teachers appreciate the autonomy but also acknowledge that it often takes more time than allotted and significant effort to develop meaningful and rigorous curriculum for all their students.

Need for Improvement

The educational field is riddled with top-down reform initiatives that have failed to address inequitable student learning outcomes for students from low socioeconomic backgrounds and students of color (Lee & Reeves, 2012; Mathis, 2010; NAEP, 2015). Over the past century, there has been a steady consolidation of decision-making power at the district, state and federal levels, far removed from the classroom and the context in which teaching and learning occurs (Berube, 1994; Bryk et al., 2015; Darling-Hammond, 1994; DuFour & Marzano, 2011). These remote education reform decisions are often constructed as a "one-size-fits-all" solutions and fail to take into account the significant variability in what counts as effective teaching and learning strategies from class to class and school to school (Bryk et al., 2015). Consequently, many reforms fall short in fulfilling their promise to improve student achievement and high school graduation rates for underserved students. Teachers, who are often the target of such reforms, experience what some call "initiative fatigue."

Many educators acknowledge that our deepest insights come from action, followed by reflection and a search for improvement. Every person who enters the field of education should have both an opportunity and an obligation to be a leader (DuFour & Marzano, 2011). Rick DuFour has committed over 36 years to improving student achievement through teacher team collaboration in PLCs. DuFour argues that a PLC is an ongoing process in which educators work collaboratively in recurring cycles of collective inquiry and action research to achieve better results for the students they serve (DuFour, DuFour, Eaker, Many, & Mattos, 2016). Despite the popularity of PLCs in today's educational initiatives, the practice of a PLC continues to represent a road less traveled in public education. Many teachers and administrators prefer the familiarity of their current path, even when it is evident that it will not lead them to their desired destination (DuFour, 2010).

Masalach and Jackson (1986) define burnout as a three-dimensional concept: emotional exhaustion, loss of a sense of personal accomplishment and depersonalization. Emotional exhaustion includes teachers' tiredness. When teachers' emotional resources are drained, tiredness develops, and depersonalization occurs. The role of teacher is arguably among the most demanding while also having the highest impact on student outcomes. Teachers cope with the numerous demands of an uncertain society and high-stakes expectations, contributing to high levels of burnout among teachers, with one third leaving the profession within five years of starting (Farmer, 2017). It seems the national focus is on everything in education that is not working (Mehta, 2017). When teachers are stressed, it not only affects their quality of life and well-being, it also impacts their teaching performance, which in turn directly impacts their students' academic performance.

DuFour and Eaker (1998) identified a number of reasons past efforts to improve schools have failed. They included "the complexity of the task, misplaced focus and ineffective strategies, lack of clarity on intended results, failure to persist, and lack of understanding of the change process" (p. 17). PLCs are different from the failed efforts of the past because they address these issues, so the improvement efforts can be sustained. As DuFour (2010) noted, "Researchers who have studied schools where educators actually engage in PLC practices consistently cited those practices as our best hope for sustained, substantive school improvement" (p. 6). Teachers are a critical component in PLCs: "Teachers contribute to sustaining learning communities when they shape practices and experiences around shared values and beliefs" (Jenlink & Jenlink, 2008, p. 315). These shared values and beliefs create a culture focused on the learner and make the PLC essential to ongoing student success.

Hattie (2009) concluded the best way to improve schools was to organize teachers into collaborative teams. Despite the fact that teacher teams are conducting this work together, student achievement across the United States continues to stagnate. To address this, many educational experts have analyzed new ways for teachers to ensure students of all backgrounds achieve educational success. The DuFour model PLC is a proven system, in which teacher teams share the workload, discuss effective instructional techniques and provide intervention and enrichment opportunities for the students who need extra supports (Hattie, 2009); however, through this system of teacher development, new problems of practice have emerged.

Although teacher burnout and lack of involvement in change efforts are one indication of the need for improvement, another indicator is student outcomes. Nationally, student performance data is not improving quickly enough, nor among the populations who have not historically been served by our schools: students of color, students living in poverty and students with disabilities. Despite the fact that teacher teams are conducting PLC work together, student achievement across the United States continues to stagnate. The 2009 PISA scores showed that 18% of 15-year-olds in the United States do not reach the PISA baseline of a level two in reading proficiency (Organisation for Economic Co-operation and Development, 2011). To put this into perspective, the National Center for Education Statistics (NCES) estimates that of the 4.1 million 15-year-olds currently enrolled in U.S. public schools (Hussar & Bailey, 2013), if 18% of these students fail to meet the baseline PISA level two for reading, it means nearly 738,000 students every year are considered incapable of "participating effectively and productively in life" (Organisation for Economic Co-operation and Development, 2011).

Testing the Change

Research on the impact of using improvement science in schools is developing and our case study contributes to the research on improvement science by examining the use of PLCs as a strategy for implementing IS. For example, in Rao's district, PLCs examine student content standards, rewrite expectations in their own words, create common assessment rubrics and then utilize the rubrics to determine if their teaching strategy was effective (DuFour, Eaker, & Many, 2006). The inquiry cycle might be a month, a term or a full year or more. Teachers ask the following questions:

1. What do we want students to learn?
2. How do we know if they learned it?

3. What do we do for those who did not learn it?
4. What do we do for those who did learn it?

Unless teachers can answer each of these questions with credible evidence, they will not be able to accurately direct their improvement efforts (DuFour, 2010). Without a sufficient number of skilled people to enact these cultural, structural and pedagogical changes, capacity-building cannot occur. In addition to providing PLCs to help expand teachers' instructional skills, school leaders provide an array of opportunities for teachers to extend their leadership expertise in conversations, coaching, mentoring, networking and new teacher instruction (Kaplan & Owings, 2017).

In order to build the organizational capacity to effectively run a PLC, the leadership needs to create the conditions in which to develop a collaborative environment. Principals cannot simply direct teachers to set up and join a PLC. For teachers' capacity to grow and positively impact students, the principal needs to ensure that certain basic structures are in place (Kaplan & Owings, 2017). First, the principal must create and sustain the school culture and conditions to support teacher and student learning. Second, the principal must develop a shared unity of purpose about the important problems the school faces. Third, the principal needs to hire educators who have (or can develop) the deep expertise in approaches to improving teaching, learning and leading (Williams, 2009).

Determining a school's primary focus requires collecting and analyzing data that regularly highlights progress toward the goals of improving teaching and learning and linking these with ongoing professional discussions about that progress. In these ways, teachers and leaders come to agree on their priorities, share norms about best practice and hold each other accountable for the results (DuFour et al., 2016). Actively participating in this process develops a sense of ownership and commitment about the goals they want to reach, making follow-through more likely.

While the structures listed above are key takeaways for educators interested in developing an improvement culture at their school site, teachers will experience challenges using the tools and methods of improvement science without a solid foundation in a collaborative culture. Using DuFour's PLC framework allows teacher teams to maintain an intentional focus on student learning while using improvement science techniques to collaboratively address problems of practice that increase teacher agency and capacity.

A concept that may increase teacher agency and capacity while also allowing for variation of context is to address challenges through what is known as "standard work" (Sharrock, 2018). In many professions, portions of the work are standardized to reduce variation. Doctors have checklists for routine procedures to ensure that a high-level standard of care is met. A set routine in a teacher's classroom that supports an already identified student behavior may be a more accessible target for iteration compared to testing out a new teaching practice. The desired student behavior provides an easily identifiable measure that teachers can collect data on as they iterate on the already established routine (Sharrock, 2018).

In some cases, the nature of the problem also causes challenges to collecting useful data. Developing student literacy, mathematical agency or vocabulary acquisition are all complex processes with a myriad of interconnected variables (Evangelista, 2017). Recognizing the significant cognitive load that a full day of teaching already demands, where does the cognitive work of data analysis fit in? What data do teachers find useful? And what data-collection methods build on teachers' already powerful classroom observational skills? And most importantly, what contributes to a teacher's sense of efficacy and fulfillment, conditions that harness their passion and cause them to thrive in their roles as teachers (Marshall, 2009; Peterson, 2014).

Implementation

Given that PLCs and IS have such high potential to create conditions for teacher success in each classroom and due to what Superintendent Rao views as complementary concepts, he is using PLCs to implement IS. For example, in the CFSD, PLC members examine student content standards, rewrite expectations in their own words, create common assessment rubrics and then utilize the rubrics to determine if their teaching strategy was effective, as described earlier in this chapter.

For the Plan stage of the PDSA cycle, each individual teacher team identifies a student learning objective to focus on. The team focuses on the PLC question "What do we want students to learn?" During this step, teachers work together to analyze the common core state standard, collectively rewrite the standard into their own words, identify individual learning targets within the standard and clarify what proficiency looks like. Clarifying what is essential that each student know and be able to do requires that collaborative teams literally become "students of the standards." Rather than each teacher trying to figure out what the standards mean, teachers study the standards with their colleagues (Mattos, 2011). Although the term "pacing guide" has inherited a negative connotation in many circles (primarily because they often become too prescriptive and rigid), collaborative teams must engage in discussions around the topic of time allocation, regardless of whether it is called "pacing guide," "time allocation guide," or in the case of the CFSD and many other districts, "backward planning." Figure 14.1 presents an example of a backward planning template we use.

During the Do stage of backward planning and implementation in the individual classroom portion of the PDSA cycle, the teachers execute their lessons with their shared understanding of the standard guiding their teaching. Individual teachers are encouraged to be creative in how they instruct and assess learning in their classrooms. Teachers collect student work samples. As individual teachers test new strategies in their classrooms, they share insights with the other members of their collaborative teams and continually look for ways to improve their instruction to meet the needs of all students. It is also during this time that the PLC team collaboratively constructs a common formative assessment. Importantly, discussions of standards should also address the question of how much data will be needed to assess proficiency and when this data should be gathered. For example, will one assessment with a significant number of

Backward Planning Assessment Design Template
2018-19

Team: 2nd Grade   Date: 10/3/18

1. Which Essential Learning Standard(s) will we address within this unit?

NBT.1 Understand that the three digits of a three-digit number represent amounts of hundreds, tens, and ones; e.g., 706 equals 7 hundreds, 0 tens, and 6 ones. Understand the following special cases:

NBTA.1.A 100 can be thought of as a bundle of ten tens- called a "hundred"

NBTA.1. B The numbers 100, 200, 300, 400, 500, 600, 700, 800, 900 refer to one, two, three, four, five, six, seven, eight, or nine hundreds (and 0 tens and 0 ones)

2. Essential Question:

How does the position of a digit in a number affect its value?

3. Develop rubric(s) for ELS(s) (link here, copy/paste, or create below):

Standard	1	2	3	4
2.NBT.A.1 Understand that the three digits of a three-digit number represent amounts of hundreds, tens, and ones; e.g., 706 equals 7 hundreds, 0 tens, and 6 ones.	Unable to understand that the three digits of a three-digit number represent amounts of hundreds, tens, and ones; e.g., 706 equals 7 hundreds, 0 tens, and 6 ones	Inconsistently understands that the three digits of a three-digit number represent amounts of hundreds, tens, and ones; e.g., 706 equals 7 hundreds, 0 tens, and 6 ones	Understands that the three digits of a three-digit number represent amounts of hundreds, tens, and ones; e.g., 706 equals 7 hundreds, 0 tens, and 6 ones	Can solve word problems/riddles to understand/ identify a number (vocab: even, odd)
Target 1: I can tell the value of an underlined digit.				
Target 2: I can draw a model to represent a number.				
Target 3: I can tell number by looking at a model.				

Figure 14.1. Backward planning example.

questions be preferable, or would shorter, more numerous, formative assessments be better? Are we looking at progress over time, or a single, summative assessment (Mattos, 2011)? In Figure 14.2, the second grade team created formative assessment questions that will be given on a mutually agreed-upon date.

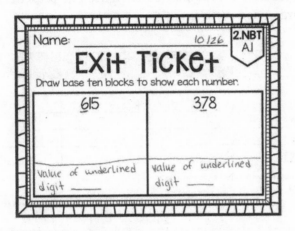

Figure 14.2. Formative assessment.

Next, teachers enter the Study phase of the cycle. Teachers use the locally created common assessment rubric to evaluate student learning and analyze the outcomes. The team focuses on the PLC question "How do we know if students learned what the standard requires?" Deep, rich discussion around the issue of common scoring ultimately leads to valuable and critical discussions about a number of related topics. For example, how will each question or parts of questions be weighted? How much weight will be given to homework or class projects? Will students be allowed, or even required, to redo work? If so, under what conditions and how much weight will be given to work that has been redone? These are but a few of the questions highly effective teams tackle (DuFour, 2010).

In the last stage of the PDSA cycle, teachers use the analysis to inform their teaching. Teachers use the common assessment rubric to evaluate student learning and analyze the outcomes. The team focuses on the PLC questions "What do we do for those who did not learn it?" and "What do we do for those who did learn it?" During the data analysis portion of the PLC, teachers determine the percentage of students proficient by target and gather their data into one document for all members of the collaborative team to view when discussing the data. Our teachers preferred to use Google Docs for ease of access for all team members. Figure 14.3 presents how CFSD teachers organized their data.

Learning Target 1

	Number of Students Below Proficiency	Number of Students at Proficiency	Number of Students Above Proficiency
Teacher 1	7	8	8
Teacher 2	7	10	5
Teacher 3			
Teacher 4	8	5	5
Teacher 6	4	5	10

Which students need more time and support?
Learning Target 1

	Students Identified for Intervention, Practice, or Enrichment	Planned Instructional Strategy
Additional time and support	26	Small group reteaching, hands on manipulatives continue math stations/games, calendar/number talks
Additional practice/enrichment	28	Continue math Stations/games, hundreds place in small group, practice with partner
Enrichment	28	hundreds place in small group, practice with partner to hundredths place, expanded form

Figure 14.3. Example of data organizer.

Looking at this initial overview of the data allows teachers to address areas of strength and areas to grow within each classroom and across the team. Teachers also can discuss any surprises in the data and make sense of the student learning in each classroom compared to the whole grade level or course. Once there is a common understanding of student learning, it is then critical to acknowledge and discuss which students are proficient and not proficient, or proficient, close to proficient and far from proficient by target. During this discussion, teachers are looking for trends among outcomes of students of color, recent immigrants and students living in poverty, as well as individual student data. They also discuss specifics regarding student work: what evidence of learning distinguished the work of proficient students from others? Next, teachers examine the evidence of the work shown by students close to proficiency and compare and contrast that student work to the work of proficient students. After this rich discussion about teaching and learning occurs among the team members, the PLC team creates a fishbone diagram identifying the problems of practice, collectively creates a strategy to engage in intervention and enrichment strategies and conducts another PDSA cycle to address the needs of each of their students. Figure 14.4 provides one example of a fishbone diagram from a teacher team attempting to address the needs of English learner students in a specific unit.

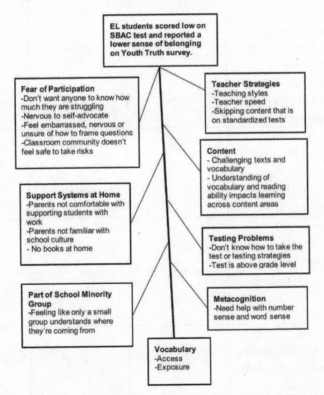

Figure 14.4. A fishbone diagram.

The Cascade Falls School District has experienced early success within one year of implementation of improvement science in their PLCs. Significant growth in student outcomes was reported in the elementary and high school levels. Furthermore, students identified for special education services also experienced substantial gains under this model. Table 14.1 presents the improvement in student achievement outcomes experienced after just one year of using PLCs to implement IS.

Table 14.1 Cascade Falls School District 2017–18 student growth in state assessment

Grade Level/School	Percent Passing 2017 State Standardized Test	Percent Passing 2018 State Standardized Test	Percent Increase
Fourth Grade English Language Arts (Ponderosa Creek Elementary)	55%	65%	118%
Fourth Grade English Language Arts (Juniper Flats Elementary)	15%	50%	333%
Fourth Grade Math (Juniper Flats Elementary)	5%	44%	880%
Fifth Grade English Language Arts (Ponderosa Creek Elementary)	20%	40%	200%
Fifth Grade English Language Arts (Juniper Flats Elementary)	40%	46%	15%
Eleventh Grade English Language Arts (Cascade Falls High School)	80%	87%	9%
Eleventh Grade English Language Arts—Students With Disabilities (Cascade Falls High School)	10%	45%	450%

In order to maintain decision-making over how students are taught and assessed on their learning, teachers need to have a shared knowledge base. A shared understanding of how learning occurs and its dependence on the individual, the collective group and the learning environment is an important framework for developing solid pedagogical practices and classroom structures that promote student achievement and equity. Challenges to developing a shared knowledge base include teachers' past experiences and current beliefs about the purpose of schooling and the isolated nature of teaching. Each educator brings a unique perspective and set of goals to their practice. At times, those goals are at odds with the broader institutional and cultural conversations around the purpose of education. Since shared knowledge is coconstructed, creating a unified goal such as equitable student outcomes require ongoing dialogue and collective consideration (Biesta, Priestly, & Robinson, 2015).

One of the hopes for improvement science is that the tools and methods can be used by teachers to engage in inquiry to achieve more equitable outcomes for all their students. In order to achieve this goal, teachers need to first recognize that the tools are useful to their practice. Using the fishbone diagram, interrelationship digraph and driver diagram tools in the initial professional development workshops provided teachers with a shared experience in which they deepened their own understanding of their identified problems of practice.

Discussion

Generating a shared knowledge base and common vision of teaching and learning while assuming responsibility for student outcomes is crucial if we are to end the educational disparities experienced by children of color, children with disabilities and students living in poverty. Teachers who feel that they are an integral part of an improvement community and that they can meet the learning needs of all their students are more likely to iterate on new and existing teaching strategies and be willing to collaborate and learn together (Marzano, 2017), thus benefiting our students.

The challenges teacher teams have experienced in generating a shared knowledge base included limited generation of sharable evidence of change ideas working and the continued silo nature of classrooms. These challenges underscore the complexity involved in developing a shared knowledge base for teaching and learning. In order to develop common practices, a shared vision for what good teaching and learning looks like must first be developed. This requires teachers to discuss common problems of teaching, their possible root causes and what student learning looks and sounds like within a given context. Improvement science tools and methods can help facilitate this process and may be enhanced if paired with other structures that support additional shared experiences within the PLC structure.

Although we do not yet have outcome data in this case, we plan to use IS strategies and tools to measure the implementation of the DuFour model PLC with IS. This use of PLCs to implement IS ensures that those closest to the problem of increasing student achievement, our teachers, are those who identify the change, measure the impact of the change and adjust—quickly—to ensure the change benefits their particular students. For us, one of the most powerful parts of IS is that these teachers, who have the deepest and richest expertise in teaching and who have made teaching their life's calling (Marshall, 2009), are respected and valued (Peterson, 2014) in an improvement effort that is more likely to succeed with their leadership and their expertise.

Discussion Questions

1. Consider an unsuccessful change process in your setting.
   a. To what do you attribute the failure?
   b. What data indicated it was a failure?
   c. Were there any positive and unintended outcomes?
2. What would you strongly encourage Superintendent Rao to consider regarding his context as he implements improvement science through PLCs?

3. What information do you still need about the context of the CFSD to ensure the successful implementation of IS through PLCs?

Class Activity

1. Examine one change effort that you engaged in within the past five years that was successful.
   a. To what do you attribute the success of the change process?
   b. What data did you use to indicate it was a success?
   c. Were there any positive unanticipated outcomes of the change process? Any negative unanticipated outcomes of the change process?

References

Biesta, G., Priestly, M., & Robinson, S. (2015). The role of beliefs in teacher agency. *Teachers and Teaching: Theory and Practice, 21*(6), 624–640.

Bryk, A., Gomez, L., Grunow, A., & LeMahieu, P. (2015). *Learning to improve: How America's schools can get better at getting better*. Cambridge, MA: Harvard Education Press.

Berube, M. R. (1994). *American school reform: progressive, equity, and excellence movements, 1883–1993*. Westport, CT: Praeger.

Darling-Hammond, L. (1994). Performance-based assessment and educational equity. *Harvard Educational Review, 64*(1), 5–30.

DuFour, R. (Ed.). (2010). *Raising the bar and closing the gap: Whatever it takes*. Bloomington, IN: Solution Tree Press.

DuFour, R., DuFour, R., Eaker, R., Many, T., & Mattos, M. (2016). *Learning By Doing: A Handbook for Professional Learning Communities at Work* (Third). Bloomington, IN: Solution Tree Press.

DuFour, R., & Eaker, R. E. (1998). *Professional learning communities at work: best practices for enhancing student achievement*. Bloomington, IN; Alexandria, VA: Solution Tree Press ; ASCD. Retrieved from http://public.eblib.com/choice/publicfullrecord.aspx?p=3404964

DuFour, R., Eaker, R., & Many, T. (2006). *Learning by doing: A handbook for professional learning communities at work*. Bloomington, IN: Solution Tree Press.

Dufour, R., & Marzano, R. J. (2011). *Leaders of learning: How district, school, and classroom leaders improve student achievement*. Bloomington, IN: Solution Tree Press.

Evangelista, V. (2017). Are your team members working together or simply working? *TD: Talent Development, 71*(4), 102–103.

Farmer, L. (2017). How to beat teacher burnout: With more education. *Education Digest, 83*(2), 13–16.

Hattie, J. (2009). *Visible Learning: A synthesis of over 800 meta-analyses relating to student achievement*. New York, NY: Routledge.

Hussar, W., & Bailey, T. (2013). *Projection of Education Statistics to 2021* (No. 2013-008). Washington, DC: U.S. Department of Education. Retrieved from https://nces.ed.gov/pubs2013/2013008.pdf

Jenlink, P. M., & Jenlink, K. E. (2005). *Portraits of teacher preparation: learning to teach in a changing America*. Lanham, MD: Rowman & Littlefield Education in partnership with the Association of Teacher Educators. Retrieved from http://catalog.hathitrust.org/api/volumes/oclc/58536702.html

Kaplan, L. S., & Owings, W. A. (2017). *Organizational behavior for school leadership: Leveraging your school for success*. New York, NY: Routledge.

Lee, J. and Reeves, T. (2012). Revising the impact of NCLB high-stakes school accountability, capacity, and resources: State NAEP 1990–2009 reading and math achievement gaps and trends. *Educational Evaluation and Policy Analysis 34*(2), 209–231.

Lewis, C. (2015). What is improvement science? Do we need it in education? *Educational Researcher, 44*(1), 54–61.

Manju, M. (2017). Relationship of emotional intelligence with secondary school teachers' burnout. *Indian Journal of Health & Wellbeing, 8*(8), 819–821.

Marshall, J. M. (2009). Describing the elephant: Preservice teachers talk about spiritual reasons for becoming a teacher. *Teacher Education Quarterly*, 25–44.

Marzano, R. J. (2017). *The new art and science of teaching* (revised and expanded ed.). Bloomington, IN: Solution Tree Press.

Maslach, C., & Jackson, S. E. (1986). *Maslach Burnout Inventory Manual* (2nd ed.). Palo Alto, CA: Consulting Psychologist Press.

Mathis, W. (2010). The "'common core'" standards initiative: An effective reform tool? http://greatlakescenter.org/docs/Policy_Briefs/Mathis_NationalStandards.pdf. Retrieved from http://epicpolicy.org/publication/common-core

Mattos, M. (2011). *Prerequisites for standards-based reporting.* Available from http://www.allthingsplc.info/blog/view/120/prerequisites-for-standards-based-reporting

NAEP - Mathematics and Reading. (2013). Retrieved November 4, 2017, from https://www.nationsreportcard.gov/reading_math_2013/#/state-performance

Organisation for Economic Co-operation and Development, National Center on Education and the Economy (U.S.), Programme for International Student Assessment, & OECD Directorate for Education (Eds.). (2011). *Strong performers and successful reformers in education: lessons from PISA for the United States.* Paris: OECD.

Peterson, D. S. (2014). A missing piece in the sustainability movement: The human spirit. *Sustainability: The Journal of Record, 7*(2), 74–77.

Reeves, D. B. (2002). *The Leaders Guide to Standards: A blueprint for educational equity and excellence.* San Francisco, CA: Jossey-Bass.

Sharrock, D. (2018). The impact of improvement science professional development on teacher agency. Retrieved from https://escholarship.org/uc/item/47t07lhx

Stamou, S., Camp, S., Stiegel, R., Reames, M., Skipper, E., Watts, L., ... & Lobdell, K. (2008). Quality improvement program decreases mortality after cardiac surgery. *The Journal of Thoracic and Cardiovascular Surgery, 136(2),* 494–499.

Williams, H. S. (2009). Leadership capacity—A key to sustaining lasting improvement. *Education, 130*(1), 30–41.

CHAPTER FIFTEEN

Implementing Professional Learning Communities

Improvement Required

JACQUELINE HAWKINS, GARY A. HENRY,
SARA J. JONES, KRISTI L. SANTI
AND KEITH A. BUTCHER
University of Houston

Abstract

This illustrative chapter focuses on an elementary school improvement team, which includes leadership and instructional members, during the initial implementation of a professional learning community (PLC) approach. The scope of the case is guided by improvement science (IS) strategies as PLC members focus on both processes and evidence-based decisions about instructional approaches that respond to the needs of students in the fourth grade. At the time of this case study, the elementary school was implementing a district-wide initiative to implement a PLC approach on every campus. As a recent innovation, albeit to the district, campuses and leaders struggled with the change in approach and how to implement the change with their personnel.

The Every Student Succeeds Act (ESSA) added pressure to leaders to improve scores while at the same time requiring leaders to provide teachers with high-quality professional development. Fortunately, there is a growing body of evidence that supports the use of PLCs within campus communities and a growing body of evidence supporting the personalization of teacher professional development. This chapter documents an applied research study that follows the principles of improvement science (IS) to provide a model of personalized professional development within a PLC structure, documents the initial outcomes for both teachers and students, recommends next steps in the improvement cycle and provides sample templates for other improvement science initiatives.

Keywords

improvement science, professional development, professional learning communities, goal setting, evidence-based practice

The Setting and Background

Donald Lewis has been the building principal at Meadow Lawn Elementary (MLE) for the past 14 years. Over that time, Principal Lewis has been well known in his district for improving the morale of his campus through effective communication with his staff, students and community to create a harmonious working and learning environment. This relatively small school has an average daily attendance (ADA) of 618 within a district that has an ADA of 35,000+ students. Principal Lewis knew the importance of surrounding himself with strong leaders and communicators who also had reputations for creating and maintaining positive relationships with others. Therefore, he made it his goal to hire, support and retain school personnel well. By his 14th year, he had changed the campus's external interactions from community reactive to community responsive, had built some teacher-expert teams and had built an internal campus communication structure. This foundation helped the campus respond to both changing demographics and state/district plans and directives that had an impact on day-to-day activities.

Demographics

Fourteen years ago, the campus received Title I funding, with 53% of the students attending identified as low socioeconomic status (SES). However, a regeneration of the community occurred over the next 10 years. Major land developers bought several apartment complexes within the school's boundaries and built larger and more expensive homes. This reduced the percentage of students with low SES to 14.4%. Currently, MLE does not have Title I status. The campus consists of 1% African American, 24.9% Hispanic, 62.1% White, 0.3% American Indian and 8.9% Asian students.

Plans

When the district passed a bond to rebuild MLE four years ago, Principal Lewis had the opportunity to engage his change management skills to improve his campus and connect with his community. Principal Lewis developed a team that included community members, staff members, local business members, representatives from city councils, district representatives and architects. He led the team from the campus design phase to the opening of the new MLE campus. This involved moving the entire school to a transition elementary campus for two years and then back to the new campus. The process of working with a team to keep the campus and the community both engaged and informed ensured a smooth transition. Consequently, Principal Lewis now serves as a model for the district as it addresses change.

Directives

Increasing teacher capacity to support diverse students was the focus; the proposed district solution was a district-wide directive to administrators (along with a book that was provided to each educator) to implement professional learning communities (PLCs) on every campus. Additionally, the state's new Texas Teacher Evaluation and Support System (T-TESS) had been introduced. Principal Lewis knew that these directives would hit home—it would require changes in how teachers worked and learned, how students were taught and what they learned and how the community understood what was happening on campus. As a seasoned principal, he had just finished reading Bryk, Gomez, Grunow, and LeMahieu's (2015) new volume on improvement science. Much of the content resonated with him and he began to recall what he had done previously in light of the structure and processes outlined. He felt encouraged that improvement science was key to moving the campus through the change process and would provide a much-needed comprehensive lens through which the campus could view education needs, rely on evidence-based practices, strengthen teams and networked improvement communities to support student success, utilize better ways to support social justice in the school and systematize better ways to inform change.

Need for Improvement

Overall, 85% of MLE's students met the state standard for academic performance for all subjects and 34% met the advanced standard. However, the 15% who did not meet the state minimum standard were most often identified as students classified as English Language Learners (ELL), low SES and/or students with disabilities. Clearly there was a gap in student outcomes and many of the same students were identified across different categories. Consequently, the district directive to engage in PLCs, coupled with the new state evaluation, provided an impetus for change.

Teachers were compassionate, kind and respectful to students and each other; 20% had master's degrees and 70% had six-plus years of experience. Informal comments about professional development (PD) often identified that the PD was not tailored to teachers' needs. After conducting an initial review of evidence-based practices in PD (Ball & Cohen, 1999; DuFour, DuFour, Eaker, Many, & Mattos, 2016; Yoon, Duncan, Lee, Scarloss, & Shapley, 2007), Principal Lewis thought that using the district directive to implement PLCs could result in changes to the current system that could improve teacher PD and, subsequently, improve long-range achievement outcomes for all students. It was a place to start a conversation on campus.

Testing the Change

Setting the stage for how to change internal processes based on an external directive is a delicate situation. Principal Lewis knew better than to try to effect change alone—accelerated and sustained improvements were the goal. Over the past year, Principal Lewis had read a lot about school improvement (Boudett, City, & Murnane, 2013; Bryk et al., 2015; DuFour et al., 2016; Mintrop, 2016). He had read about the cornerstones of the improvement science process (Figure 15.1) by Bryk and colleagues (2015) and had concluded that campus work had to focus on a problem of practice that was embraced by the school (i.e., how to implement PLCs); different people at different places in their PD would focus on different things at different levels (i.e., it's personal); teachers had to see how it all fit together in a system (i.e., probably would need examples/experiences and templates/graphics would help); student outcomes were the ultimate measure of the impact of PLCs, but teacher changes also needed to be assessed throughout the process; Plan, Do, Study, Act cycles of inquiry could drive improvements in teacher capacity; and educators and leaders had to come together as a network to improve their community.

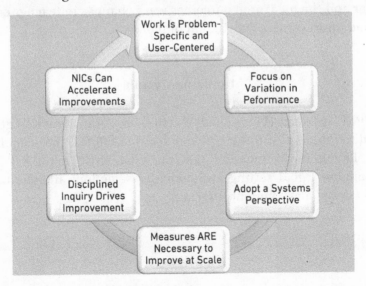

Figure 15.1. Improvement Science process.

Fortunately, the Special Education Team (SET) at the campus had begun a process called personalized student improvement (PSI) the previous year. The major tenets of that process could align with the district's PLC directive and the improvement recommendations by Bryk and his colleagues (i.e., a minor rather than a major leap). Ongoing discussion with the SET members identified a willingness to adjust the focus of PSI to the PLC components (i.e., some minor changes in the lexicon and other more substantive modifications to the structure and processes) and deliver some initial staff development. The SET led the discussions that generated an emerging change management plan for the campus. Teachers wanted to survey the campus to determine what was needed; to use the T-TESS Teacher Self-Assessment to identify what each specific teacher wanted to learn in a PLC; to gain release time in order to work on the PLC—especially grade-level PLCs; and to focus on student data to ensure that the PLC content had the capacity to drive changes in student measures. Engaging key community members early in the process allowed the district directive to be embraced by the campus and the implementation of PLCs to occur organically. A network improvement community (NIC) was born, the PLC process was the driver and the measured outcomes were changes in teacher capacity and improvements in student outcomes.

Implementation

The PLC approach (Figure 15.2) was the core component that guided the development of the other four focused efforts: the school survey; "Laying the Foundation" (DuFour et al., 2016) and the T-TESS self-analysis; goal setting and activities selection; and the use of professional development (PD) logs.

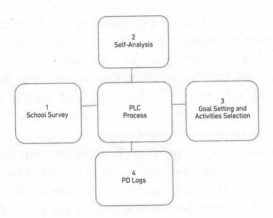

Figure 15.2. PLC case study approach.

The school survey tapped into teacher (anonymous) results for the entire campus (Table 15.1). The survey results coincided with research surrounding the notion of the effect of teachers working together (Bryk et al., 2015). Clearly, team planning is important to both teacher and student success, influencing student academic progress and facilitating better teacher performance. However, what teachers spent their time doing was in question. A majority of teachers indicated that although they did meet on a weekly basis, oftentimes planning was spent on tasks such as organizing activities (e.g., field trips, guest speakers, etc.).

Table 15.1. School Survey Results

School Survey Results*	D	N	A
Team planning is spent primarily on organizing activities such as field trips, guest speakers, etc.	9	10	8
The time I spend planning with my team is important to the success of my students.	0	2	25
The time I spend planning with my team is important to my success as a teacher.	0	2	25
The planning I have with my team has minimal influence on my students' academic progress.	21	3	3
I am a better teacher when I plan with my team.	0	4	23
* Disagree (D); Neutral (N); and, Agree (A)			

A more robust structure of team meetings could justify the focus on PLCs. If team planning is valuable to success, then changes in how team time is managed could help improve outcomes. Further discussion found that multiple different teacher teams were needed—community, campus educators and within and across grade level teams. Teachers proposed to the leadership team that these changes in team time should occur.

This information was vital to the leadership team that provided the data to support the need for more activities. These included reflecting on what they needed to learn, sharing effective practices and communicating better—within grade levels and across the school. Faculty meetings changed from leadership team presentations to PLC-led meetings about specific topics that directly related to student outcomes.

Informal communication encouraged open dialogue and, as a seasoned leader, Principal Lewis knew his teachers: whom to talk with, how to talk with them and how to listen for feedback and identify needs for support. This informal "temperature taking" of the campus helped to determine that is was time to review the school's vision, mission and goals and communicate those clearly to the entire network. Implementing the PLC process seemed like a good time to conduct a review. After the campus developed the mission, vision, values and goals, the educators completed self-assessments.

For the initial self-analysis component the campus utilized the Laying the Foundation continuum framework provided by DuFour and colleagues (2016) and T-TESS. Sparks (2013) discusses the importance for teachers to not only discuss student work samples within their team meetings; he also suggests the importance of teachers sharing and discussing their own evaluations and self-assessments of their own teaching. The teachers completed a self-analysis at the beginning of the year as a component of their personal goal setting prior to conferences with the principal. Subsequently, they shared their self-analysis results with each other as a component of the PLC process. This enabled teachers to collaborate on both individual and team professional development activities that would be most beneficial. Subsequent self-assessments were conducted during the midstages of implementation (January) and then at the end of the school year (May). At each assessment point, team members discussed and collaborated on where the team felt they were on the continuum and self-reported improvements in many areas. This provided leaders with a measure of implementation for the school as a whole and each grade level team separately. Figure 15.3 provides an example from fourth grade that indicates the stages at which the team identified their implementation status at each of the three points in time. Clearly, the fourth grade team has moved from the initiating phases to the developing phase on most indicators. The team is a work in progress. By May, members report that they are likely able to sustain common school goals.

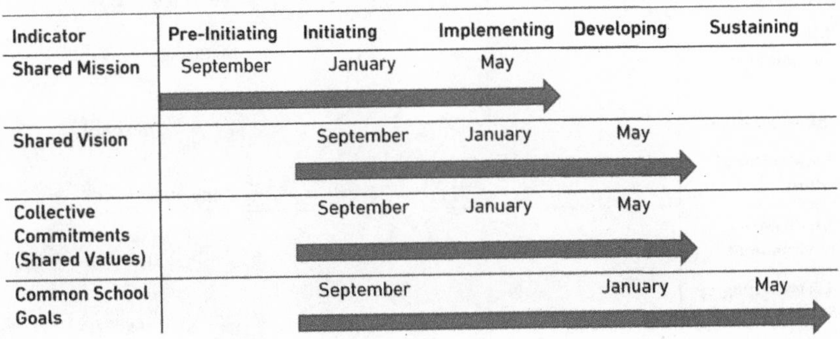

Indicator	Pre-Initiating	Initiating	Implementing	Developing	Sustaining
Shared Mission	September	January	May		
Shared Vision		September	January	May	
Collective Commitments (Shared Values)		September	January	May	
Common School Goals		September		January	May

Figure 15.3. Fourth grade team PLC implementation results (September, January, May).

T-TESS was implemented by the State of Texas during the 2016–2017 school year. The tool consists of four domains and several dimensions associated within each domain. The T-TESS rubric can be located at https://teachfortexas.org/ and results of sample self-analysis outcomes are provided in Table 15.2. Results show changes in some areas and, in areas where there was no change, the initial levels were self-reported as Proficient or Accomplished.

Table 15.2. September to May Improvement on T-TESS Self-Analysis Rubric

Domains & Standard	Improvement Needed	Developing	Proficient	Accomplished	Distinguished
1.1: Standards & Alignment				No Change	
1.2: Data & Assessment			No Change		
1.3: Knowledge of Students				No Change	
1.4: Activities		Increase →			
2.1: Achieving Expectations			Increase →		
2.2: Content Knowledge & Expertise				Increase →	
2.3: Communication				No Change	
2.4: Differentiation					Increase →
2.5: Monitor & Adjust			Increase →		
3.1: Classroom Environment					Increase →
3.2: Managing Student Behavior					Increase →
3.3: Classroom Culture					Increase →
4.1: Professional Demeanor & Ethics				No Change	
4.2: Goal Setting			Increase →		
4.3: Professional Development			No Change		
4.4: School Community Involvement				Increase →	

Goal setting and activity selection are documented on the T-TESS. Teachers documented their goals, how they planned to fulfill them and shared them with administration and their team members. A sample is provided in Table 15.3 and further explanation of the process is described in the Plan, Do, Study, Act log in Table 15.4.

Table 15.3. Goal Setting and Activity Selection

	Professional Goals
1.2: Data & Assessment:	Attend training on guided math and create a guided math binder to keep track of student data and performance.
4.3: Professional Development:	Provide opportunities for novice teachers to visit classroom in order to model best practices.

Table 15.4. Sample Professional Development Logs–Plan, Do, Study, Act

Month	Goal	Activity	Implementation
September 2016	T-TESS Self-Analysis	Goal Setting—create student data binders in PLC	Implementation of student data binders in PLC
	Model Lesson	Prepare Math lesson in PLC with novice teacher visit focusing on classroom management	Model Math lesson for novice teacher; discuss/collaborate in PLC
	Peer Observation	Collaborate with novice teacher in PLC focusing on classroom management—prepare lesson for observation	Observe novice teacher Math lesson focusing on classroom management—provide feedback in PLC
October 2016	Analyze Student Data	Meet with PLC to review math and reading benchmark assessments to differentiate instruction for students	Implement differentiated math instruction to students in small group settings
	Model Lesson	Prepare math lesson in PLC for novice teacher visit focusing on transitions	Model lesson for novice teacher focusing on transitions—discuss/collaborate
	Peer Observation	Plan lesson in PLC with novice teacher focusing on transitions	Provide feedback to novice teacher after observing lesson focusing on transitions
	Plan for Parent Conferences	Collaborate on parent conference agenda in PLC	Role play challenging parent conference in PLC

Month	Goal	Activity	Implementation
November 2016	Model Lesson	Prepare math lesson in PLC for experienced teacher (Teacher 2) focusing on classroom management	Model lesson for experienced teacher (Teacher 2) focusing on classroom management—discuss/collaborate in PLC
	Peer Observation	Plan lesson in PLC with experienced teacher (Teacher 2) focusing on classroom management	Provide feedback to experienced teacher (Teacher 2) after observing lesson focusing on classroom management
	Analyze Student Data	Update student binders, collaborate on results, plan next steps with PLC	Implement structure of delivery of math instruction
December 2016	Participate in book study with PLC	Read *"Who's Doing the Work?"* in preparation for PLC discussion	Discuss and collaborate with PLC elements in book
January 2017	Analyze Student Data with PLC	Collaborate on results with PLC and special ed. team regarding student Math benchmark results—plan next steps	Implement Response to Intervention strategies
	Peer Observation	Discuss/plan with PLC Third Grade specialized reading lesson (Neuhaus)	Observe Third Grade specialized reading lesson (Neuhaus)—provide feedback and collaborate
February 2017	Analyze Student Data/Work	Review samples of student work and data during PLC meeting	Collaborate with PLC next steps after reviewing student work
March 2017	Plan for STAAR	Review practice STAAR results with PLC and implement next steps	Implement student lesson delivery rotation in preparation for STAAR
	Analyze Student Rotation	Review student data and make adjustments to rotation as needed	Implement updated rotation schedule for differentiation
April 2017	Plan for Parent Conferences	Collaborate on parent conference agenda in PLC	Role play challenging parent conference in PLC
May 2017	Review End of T-TESS Self-Analysis	Collaborate with PLC; T-TESS Post Self-Analysis	Complete T-TESS self-analysis to be share with appraiser

Goal setting was linked to professional development logs that were implemented in the PLC setting. A Plan, Do, Study, Act format was applied to lesson planning and was directly linked to the specific needs of the PLC members. During the planning stage, teachers collaborated on the lesson to be delivered (Plan); watched a target teacher in the PLC deliver the lesson (Do); provided feedback and guidance for next steps (Study); and then replicated the lesson, with or without adjustments (Act).

From Isolation to a Team

Teachers collaborated within their PLC structure to plan professional development activities they felt would improve their effectiveness. They participated in book study, classroom visits, data analysis, student work examination, focused conversations, peer coaching and mentorship. They collaborated closely with one another as opposed to working in isolation. They studied initial outcomes, revised next steps and enacted the process again. PDSA activity cycles met the definition by Bryk and colleagues (2015) of Level B learning—learning that sticks—learning that actively engages the learner. Additionally, activities chosen further confirm research findings related to adult learning theory; it is more effective and desirable to learn while interacting with other professionals (Cohen & Ball, 1999).

Student Outcomes

In Texas, student outcomes are assessed using the STAAR exam. This project relied on student data over a two-year period. However, there were challenges in the format of the state data. From the first to the second year, the metric for the test had changed, the cut scores had changed, the number of items on the tests had changed and the type of standard scores had changed (and means and standard deviations were not provided to allow comparisons of different standard scores). Traditional statistical comparisons were not possible. The campus, therefore, relied on what was important to parents and students—did students' scores go up, stay the same or drop? Table 15.5 provides that summary for the fourth grade students who had been in the school in the third grade. By March of the first year of PLC implementation 85% of students were improving or had similar outcomes over time; 15% of students declined over time.

Table 15.5. Summary of STAAR Results

Student Status	%
Improving from 2016–2017	25%
Showing similar growth from 2016–2017	60%
With declining scores from 2016–2017	15%

These percentages look remarkably similar to the passing rates for the school as a whole. As the work from third grade to fourth grade accelerated in rigor, about 3 in every 20 students in a class fell a little behind. Therefore, based on the student metrics used and results found, it is difficult to ascertain if the implementation of these early PLC activities had a positive impact on the achievement of students. Most likely, it is too soon to tell but the information that we have, on balance, shows some benefit. Additional PLC analyses of the student data, the student actual scores, the number of points changed and the interventions that the PLC teams implemented need evaluation.

Discussion

Seasoned leaders can rely on their experiences and their abilities to support people and they must have a plan. Changing a system, involving a team, developing a focused effort to drive improvement, measuring outcomes and communicating both the plan and the outcomes are all integral to improvement. Leaders can have an initial plan or a basic understanding of a directive but need their network improvement community (NIC) to flesh out a team-building plan that makes it user-centered and problem-specific while helping to generate the implementation steps and measured outcomes in the change management plan; they must also determine a communication plan that provides the information, feedback loops and urgency of purpose to meet the target and keep energies focused. Seasoned leaders also likely know that change will not occur in a single cycle. Systemic changes occur with thoughtful and systematic attention to detail and adherence to a long-range improvement plan. The Plan, Do, Study, Act cycle is not just for the implementation of a specific disciplined inquiry—it is the focus of the sum of an improvement science initiative. MLE has begun that process and, like many systems' change efforts, finds that its work is not done after a one-year implementation. However, MLE learned some guiding principles for moving forward.

Overall, the initial outcomes of this improvement science project identified that the PLC process changed meetings, discussions, planning, review of student data, what to focus on in a PLC and what is important—and what is not—at MLE. PLC meetings, often run without the leader, became an integral part of the culture of the campus and are driving review of student data.

Teachers changed and used self-assessments to study both themselves and others on their team to determine where they needed to develop professionally. They engaged in Plan, Do, Study, Act cycles that helped them to realize some of their goals. Some of the greatest changes were in teacher connections with one another and their abilities to work as a team. The long-range goal for PLC teams would be to reach the sustaining stage on the continuum. Reaching this level would indicate the commitment of the team to work collaboratively and effectively while consistently reviewing practices and the impact those practices have on student achievement (DuFour et al., 2016). After a year's use of a PLC approach, based on the implementation assessment, the teachers moved from the pre-initiating stage (early fall) toward the developing stage (late spring) on the continua. These results are important since the tool is used for the team members to self-assess their group in terms of readiness toward working collaboratively. Bryk and colleagues (2015) discussed the importance of moving teachers from Level A learning (professional development activities in complete isolation) to Level B learning (professional development activities where teachers work collaboratively). Results are clear that teachers who engaged in the PLC process are shifting from Level A learning to Level B learning.

Time is an important factor in change management. The campus was directed to begin implementing a PLC structure at the beginning of the school year. Research indicates that it takes a rather lengthy time to establish an initial professional learning community.

Utilizing frameworks designed by DuFour and colleagues (2016), the campus worked quickly to establish PLCs from scratch—without an already-established PLC structure on the campus. The campus worked hard at the beginning of the year defining the professional learning community structure, identifying norms for behaviors and establishing a vision, mission and goals. Those components took a considerable amount of the first half of the year to establish as a community. Following those components, they began to establish the PLC structure that would plan and evaluate student work.

Student outcomes are the direct effects of the PLC and are difficult to determine at this early phase. Most students (85%) are doing as well as, or better than, they did the previous year—even with more challenging materials. However, the remaining students lost ground on the standardized test. Although there's more to students than standardized test scores, they're an integral part of accountability models. Adding more student measures, with greater reliability and validity, would help to determine the impact of the PLC process. Also, working with deidentified student data could help campuses conduct descriptive analyses of student outcomes in light of demographics, other variables (e.g., health, welfare, attendance) and actual scores rather than categorical outcomes (e.g., pass, fail, commended). On the bright side, changes in teacher behavior afford hope for future improvements in student outcomes.

In sum, ongoing engagement with the change management process supported by PLCs likely will continue to support team collaboration and communication. These ongoing efforts can change teacher practice and improve student outcomes. All being well, this improvement science process will never be over. There will always be more opportunities to "rinse and repeat" on the path of *Improvement Required*.

Key Concepts

Improvement science—a concept that explores how to apply research methods to help understand what impacts quality and improvement

Professional development—the process of learning professional skills

Professional learning communities—a group that meets regularly to share their expertise, experience and work samples to improve their teaching skills and student outcomes through a collaborative process

Goal setting—the process of identifying a target outcome to be attained and setting a process, a timeframe and a measure that determines the degree to which the target has been met

Evidence-based practice—decision-making with a basis in available evidence that informs practice

Discussion Questions

1. Identify the key challenges faced by Principal Lewis. How did his approach align with the PDSA improvement cycle? What next steps should Principal Lewis and his school take to continue to grow to better meet student needs?

2. Discuss what steps your campus currently takes to build staff members' capacity to respond to the needs of students? What additional steps could be taken to ensure that faculty members are equipped to identify the professional development necessary to support students? What additional internal and external sources (e.g., people, data, technology tools) could your campus draw upon to augment the current campus capacity to respond to the needs of students?

3. Have you experienced professional development that did not meet your needs? Provide an example of professional development that failed to meet your needs and describe why it did not meet your needs. Oftentimes, PD fails to identify what is important content and skills to be learned and why they are

important. Discuss how a professional learning community (PLC) approach could help individuals to identify, develop and implement important factors that could promote teacher capacity and improve student outcomes.

4. What types of leadership challenges have you faced, or might you face, in responding to modifications in a district's or group's mandate for change in how members engage in professional development? As you identify members who can help you in your network of change agents, what knowledge, skills and dispositions might you harness in different people and why?

Class Activities

1. Look back at the case study to complete the team-building plan. Be sure to include the factors that you feel supported positive team-building and areas where you feel that the team-building process could be improved.

2. Recall a successful attempt at team-building that you have experienced or witnessed on the part of a campus, organization or group. Use your recollection and the template in the Appendix to develop a team-building plan. Please ensure that your plan includes what you think made the experience successful and any changes you would suggest to improve the process.

3. Recollect a successful attempt that you have experienced or witnessed on the part of a campus, organization or group to prepare its members to engage in a change process. Use the template in the Appendix to develop a change management plan. Please ensure that your plan includes the relevant features that you believe helped the group to work together toward a common goal.

4. Professional development initiatives can gain more traction when members of an organization feel that they have a voice in identifying the challenges and how challenges might be resolved, with a reliable source of communication throughout the process. Use the template in the Appendix to develop a communication plan. Please ensure that your plan includes

how technology infrastructure or communication tools might be engaged to guide members, document milestones and celebrate members' accomplishments along the way.

References

Ball, D. L., & Cohen, D. K. (1999). Developing practice, developing practitioners: Toward a practice-based theory of professional education. In L. Darling-Hammond & G. Sykes (Eds.), *Teaching as the learning profession: Handbook of policy and practice* (pp. 3–31). San Francisco, CA: Jossey-Bass.

Boudett, K. P., City, E., & Murnane, R. (2013). *Data wise: A step-by-step guide to using assessment results to improve teaching and learning.* Cambridge, MA: Harvard Education Press.

Bryk, A. S., Gomez, L. M., Grunow, A., & LeMahieu, P. G. (2015). *Learning to improve: How America's schools can get better at getting better.* Cambridge, MA: Harvard Education Press.

Cohen, D. K. & Ball, D. L. (1999). *Instruction, capacity, and improvement* (CPRE Research Report Series RR-043). Philadelphia, PA: Consortium for Policy Research in Education, University of Pennsylvania.

DuFour, R., DuFour, R., Eaker, R., Many, T. W., & Mattos, M. (2016). *Learning by doing; A handbook for professional learning communities at work.* Bloomington, IN: Solution Tree Press.

Mintrop, R. (2016). *Design-based school improvement: A practical guide for education leaders.* Cambridge, MA: Harvard Education Press.

Sparks, D. (2013). *The 6 fundamental ingredients of robust professional development.* Available from: https://dennissparks.wordpress.com/2013/11/26/the-6-fundamental-ingredients-of-robust-professional-development/

Yoon, K.S., Duncan, T., Lee, S.W., Scarloss, B., & Shapley, K.L. (2007). Reviewing the evidence on how teacher professional development affects student achievement. (Issues & Answers Report, REL 2007-No. 033). Washington, DC: US Department of Education, Institute of Education Sciences, National Center for Education Evaluation and Regional Assistance, Regional Educational Laboratory Southwest.

Appendix: Templates

Team-Building Plan

Team Purpose: *What was/is the purpose or reason for the team?*

Team Creation Process:
Describe how the team was/will be formed. Is there a leader? How are people included (invited, appointed, volunteered, etc.)?

Team Urgency:
Describe how a sense of urgency to build a successful team was/will be conveyed to and understood by all team members?

Task Activities:

What activities did/will the team members engage in during this process? Which team members will engage in each activity?

ACTIVITY	TEAM MEMBER(S)
1.	
2.	
3.	
4.	
5.	
6.	
7.	
8.	
9.	

Team Accountability:

Describe how team members were/will be held accountable for their interaction in the team.

Key Features of the Improvement Process:

Improvements:

Change Management Plan

Change: *Briefly describe the change and how it was initiated.*

Relationships: *Describe who was/will be involved in the change and how they are related to each other.*

Progress Monitoring: *Describe how change was/will be measured and how frequently.*

Keys to Success: *Describe the relevant features that help(ed) the group work together toward a common goal.*

Organizational Communication Plan

Input and Feedback:
List the key stakeholders and how you will elicit feedback from them.

STAKEHOLDERS	MODES OF COMMUNICATION
1.	
2.	
3.	
4.	
5.	
6.	
7.	
8.	
9.	

Decision-Making Process:
Describe how decisions will be made in the group or organization. Include a process for resolving disagreements within the group.

Dissemination Process:
Describe how and when decisions will be communicated to the group or organization.

Existing Infrastructure:

Describe how current technology and organizational infrastructure will support the communication process. Include specific ways that infrastructure might be engaged to guide members, document milestones and celebrate members' accomplishments along the way.

Infrastructure Needs:

Assess what additional processes or infrastructure may need to be acquired and/or developed to facilitate communication more effectively.

CHAPTER SIXTEEN

Applying the Plan, Do, Study, Act Framework to Building a Social-Emotional Student Support Framework

KEN FACIN AND PATRICK DAILEY

Hoosick Falls Central School District

Abstract

Mental health can be supported at the school district level. This chapter's case study will share some of our experiences implementing a large-scale social-emotional development (SED) initiative in a rural New York school district with the support of PEAR Institute, Partnerships in Education and Resilience, a translational center connecting research to practice at McLean Hospital. Finding resources to support youth mental health in rural areas is an ongoing issue. A study by the National Rural Health Association found that three-fourths of the rural counties they examined lacked a psychiatrist and 95% lacked a child psychiatrist. Traditionally, much of the pressure for mental health care falls to schools, and although school-based interventions have proven to be effective, schools have reported that long wait lists of students and a lack of available providers have been huge barriers to treatment (Smalley et al., 2010). This partnership was formed under the shared belief that a strengths-based, developmental approach to mental health was key to effective promotion of SED, prevention of emerging mental health challenges and intervention for students who need additional mental health support. The goals of this collaboration were to leverage systems and programs already in place in the school district; to treat students as partners in this process and give them an opportunity to directly communicate their needs through self-report; to reframe the schools' relationship with data beyond end-of-year evaluation to a tool designed to know every child at the beginning of the year; and to center the district on a common language and framework for SED that is supported by student data. In addition, this case utilized the PDSA framework as a delivery system for ongoing examination of data and programmatic feedback. This unified SED approach to mental health is also applicate and scalable to urban and suburban schools.

Keywords

resiliencies, trust, action orientation, emotional control, reflection, relational therapy

Setting/Background

This school district serves children, pre-K through grade 12, from five different townships in a remote rural section of the county. Adjacent to two states, it is located in the easternmost portion of the Greater Capital Region of the State of New York. Multiple generations have raised families here and want their children to remain living in the area. However, owing to economic distress, newly identified municipal issues and localized natural disasters that have taken place over the last several years, it has become increasingly difficult to maintain a financially stable household.

The school district plays a major role in keeping families together while serving youth in the community. It has kept up with technology and provides a cutting-edge education to all students, allowing them to compete on an equal footing with larger school districts that have more community assets and funding. The district functions as one team across grade levels, assisting students and families, not only educationally but by providing social structure on a daily basis.

The community population was 3,501 at the 2010 census. The Capital District Regional Planning Commission projected a decline in population after 2010 and beyond, but that prediction has not happened as a growing population of younger families have been attracted to the school district and rural lifestyle. The village center is listed on the National Register of Historic Places, local artists have become internationally famous and the surrounding lands are steeped in American history as the site of British entrenchments during the American Revolution. However, in the year 2018, it faces life-changing issues that could erode its place in history. Flooding and water contamination by local manufacturers have plagued the local area, but the citizens are strong and are turning the community around as a safe, healthy rural environment to raise children to be as successful as their major city counterparts.

The district has approximately 1,108 students enrolled, 7% from minorities and 51% identified as economically disadvantaged (see Table 16.1).

Table 16.1. Demographic Information for the School District

District enrollment	1,108	Economically disadvantaged	51%
Jr./Sr. high school enrollment	530	Free and reduced lunch	>51%
Elementary enrollment	578	Attendance rate	94%
Minority population	7%	Student suspensions	7%
SWD population	136	Graduation rate	88%

Introducing the PDSA Framework

In previous years, the school district received funding for a New York State Education Department Homeless Youth Program, reflecting a growing teen pregnancy rate, youth living with nonparents, youth living in apartments in the village with friends and youth coming from adjacent states unable to provide the legal documentation for a proper residence. These issues were addressed and now reflect a stable student base. However, rural poverty continues to plague the community and to undermine students in succeeding academically, socially and emotionally. Thus, the school district has created programming to expand learning beyond an academic-centric school experience by placing an emphasis on whole child development.

The goal of the district is to develop and implement meaningful social-emotional supports for students through innovative programming that focuses on relationship-building. For the past century, public schools have used subject matter as the pedagogical basis for relationship-building with students. This has created an environment where tension exists between the teacher and the student at the expense of the academic subject. Through the development of unique social-emotional supports, students and teachers are now establishing strong, meaningful relationships complementary to subject matter learning. The tension should only exist between the subject matter and the learner. By alleviating the tension between the learner and the teacher, students develop greater resiliencies for learning.

This approach extends beyond the classroom and has great value in reconstituting counseling approaches in schools. By using a clinically researched survey instrument, the Holistic Student Assessment (HSA), the social-emotional needs of students became evident. Using student responses, this self-reporting instrument creates a unique social-emotional profile based upon 19 essential SED elements.

The HSA was created by the PEAR Institute's Partnerships in Education and Resilience at McLean Hospital, a Harvard Medical School affiliate. It is a data-driven tool administered to students in grades 5–12 and used to promote social-emotional development. Research has shown that students younger than fourth grade do not fully comprehend the questioning on the instrument. Using student responses on a questionnaire, it provides a "portrait" of the unique strengths and challenges in different social-emotional domains of each student taking the assessment.

The instrument is based on the PEAR clover model, which describes child and adolescent development as a holistic interaction between four core human developmental needs: active engagement (engaging the world physically), assertiveness (expressing voice and choice), belonging (social connection and relationships) and reflection (thought and meaning-making). Based on self-responses, a portrait for each participant provides information about the student's social-emotional balance. This information can then be reported at individual, classroom, school or district levels.

Plan

As part of the planning process the district administered the HSA to students in grades 5–12. The results of the HSA showed 411 students at Tier 2 and 249 students at Tier 3. There were 139 special education students in grades K–12 in fall 2016. At a minimum, the number of students in grades 5–12 indicating a need for Tier 3 support was over 50% greater than the total number of students in special education across the district. The data provided by the HSA was concerning for the following reasons: (a) the number of students identifying at a Tier 3 level was almost 30% of the student body, (b) this number was significantly higher than the number of students involved in disciplinary referrals and counseling sessions combined, (c) the information provided was self-reported by the students and (d) the school district was not prepared to handle such a large number of issues identified by the HSA.

Do

Based on the data from the initial administration of the HSA, a plan was developed and implemented. Response to intervention (RTI) teams instituted programming to address the needs of Tier 2 students, including adopting mindful practices (daily meditative breathing), increased physical engagement for learners (yoga in the classroom), restorative homeroom (presetting students at the beginning of each school day), increased counselor resources, enrollment in a social-emotional learning program and introduction of canine therapy. A concerted effort was made to connect students of the school with a rich offering of clubs and activities that offered engagement and student voice. We have begun our shift from talk therapy to nontalk therapies (relational therapies) steeped in creative arts, interactions with nature, animal relations and equine experiences.

To address the underlying social-emotional needs of Tier 3 students, the school district initiated an Equine Therapy Program at a local farm. Equine therapy is a form of relational therapy that involves interactions between a horse and an individual. Activities do not include riding a horse but rather, under the supervision of an equine specialist and a mental health professional, groups of students perform project-based learning activities with horses. Through these activities, students develop relationships with horses. These newly acquired relationship skills are transferable to the challenges the students have in human relations.

Equine therapy is one example of relational therapy available to students in the school district. The RTI team was charged the task of reviewing each Tier 3 student's records to determine whether this type of therapy would be a viable option. The team focused on the relationships and resiliency portion of the HSA: assertiveness, belonging, trust, empathy, emotional control and action orientation. They reviewed academic grades, disciplinary records and the demographic information of each student.

The high school psychologist engaged in professional development on equine therapy, visited programs in and out of New York State and worked with the local farm to help create the program. The psychologist was also certified in Equine Assisted Growth and Learning Association (EAGALA) horse therapy. EAGALA certification assisted the psychologist and team in developing a unique school-based program. Historically, RTI teams help develop strategies for use by teachers in the classroom, make recommendations for additional academic services or even recommend testing for special education services based on learning discrepancies. Equine therapy was a new option to the RTI team and required additional professional development for counselors and school leaders. A key component was participating in a simulated therapy session at the farm, meeting and working with the horses. The adults reacted no differently than students would have, giving the team insight into the program, how the horses react, how individuals react and the protocol followed during a session at the farm.

After it was determined a student would benefit from participating, the high school psychologist would contact the parent/guardian, review the program and attain the appropriate permission. To this day, all students chosen for the program have been given permission by their parent/guardian. Once permission was received, the high school psychologist would set up a meeting with the student to review the program and encourage participation if necessary.

To efficiently run the Equine Therapy Program, the high school psychologist was given the authority to make administrative decisions for the school district and manage the program. She acted as a liaison between the school and farm, organized transportation and determined the number of students in each session, which students would work together and the amount of time a student was at the farm and away from the classroom. A weekly schedule was created and distributed to administration and staff. Students were not forced to participate in the program, but were not also allowed to skip or "opt out" if they did not want to go.

Students are scheduled to attend the farm in small groups, once per week on a six-week cycle. Including travel time, each session takes approximately 90 minutes. From a classroom perspective, the students would be missing just over two periods each time they attend. To minimize the academic impact of missing class, sessions would use a rotating schedule. The program was reviewed with the teaching staff at both faculty meetings and team/grade level meetings before the start of classes at the beginning of the school year.

Study

The Equine Therapy Program's six-week cycles provided a natural "mechanism" to use short data-collection cycles (Bryk, Gomez, Grunow, & LeMahieu, 2017; Langley et al., 2009; Mintrop, 2016). Attendance, discipline referrals and grade point average of small cohorts of students were continuously examined each quarter in order to determine if equine therapy was working in the short term. Evidence suggested that students participating in the program were showing initial improvement. This short-cycle data helped to ensure to the RTI team that students should continue in this program.

Equine therapy is not based upon talk therapy but rather a relational therapy based on creating meaningful relationships with animals and nature. It places students in an environment where they have to develop resiliencies based on their own emotional and physical actions. Horses do not positively respond solely to a voice or command. They can only respond positively when people have emotional control, are calm and reflective. A positive horse-human relationship is built upon empathy, emotional control and trust. Horses do not respond to voice control like pets. To work with horses, you have to build a relationship. These relational attributes can then be applied to interactions with individuals in a student's life. When students understand and make this connection, mutual trust increases, friendships are formed, discipline referrals and absences decrease and academic performance increases.

Act

Based on data collected from the initial Study phase, student data were then tracked over the next two years. The Equine Therapy Program was instituted in fall 2017. Data from the 2016–2017 school year is prior to student enrollment in the program. Absences decreased a minimum of 40% for all students, almost 80% for students 2 and 3, for a combined average rate of 68% (or an average rate of 58%) once students were enrolled in the program. The information from one cohort of five students is shown in Figure 16.1.

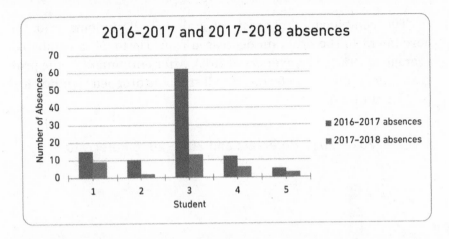

Figure 16.1. Impact on student absences.

The grade point average (GPA) of all students increased at least 10 points, with an average increase of 23 points. Prior to enrollment in the program, four of the five students had an overall GPA of below 65, with only one student maintaining a passing average of 66. After enrollment, all students maintained a passing average for the year with an average GPA of 81 (see Figure 16.2)

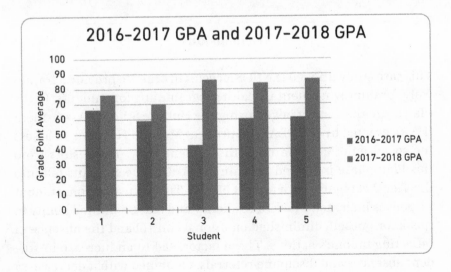

Figure 16.2. Impact on GPA.

The combined number of referrals for all students prior to enrollment in the program decreased from 114 to 24, a combined average of 79% (or an average of 78%). After enrollment in the program, the number of referrals for all students dropped significantly (see Figure 16.3).

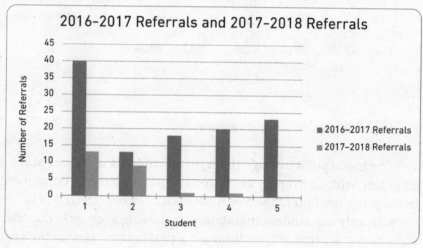

Figure 16.3. Impact on referrals.

Conclusions

This case study utilized the PDSA cycles in order to provide a framework for improving mental health programming for students. In the Plan stage the district began using the Holistic Student Assessment (HSA), created by the PEAR Institute at McLean Hospital, to assess the social-emotional status of the student body. The results from this Plan phase indicated that almost 60% of the students fell into the Tier 2 category, with almost 30% in Tier 3. In addition, student responses indicated a lack of resiliency and trust, a limited ability to speak for oneself, diminished emotional control and the absence of reflecting on one's actions. These factors led to an increase in student absences and discipline referrals, combined with a decrease in academic performance.

In the Do phase, the school district initiated a proactive social-emotional agenda to address the stressors facing the student body. Initial Tier 2 supports included mindful practices such as meditative breathing, yoga in the classroom, restorative homeroom, an increase in counselor resources and the introduction of canine therapy. Activities were focused on nontalk (relational) therapy using a naturalistic approach to student support. In fall 2017, an Equine Therapy Program was piloted with small groups of students in 90-minute six-week cycles. These six-week cycles provided the natural "backdrop" for studying the piloting of the program, something that experts in IS note is critical to real school improvement. Data on absences, discipline referrals and grade point average were collected on students enrolled in the program. Analysis of these data points revealed that students in the program were making some favorable gains.

Based on this promising evidence, the district continued the Equine Therapy Program and monitored students long term over the next two years. Results from this extended effort showed fundamental growth and positive change for students in all three areas: on average, absences decreased 68%; discipline referrals decreased 79%; and GPA increased 23 points. In addition, the results of these studies indicate that, although the program is highly effective when actively engaged, student performance and behavior does not remain consistent once removed. Overall growth was observed from enrollment in the program but also revealed lapses in data sets as participation was removed and the school year progressed.

As part of the Study phase the district has learned that the success of the students while enrolled has shown the efficacy of the program. The school district is not looking to make fundamental changes in program design in the second year. Instead, changes in the frequency, length of session and/or student group dynamic will be considered. The six-week cycles of interaction show significant gains for all students enrolled, but a decrease once disengaged. Increased GPAs also showed that 90-minute sessions did not have a negative impact on academic performance. Future considerations to sustain or improve system growth include increasing the length of the cycles, retaining the initial six-week cycle and returning later in the year for a second cycle, increasing the length of each session or adjusting the makeup of the students in each group between cycles.

Discussion Questions

1. What are some of the challenges schools face with providing mental health services to students?
2. How does the district work to gather initial data about its student body's social-emotional development? And what does this data tell school administrators?
3. What are the major components/activities for each section of the PDSA framework in this case? What are the final results of the pilot and how will the district move forward based on what it has learned?

Class Activities

1. What is social-emotional development? Who are the main developmental theorists whose work underpins the study of adolescent social-emotional development and well-being? Break the class or group into teams. Have each team conduct research about theorists who would support this type of development. Have each team present a theorist and his or her theory.
2. There are many different metrics and assessments that have been developed to measure social-emotional development of students. Break the class or group into teams and have each team research assessments that measure social-emotional development. Have each team report out at the end of their research what these different measures do, their purpose, the subscores or subconstructs they measure and how the data/results are to be interpreted and applied to school settings. Also, each team should be prepared to address the benefits and the limitations of the measure they have selected.

References

Bryk, A. S., Gomez, L. M., Grunow, A., & LeMahieu, P. G. (2017). *Learning to improve: How America's schools can get better at getting better.* Cambridge, MA: Harvard Education Press.

Langley, G. J., Moen, R. D., Nolan, K. M., Nolan, T. W., Norman, C. L, & Provost, L. P. (2009). *The improvement guide* (2nd ed.). San Francisco, CA: Jossey-Bass.

Mintrop, R. (2016). *Design-based school improvement: A practical guide for education leaders.* Cambridge, MA: Harvard Education Press.

Smalley, K. B., Yancey, C. T., Warren, J. C., Naufel, K., Ryan R., & Pugh, J. L. (2010). Rural mental health and psychological treatment: A review for practitioners. *Journal of Clinical Psychology, 66*(5), 479–89. doi:10.1002/jclp.20688

CHAPTER SEVENTEEN

The Methodology
for Educational Leaders

DEAN T. SPAULDING
Z Score Inc.

BRANDI NICOLE HINNANT-CRAWFORD
Western Carolina University

As demonstrated by the chapters in this book, improvement science (IS) is a welcomed approach to school improvement. Prior to the IS movement, school leaders were severely limited in the approaches they employed. As you read in earlier chapters, leaders who wanted to make improvements in their organizations were faced with using traditional research methods and designs as a way to investigate problems and issues. Whereas these traditional designs were effective for what they allowed researchers to do, they were not effective for helping school leaders make ongoing programmatic decisions and improvements.

The Educational Leader's Guide to Improvement Science has helped to address this void between traditional research and pragmatism. Although this is only one step in an otherwise long journey, it is a beginning. The tools and approaches presented in this book will no doubt spark educational leaders thinking about improvements they want to make in their organizations and give them a set of tools to explore and address those goals and objectives; however, despite the use of the IS approaches presented in this book, school leaders will have many challenges as they try to improve education for all students, especially those who are underrepresented.

This book provides both the school-leader-in-training, as well as those already in service, with an overview of various approaches and an in-depth perspective about how to apply them. You most likely have found that these approaches are practical in nature, utilizing what you already know about data collection (both quantitative and qualitative) and applying that knowledge to new IS tools that you may have not been aware of. Run charts, driver diagrams, process maps, fishbone diagrams, the five whys approach and the PDSA framework are a few examples of IS tools and frameworks that you now have at your disposal. These tools will be invaluable in helping you identify problems and issues within your organization and laying out a practical and logical method for systematically addressing them.

In addition to these approaches, two main organizations are focused on in this book: K–12 schools and higher education institutions (IHEs). In IHEs, there are multiples issues that need to be addressed regarding IS. First, there is the training of current faculty about IS and how to teach IS. The training of faculty will require IHEs to provide faculty with considerable support and resources. Faculty will have to attend professional development opportunities in IS and begin to integrate IS into their perspectives. Once faculty are trained, they will then need further support as they begin the long and difficult task of developing new coursework in educational leadership that reflects the core IS values. We know that this takes time; however, all of this will have to take place if IHEs are truly going to create leaders of tomorrow who will go out and become critical change agents.

K–12 schools, especially those that are falling behind and not adequately serving all students, need to also step back and reflect on their practices. In these settings, IS can be implemented in two ways: hire new school leaders, fresh from educational leadership programs that are IS focused, or retrain current leaders already in service to adopt an IS mindset and implement IS tools.

Although there are certainly challenges that are external, school leaders will also be met with barriers to implementing IS approaches from within their buildings. In order for the improvement process to be a complete success, everyone within the organization has to be on board. Although IS approaches and tools have been shown to be effective methods for ongoing school improvement processes, a school leader also has to convince those working within the organization. School leaders will also have to learn how to motivate staff who are reluctant to learn about IS. Perhaps, they think like many initiatives that have come and gone, that this too shall pass. Certainly, this book profiles a few case studies where leaders can be visibly seen needing to work with their staffs in order to fully implement the IS process.

Improvement science is different. And different may experience pushback, especially from those trained in traditional methods of research. Scholars will raise concerns about the rigor and validity of improvement science as a method of continuous improvement. In education, we have become obsessed with evidenced-based practice; as Slavin (2002) reminds us, scientifically based research was mentioned 110 times in No Child Left Behind. In his 2002 address to the American Educational Research Association, he explained that scientifically based interventions were not enough. He argued that "there needs to be a strong effort to invest in the development and evaluation of reputable programs in every area, so that eventually legislation can focus not on programs based on scientifically based research but on programs that have actually been successfully evaluated in rigorous experiments" (2002, p. 19). He advances two ideas: (a) implementation is critical and (b) experiments, the gold standard of research, are the best way to determine effectiveness. Experiments tell you if an intervention can work, whereas improvement science tells you how it works and under what circumstances.

Cohen-Vogel and associates (2015) outline three distinctions between improvement science and traditional research that every educational leader engaged in improvement science work should be able to articulate. The first is the amendable nature of improvement research; as you go through the cycles you may amend your intervention or the way you collect data. Such practices are unheard of in traditional research, but improvement science encourages you to adapt to what you learn in the moment. Second, scholars engaged in improvement science work are interested in studying the methodology itself. And third, improvement science is largely evaluation completed by internal stakeholders. In discussions at our university with the Institutional Review Board about improvement science, where concerns were raised about coercion when educational leaders are leading and evaluating initiatives in their own organizations, we explained how improvement science was a methodology that aimed to change organizational culture (see Figure 17.1).

PreTest-PostTest Design with External Researcher

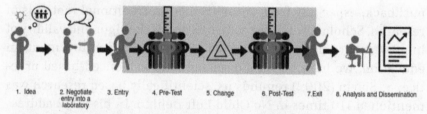

1. Idea   2. Negotiate entry into a laboratory   3. Entry   4. Pre-Test   5. Change   6. Post-Test   7. Exit   8. Analysis and Dissemination

Continuous Improvement Research Design with Internal Researcher (Organizational Leader)

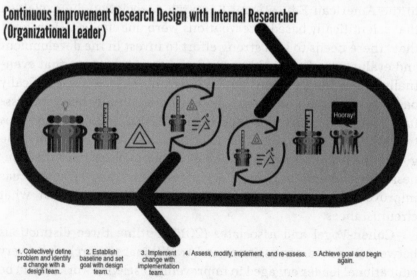

1. Collectively define problem and identify a change with a design team.   2. Establish baseline and set goal with design team.   3. Implement change with implementation team.   4. Assess, modify, implement, and re-assess.   5. Achieve goal and begin again.

Note: Color change is indicative of organizational change. Every ruler is a different point of data collection. Data are collected at multiple time points.

Figure 17.1. Research timelines.

Our communication with the IRB illustrates the education that you have to be willing to engage in to help others understand the distinction between improvement science and traditional research.

Improvement Science as the Methodology of Scholar-Practitioners

Educational leaders in all sectors are required to be more than managers or instructional leaders—they have to be problem-solvers. Scholar-practitioners bridge the gap between theory and practice; they embody practice informed by scholarship. Improvement science methodically aids in the ability to solve problems and continuously refine the processes and practices within an organization. There are distinctions between scholar-practitioners and researchers. There are epistemological differences, axiological differences and methodological differences. Yet the two are not in competition with each other, nor does one hold more value than the other. Traditional scholarship has its place, but usually it is not the most useful exercise for educational leaders. Remember and explain the distinctions to those who question the merit of improvement science.

Improvement to What End?

After all of our discussion of root cause analyses, practical measures, PDSA cycles and theories of improvement, at the end of the day, improving our educational institutions is about improving the opportunities of the students we serve. Improvement science allows practitioners to closely examine the systems we create (or uphold) and how our decisions impact our outcomes. In a time where it is easy to blame external factors for poor outcomes or employ deficit ideologies advancing the notion that our failures lie within our students, improvement science reminds us that every system is designed to get the results it gets. It forces us to take control over the drivers we can

WHAT THEY ADDRESS

CAN IT WORK IN MY CONTEXT?

CAN IT WORK?

Problems of Practice

After noticing an issue in organizational outcomes or organizational efficiency, a practitioner-scholar assembles a group of stakeholders to determine if the problem is truly a problem.

Problems in Literature

After conducting a thorough literature review, a traditional researcher asks what questions remained unanswered. Their research is used to address gaps or inconsistencies in the literature.

WHAT THEY VALUE

Complexity

Scholar practitioners are trained in systems thinking. They seek not to understand the essence of a phenomena but all the complexities that interfere with the phenomena in its current context.

Simplicity and Parsimony

Traditional researchers (particularly positivists) look for causal relationships between variables. The goal is to explain the essence of the relationship as simply as possible and to extract that essence from noise unique to a particular context. The goal is generalizability.

WHAT GUIDES THEIR INQUIRY

Theory of Improvement

Scholar practitioners develop a "Theory of Improvement" by consulting research literature on interventions, theoretical literature related to the problem of practice, the actions of similar organizations, and the expertise of a wide variety of stakeholders. Rarely do they adopt a theory as is, instead they develop a working theory and test it.

Theory

Traditional researchers look to pre-established theories found in the literature to serve as guidance for understanding the phenomena under investigation. Some researchers (primarily qualitative) seek to generate theory through iterative inquiry.

HOW THEY CONDUCT RESEARCH

Cyclical Research Designs

Many scholar practitioners engage in improvement science or similar continuous improvement methodologies. One such framework is the Plan, Do, Study Act 90-day-cycle. Such methodologies require scholar practitioners to test new interventions RAPIDLY and modify the intervention based on the results of each test. The process is cyclical and in the end they determine whether or not to adopt, adapt, expand, or abandon a particular intervention.

Linear Research Designs

Traditional researchers follow modified versions of the scientific method. They began with explicit questions and background research, develop hypotheses and test those hypotheses. Traditional research in most paradigms is linear in nature. Interventions cannot be modified during a research process due to threats to validity.

HOW THEY MEASURE SUCCESS

Practical Measurement

Practitioner scholars use multiple measures to determine the success of an intervention. In an attempt to understand the impact of the intervention on all parts of the system, they use outcome measures, process measures, and balancing measures.

Significance

To establish causation in traditional research, scholars rely primarily on research design (experiments with random assignment). However, to measure impact they rely on statistical significance (likelihood of the result being due to chance) and practical significance (the magnitude).

HOW THEY SHARE WHAT THEY FIND

Network Improvement Communities

Practitioner scholars share their findings through Network Improvement Communities. Individual practitioner scholars try to address similar issues in their particular context and share context specificity with others within the network.

Dissemination

Traditional researchers disseminate their findings in peer-reviewed journal articles and through conferences. Occasionally, they also share findings in practitioner oriented journals.

Figures 17.2, 17.3 and 17.4. Distinctions between scholar-practitioners and researchers.

influence and be strategic in our decision-making. If we are going to get better at getting better, we have to do something we have not done before and improvement science gives us a framework to do just that. This is the task set before educational leaders in the 21st century.

References

Cohen-Vogel, L., Tichnor-Wagner, A., Allen, D., Harrison, C., Kainz, K., Socol, A. R., & Wang, Q. (2015). Implementing educational innovations at scale: Transforming researchers into continuous improvement scientists. *Educational Policy, 29*(1), 257–277.

Slavin, R. E. (2002). Evidence-based education policies: Transforming educational practice and research. *Educational Researcher, 31*(7), 15–21.